T0197331

ENDORSEMENTS

Get ready! You are about to take a journey into what the author calls, a "high-speed connection to God's heart" and the "broadband capacity to link up with the mind of God." Can you imagine yourself possessing exceptional passion, endless energy, and the inner-capacity to receive regular, prophetic, supernatural "downloads" from your headquarters in heaven? Can you envision what your life would be like if you had a source of inside information and advance intelligence? And what if your confidential Source was the Creator Himself? That's what this book is about. Others may be deluded into believing they can access wisdom and guidance without God, but you know better. That's why you have this book in your hands now. Jennifer is delightfully prophetic, uncommonly upbeat, and overflowing with authentic faith. And you, my friend, are about to receive that same impartation as you read *Spiritual Intelligence – The Original.*

Dr. Dave Williams
Bishop - Mount Hope Church Network
www.DaveWilliams.com
Author of *The Art of Pacesetting Leadership*
Founder of Center for Pacesetting Leadership

Jennifer Palthe offers a thought-provoking and eye-opening investigation into the phenomenon of spiritual intelligence – giving us a timely word from the Father's heart for this generation. Her book integrates ancient Biblical truths with contemporary intelligence research, and helps readers to sharpen their spiritual smarts God's way. In her engaging teaching style, she offers multiple analogies and practical strategies for developing it. During an era marked by self-indulgence and counterfeit knowledge, our global community is desperate for *authentic* spiritual intelligence, sourced from the mind of an all-powerful and all-knowing God. We need a greater revelation of God's profound majesty, His remarkable holiness, His extreme wisdom, and His amazing love. Her book is sure to inspire, equip, and provoke the emerging generation of Christ followers to hunger for a greater measure of God's intelligence, and to propel readers across the globe to new levels of intimacy with Him.

Lee M. Cummings
Senior Leader of the Radiant Network
Founding Senior Pastor of Radiant Church
Author of *Flourish, Be Radiant,* and *School of the Spirit*

What a tremendous book! Jennifer Palthe's comprehensive and thorough study in Spiritual Intelligence will launch you into high level spiritual discernment and will equip you to distinguish between the gloriously original mind of Christ revealed in Scripture and every subtle counterfeit on the market today. With the rise of a new Gnosticism in our midst we urgently need to get back to the original mind of Christ that flows from the very heart of the Father. Out of the abundance of the Father's heart, Jesus has clearly spoken! The Father has shared His extreme intelligence with us and His name is Jesus! I cannot more highly recommend this book.

Phil Mason
Author of *Quantum Glory*,
***The New Gnostics*, and**
Royal Heart Therapy

What if you could connect with God's heart and mind so intimately that it changed the way you lived and related to others? What if revelation knowledge flowed to you so that you could walk more like Jesus every day? Is this stuff reserved for only the mystical or deeply spiritual among us? Good news: spiritual intelligence is not only for every believer, it's your birthright! As a true prophetic teacher, Jennifer walks us through the Scriptures bringing refreshing application and instilling a deep desire to *both* hear God and to know what to do with what He imparts. Raising the virtues of discernment, humility, love, holiness, and the fear of the Lord, Jennifer hits the mark on both the *path* and the *purpose* of spiritual intelligence. Get ready to have your spiritual sensitivity raised to a new level…"For those who are *led by the Spirit of God* are the children of God." Romans 8:14.

R. Sonny Misar
Director of the Radiant Network
Founder of Journey Ministries, LLC
Author of *Journey to Authenticity* and *Journey to the Father*

SPIRITUAL
INTELLIGENCE
The Original

Dr. Jennifer Palthe

WESTBOW
PRESS®
A DIVISION OF THOMAS NELSON
& ZONDERVAN

WestBow Press books may be ordered through booksellers or by contacting:

WestBow Press
A Division of Thomas Nelson & Zondervan
1663 Liberty Drive
Bloomington, IN 47403
www.westbowpress.com
844-714-3454

ISBN: 978-1-6642-2498-8 (sc)
ISBN: 978-1-6642-2500-8 (hc)
ISBN: 978-1-6642-2499-5 (e)

Library of Congress Control Number: 2021903710

Print information available on the last page.

WestBow Press rev. date: 06/16/2021

I dedicate this book to the supremely intelligent One.

Holy Spirit

I love You beyond words and appreciate Your profound generosity, Your immeasurable and boundless brilliance, Your inexhaustible guidance, and Your precious counsel and extravagant, enabling power. You indeed are the Spirit of God, the Spirit of wisdom and understanding, the Spirit of counsel and might, the Spirit of knowledge and of the reverential and obedient fear of the Lord, the Source of all true wisdom and intelligence.

Jennifer Palthe, PhD

TABLE OF CONTENTS

FOREWORD

Years ago, I stood in a long line waiting to attend a conference at a popular church known for having a supernatural movement around the globe. I was an emerging leader and frustrated with my obvious limitations and inexperience in leading ministry and ministry teams successfully. As I stood patiently in line, I clearly saw an angel approach me with something in his hand. The angel was the size and build of a tall man, but glistening white in appearance. It held in its hand something that looked like a grid. The grid was about ten inches long and wide and then very thin in height much like a disc that you would insert into a computer. The grid was army green in color and held several floating horizontal and vertical lines perfectly ordered about ¼" from its base. He then threw the grid inside of my mind and I felt something structural and organizational get released.

That same night as I slept, I had a dream. I saw a hand reach down from heaven and drop a "living" mathematical equation inside of my mind. I describe it as living because it had some kind of life-giving power on it and it was something discernable. When I woke up, I literally thought different thoughts and could see things from a broader and bigger perspective. Until this encounter and dream, I often felt lost, unfocused, and scattered in my organizational abilities. I struggled with planning and strategy and couldn't hold ideas together properly. When I went home, the very first thing I did was to reorganize my staff into something more efficient. I could now see where everything needed to be placed for optimal results and it just took off from there. This was the beginning stage of organizing and strategizing a supernatural and global thrust myself that would serve to impact the nations. I believe there are grids, math equations, tech solutions, wisdom solutions and divinely inspired systems just waiting to be released to you and I by the Holy Spirit. Will you be a receiver? If so, your world will shift and then you'll shift the world in response.

Jesus is the door to all wisdom, intelligence, and solutions needed to advance and perfect every system and structure in the earth. He is always the perfect answer for whatever we need personally and for every need in the earth. Like the Apostle John, He joyfully invites you and I to "come up higher" and reassess what we see and what we believe is possible in Him. Additionally, He delights to prophetically reveal the things coming upon the earth to us, His children, and then how to infuse the future with His higher thoughts and higher ways. We are His created ones, created with His divine design, wisdom, and mind. This makes us receivers of God's spiritual intelligence and distributers of His divine creativity and reformation in every area of society.

In Jennifer Palthe's new book, Spiritual Intelligence – the Original, she beautifully languages the possibilities and exciting realities of joining with God's wisdom and intelligence. She describes how true spiritual intelligence is the by-product of relationship with God and infers that spiritual intelligence is unavoidable for those who love God with all their "passion, prayer, and intelligence."

I'm so glad Jennifer wrote this book. Jennifer not only presents spiritual intelligence in a meaningful way, but she enthusiastically models it. For her, spiritual intelligence is not just a trendy sounding theory. It's her entire life, which is why she presents it with such depth. Read her book from cover to cover, use highlighters, take notes, and share her prophetic revelation with others. It's time for thought leaders to emerge who truly hold kingdom solutions and live it and demonstrate it. Jennifer Palthe is that leader.

Jennifer Eivaz
Founder, Harvest Ministries International
Co-Pastor, Harvest Church Turlock California
Author of *Prophetic Secrets, Glory Carriers,*
Seeing the Supernatural,* and *The Intercessors Handbook

ACKNOWLEDGMENTS

I want to thank my amazing husband, Tako, for his phenomenal support while I wrote this book. He is the love of my life and my best friend. His constant encouragement and belief in the significance of the topic and the need for people worldwide to develop it have been extraordinary. Thanks for all your love, patience, and understanding as I invested hours of our time studying for this project.

To Daniel, my oldest son, thank you for the continued guidance with the etymology of words and your wisdom on matters pertaining to history and theology. To Justin, my middle son, thank you for always reminding me to take note of the details, to strive for accuracy and authenticity, and to be adventurous. To my youngest son, Joshua, I want to say a special thank you for the hours of debriefing and endless discussions about what God was revealing to me as I wrote this book. Your capacity to grasp the knowledge presented with such speed and precision is a testament to your remarkable spiritual intelligence.

To my students and mentees over the past twenty years of being a professor, thank you for constantly reminding me of the beauty of a teachable mind and unbiased curiosity. While I haven't been able to teach you specifically about spiritual intelligence in our classes, I trust that, as you read this book, you will appreciate the importance of the subject and how to harness it's life-transforming benefits.

I also want to thank my mentors, both near and far, whom God has used to guide my understanding of His Word. For decades, John and Lisa Bevere have served as incredible spiritual parents to so many of us throughout the world. Their God-centered ministry and many Holy Spirit–inspired books continue to rescue people from spiritual dormancy and ignorance. I am forever grateful for their influence in my life.

I am particularly thankful to Dr. Dave Williams, a spiritual father to me and thousands around the globe. I want to extend special thanks to him for his strong support of this book and for his divine wisdom and wit during numerous formal training classes and informal mentorship. To Jennifer Eivaz, who has written some of my favorite go-to books, I am thankful for her mentorship and formal support of this book. I also appreciate that she's such an excellent role model for women authors. To my pastors, Lee Cummings and Jon Zondervan of Radiant Church Kalamazoo, thank you for your exemplary change leadership and for brilliantly demonstrating to the world what an authentic praying church looks like. To Cory Asbury and Caleb Culver, my worship pastors at Radiant, for writing and releasing the song "Reckless Love." I listened to it repeatedly while writing and it became the unofficial anthem of this book. The lyrics serve as a powerful reminder of the overwhelming love of God towards humanity. It captures the essence of the Father's heart toward a world desperate for authentic love and a genuine revelation of Him.

I am most thankful to my heavenly Father, Adonai, for giving me the privilege of being one of His daughters. I was fatherless at a young age, but You adopted me as Your own. Your constant love and generosity have made me accomplish things that otherwise would've been completely impossible. I also want to thank my Messiah and Lord, Yeshua, for being such a phenomenal leader, teacher, and friend. I marvel at Your brilliance. I could not have written this book without Your wisdom and input. To Holy Spirit, Ruach Elohim, I extend my deepest appreciation for giving me so much revelation, understanding, and counsel as I wrote. I am in awe of You and so thankful for Your profound love and empowerment. Finally, I want to thank the many people who have prayed for me and encouraged me to write this book. I'm especially thankful for my personal prayer partners because of their ongoing encouragement and continued prayers for me and for those who will read this book. Thanks to each of you for your faithfulness to pray for what God wants to achieve through *Spiritual Intelligence*. May you reap an eternal reward for your investments of time and travail in this project. I love you all.

Intelligence: Acquisition and Application of Knowledge

A person who acquires *intelligence* loves his life. A person
who *guards* understanding finds a good thing.

—Proverbs 19:8 (EHV; emphasis mine)

Imagine if you were able to discover and develop the spiritual broadband
capacity to link up with the mind of God. What would it be like to have
high-speed access to His heart and the ability to tap into His thoughts and
perspective? What would life be like if you were able to get a glimpse of His
perspective and plans for your life, organization, or nation? What if you
could access answers to the most perplexing questions and find solutions
to the most complicated problems?

If you could have a sense of the speed and strength of your connection
to Him, how intense and how fast would it be? How determined are
you to discover your genuine spiritual intelligence? How exhaustive and
thorough are you prepared to be in examining the real state of your
spiritual condition? How sure are you that your spiritual aptitude is at the
level it was designed to be?

This is a book that is going to challenge you to think about your spiritual intellectual quotient, test your assumptions about your spiritual aptitude, and examine the nature of your connectivity with the spiritual realm. This book isn't intended to be a vehicle to make you more religious or self-righteous. Nor is it a tool to gather tips to merely enhance your current way of living. The ever-increasing plethora of self-help books can assist you with that. Irrespective of where you are in your spiritual journey, I invite you to venture with me as we explore the phenomenon of spiritual intelligence—why it's so vital, what its dimensions and degrees are, what the knock-off brands look like, and what the keys to developing and maintaining high levels of it are.

Many of us throughout the world have the privilege of enjoying wireless internet access to a seemingly unlimited supply of information. We've come to appreciate continuous, high-speed connectivity with its many advantages and features, which offer better navigational tools, more current and real-time information, and better predictive data. These ever-increasing functionalities have helped us to have access to real-time data, which continue to help us make better everyday decisions. We can easily locate people and places, identify the perceived quality of products and services, and instantly interact with people and organizations around the world.

Imagine for a moment that you could experience this same level of connectivity with the ultimate Source of all knowledge, that you could shift your limited knowledge source from yourself and this world to a dimension and realm that is unlimited? What if you could shift your thinking processes and spiritual aptitude from a single-dimensional analogue system to a multidimensional network system that is unconstrained by time, education, or location? What could the implications be for your relationships, choices, strategic life decisions, or career and calling? Why, if your eternal destiny depends on it, wouldn't you at least be curious about acquiring and developing it?

A NEW ERA

At the dawn of the intelligence era, the speed and accessibility of knowledge have escalated at an unprecedented rate. No prior era has been able to convert information and translate it into working knowledge across such immense distances with such speed. Unquestionably, the rate and scope of this accessibility to knowledge have had a profound effect on how humans perform even the most essential everyday activities. Virtually instantaneous answers to fundamental questions regarding location, distance, time, and temperature are readily available.

Ironically, however, the overabundance of knowledge hasn't produced a substantial increase in authentically intelligent action. While our access to and awareness of intelligence has increased, there are still people everywhere who are desperate for answers, solutions, foresight, and truth. Even our deeper appreciation for the value of things like emotional intelligence and cultural intelligence have not solved our growing global social crises. The commodity of genuine wisdom in action appears scarce if we look at the state of the world. With all our advancements and the surge of accessibility to knowledge, so-called smart has turned out to be quite stupid because it is devoid of true intelligence.

> Don't fool yourself. Don't think that you can be wise merely by being up-to-date with the times. Be God's fool—that's the path to true wisdom. What the world calls smart, God calls stupid. It's written in Scripture, He exposes the chicanery of the chic. The Master sees through the smoke screens of the know-it-alls. (1 Corinthians 3:18 MSG)

Could it be we have been duped into thinking we could obtain wisdom outside our Maker? Have we ignored the ancient proverbs, which implore us to call out for intelligence from the Source of it?

> Call out for *intelligence*,
> if you raise your voice for *understanding*,
> if you search for it like silver,
> if you hunt for it like hidden treasure,
> then you will understand the *fear of the Lord*,
> then you will find the *knowledge of God*,

because the Lord gives *wisdom*.
Knowledge and understanding come from his mouth. (Proverbs 2:1–6 EHV; emphasis mine)

It seems like all creation is at a tipping point, and there is a growing global sense that we are approaching something of eternal finality. Are we ready? Have we exhausted the depths of true wisdom? Where do intelligence and spirituality intersect? Have we applied to spiritual intelligence the same level of attention we've given to academic intelligence and artificial intelligence? Have we simply been accumulating knowledge but missed the Originator of it? Have we overly embraced rationality and the material world at the expense of a personal relationship with our Maker? If our technological innovations have produced such advancements, why is our world experiencing all-time record levels of crises? Could it be that we've been conned into consuming a counterfeit through our neglect of our Creator? Could this be why we've been so spiritually naive and gullible as a global society?

Before we examine spiritual intelligence more closely, let's take a look at the phenomenon of intelligence more broadly, both theologically and theoretically.

INTELLIGENCE

Intelligence is the capacity to acquire and apply knowledge and is vital for human functioning and well-being.[1] *Merriam-Webster's Dictionary* defines it as "the ability to learn or understand or to deal with new or trying situations, the skilled use of reason, the ability to apply knowledge."[2] It involves perceptual awareness, the act of grasping, and the capacity to practically apply what's comprehended.

All intelligence involves superior understanding and secret information. It therefore entails a reasonable number of important areas of thought, reflection, problem solving, choice making, and action. For someone to possess any type of intelligence, they should be able to offer practical solutions and solve problems that someone without it couldn't.

At its root, intelligence advances the speed and pace at which knowledge is translated into understanding and subsequent action. It is a class of mental processes that form the subset or species of the genus of the mind. In other words, the two are inseparable. The mind involves a flow of thoughts, feelings, and perceptions (visual, auditory, olfactory, gustatory, tactile), and intelligence involves the evaluation and ordering of them to make decisions, solve problems, and act on them. The mind accumulates, stores, visualizes, and assesses objects and ideas; and it is the seat of our emotions. Intelligence decides among the collection of perceptions, thoughts, and feelings what action needs to be taken, thereby providing clarity to the mind and wisdom to action.

The Hebrew word for "intelligence" is *sakal* or *sekel*, which means to be prudent, act wisely, comprehend, show discernment, and understand.[3] It denotes one's capacity to get right to the heart of a matter, to cut through the irrelevant minutiae, to intuitively identify the crux of a matter, and to act on it. It involves understanding the essence of what needs to be done, doing precisely the right thing, and quickly achieving the most desirable outcomes.

Jesus, our Jewish Messiah, had phenomenal *sekel*! He had (and still has) the ability to cut through trivia, religious jargon, and highfalutin heresy with absolute ease. He was (and still is) totally brilliant, authentic, and unpretentious. In addition to all the profound miracles He performed, people marveled at His intelligence.

> All who heard Him were amazed by His *intelligence* and His understanding and His answers. (Luke 2:47 AMP; emphasis mine)

> And on the Sabbath He began to teach in the synagogue; and many who listened to Him were utterly astonished, saying, Where did this Man acquire all this? What is the wisdom [the broad and full *intelligence* which has been] given to Him? What mighty works and exhibitions of power are wrought by His hands! (Mark 6:2 AMPC; emphasis mine)

> The religion scholar said, "A wonderful answer, Teacher! So *lucid and accurate*—that God is one and there is no other. And loving him with all passion and *intelligence* and energy, and loving others as well as you love yourself. Why, that's better than all offerings and sacrifices put together!" (Mark 12:32–33 MSG; emphasis mine)

Look at how Jesus admired the scholar of religion's intelligent answer, noting he was close to the kingdom of God because of it. "And when Jesus saw that he answered *intelligently* (discreetly and having his wits about him), He said to him, you are not far from the kingdom of God. And after that no one ventured *or* dared to ask Him any further question" (Mark 12:34 AMPC; emphasis mine).

The Greek word for "intelligence" is *phronimos,* which means a type of wisdom relevant to practical action, a practical virtue that incorporates both good judgement *and* excellence of character and prudent habits.[4] The Bible is very clear on the importance of seeking and acquiring wisdom. Intelligence is a type of wisdom applicable to real-world, hands-on, everyday action. So when the Bible encourages us to seek true wisdom and ask God for it, we are essentially also pursuing spiritual intelligence, because wisdom and intelligence, while distinct, are inseparable. Read how the Bible encourages us to *ask* for wisdom. "If any of you lacks wisdom, you should ask God, who gives generously to all without finding fault, and it will be given to you" (James 1:5 NIV).

In the Old Testament, we see how Solomon asked God for a hearing heart and a wise, understanding mind so he could judge and lead effectively. Solomon called for a heart that was perceptually aware and a mind that could discern and translate what he was sensing into productive action. God was so impressed with his request that He granted it to him at an unprecedented level, together with riches and honor. Through a prayer, Solomon was given the unrivaled ability to translate wisdom into action. Can you see the connection to intelligence? He didn't just have a revelation of God's justice and wisdom but the ability to practically apply them in the way he led others.

So give Your servant an *understanding mind* and a *hearing heart* to judge Your people, that I may discern between good and bad. For who is able to judge and rule this Your great people? It pleased the Lord that Solomon had asked this. God said to him, Because you have asked this and have not asked for long life or for riches, nor for the lives of your enemies, but have asked for yourself understanding to recognize what is just and right, Behold, I have done as you asked. I have given you a wise, *discerning mind*, so that no one before you was your equal, nor shall any arise after you equal to you. I have also given you what you have not asked, both riches and honor, so that there shall not be any among the kings equal to you all your days.

(1 Kings 3:9–13 AMPC; emphasis mine)

ULTRA INTELLIGENCE: ONLY ONE ORIGINAL

The capacity of God's mind transcends all the intelligence on this earth. It has the power to solve any medical, mathematical, societal, linguistic, geographic, or cultural challenge. It has the memory aptitude and processing capacity to analyze and accurately resolve any algorithmic, geometric, or arithmetic challenge known to humankind. There is no problem it cannot solve, no question it cannot answer, and no theorem it cannot compute. In sharing it, we are empowered to apply wisdom and solve life's most challenging problems. God doesn't want people to be devoid of spiritual information and how best to apply it. Ignorance is costly and robs us of knowing His will and living it out. God wants people to progressively be tapping into His mind and increasingly growing in their understanding of His perspective and thoughts.

> God wants us to use our *intelligence*, to seek to understand as well as we can. For instance, by using your *heads*, you know perfectly well that the Spirit of God would never prompt anyone to say "Jesus be damned!" Nor would anyone be inclined to say "Jesus is Master!" without the insight of the Holy Spirit. (1 Corinthians 12:1–3 MSG; emphasis mine)

With all our searching and procuring in life, we need to pursue and imitate all of Him. He is the personification of wisdom and is supremely intelligent. Accessing His mind involves actively pursuing knowledge of

Him, understanding, discernment, comprehension, and interpretation of His Word and will. God doesn't want people to be uninformed or spiritually dense and unintelligent. He wants us to eagerly and conscientiously be striving to emulate Him and share in His intelligence.

> Therefore, become *imitators* of God [copy Him and follow His example]. (Ephesians 5:1 AMP; emphasis mine)

> But our God formed the earth by his power and wisdom, and by his *intelligence* he hung the stars in space and stretched out the heavens. (Jeremiah 10:12 TLB; emphasis mine)

> The beginning of wisdom is: Get skillful and *godly* wisdom, it is preeminent! And with all your acquiring, get understanding, actively seek spiritual discernment, mature comprehension, and logical interpretation. (Proverbs 4:7 AMP; emphasis mine)

Our brains and logical reasoning are useful but alone will never provide us with the power to fully fathom the spiritual realm or tune in to the thoughts of God. Systematic human reasoning and even common sense are literally incapable of such a feat. Only through the Holy Spirit are they divulged to us who are born of the Spirit of God through Jesus. When we connect with God's mind, we can begin to gain the capacity to understand and speak about things larger than what we can humanly think or imagine.

Visualize yourself having extraordinary passion, energy, *and* spiritual intelligence. Consider how radically different your life could be if you loved God and others with such intensity and intelligence that those who didn't yet know Him could at least be curious as to the source of your compassion and spiritual smarts. What would this world look like if there were more people who reflected the intelligence of God and loved Him and humanity with passion and brilliance? So much has been destroyed, nullified, and voided because of people failing to love passionately, prayerfully, *and* intelligently. Apathetic "love," half-hearted devotion, and spiritual naivety and stupidly are perhaps more characteristic of how people have expressed their love toward God and humanity over the course of history. No wonder there is such carnage, confusion, and complacency around the globe.

People everywhere are lacking spiritual intelligence, divinely sourced knowledge and information, and the capacity to accurately process and appropriately dispense that knowledge.

Our Messiah, who called Himself the Way, the Truth, and the Life (John 14:6), said that to inherit eternal life, we ought to habitually love God with all our passion, prayer, *and* intelligence. Read how The Message Bible precisely captures this. "Love the Lord your God with all your passion and prayer and muscle and intelligence—and that you love your neighbor as well as you do yourself" (Luke 10:27 MSG).

Meditating on this verse should immediately reveal the multidimensionality of what is vital in life, who it should be extended to, and how it should be expressed. Without question, love is the most important thing we were created to do. What this verse is also emphasizing, though, is that how you express that love and whom you express that love to have a profound effect on your eternal destiny. We are all wired to love, but the question is, who and how? Do we love God with a first love, which can come only from genuinely knowing Him through personal acquaintance? Do we genuinely love others? When we love, do we do so with all our passion, prayer, *and* intelligence? Maybe we've overdone the passion part to the neglect of prayer. How about intelligence? Have we genuinely loved God and others with *all* our minds, not just our hearts? Have our thoughts, emotions, and choices truly captured our love for Him? If our world is so divided, could it be that we've traded the authentic for a deceptive copy of the original? How can we make the shift?

MAKING THE SHIFT

In the intelligence era, broadband technological connectivity is virtually ubiquitous worldwide. Humanity is making the technological shifts from analogue to artificial intelligence with immense pace and ease. Likewise, in this zenith epoch, it's high time for humanity to make tectonic shifts from spiritual lethargy and gullibility to advanced levels of spiritual connectivity to God's mind. Notice how the Bible emphasizes the very thoughts of Jesus. "For who has known the mind and purposes of the Lord, so as to instruct Him? But we have the *mind* of Christ [to be guided by His *thoughts* and purposes]" (1 Corinthians 2:16 AMP; emphasis mine).

The enormity of 1 Corinthians 2:16 is almost too great to be practical. Its implication is stunning. It implies that everyone who is genuinely connected to God is empowered to access His intelligence and be guided by His thoughts and purposes. Read how The Passion Translation captures it and emphasizes possession of Messiah's very perceptions. "For Who has ever intimately known the mind of the Lord Yahweh well enough to become his counselor? Christ has, and we possess Christ's perceptions."

The capacity to perceive and accurately process and apply spiritual information through a connection to the mind of God is the essence of spiritual intelligence. As we progressively share more and more of the mind of our Messiah, we begin to perceive as He perceives, develop inferences from things observed using His perspective, and feel and sense things in ways increasingly congruent with how He views things. His intelligence helps us to regulate, arrange, and process the information we gain through studying His Word, praying, and spending time in His presence. We progressively adopt His mental faculties of reasoning, comprehension, and expression as our minds are renewed. This revitalization of the mind is as much a part of our inheritance as having the capacity to be led by the Spirit of God. This mental renewal capability is not only a gift but also an explicit instruction. Note that the Bible isn't subtle in its directive.

> And be constantly renewed in the spirit of your *mind* [having a fresh mental and spiritual attitude]. (Ephesians 4:23 AMP; emphasis mine)

> Do not conform to the pattern of this world, but be transformed by the renewing of your *mind*. Then you will be able to test and approve what God's will is—his good, pleasing and perfect will. (Romans 12:2 NIV; emphasis mine)

Romans 12:2 essentially illustrates the transformational power of mind renewal, and Ephesians 4:23 highlights that the process is ongoing. Transformational change isn't the same as minor, incremental change.

It involves radical rethinking, dramatic rejuvenation, and sometimes extraordinary reassessments of past assumptions and viewpoints. Because intelligence is the part of the mind that involves the evaluation and ordering of thoughts to solve problems, spiritual intelligence is vital for mind renewal and relearning. Simply reflecting on mental thought processes, emotions, or perceptions isn't sufficient for mind renewal. Merely employing new thinking strategies will also not suffice. Only by genuinely accessing the mind of God and employing authentic spiritual intelligence through a close relationship with God can long-term mental transformation be achieved. Given the significance of this reality, we will further explore the topic of mind renewal later in this book.

Without the mind, the eye is blind, the ear is deaf, the body is dysfunctional, and normal behavioral responses are impossible. This intricate relationship between the mind and the body is unquestionable and reflective of the relationship between the body of Messiah and Jesus Himself. Without His mind and its intelligence faculties, we are dysfunctional. Scientists claim that the most complex and mysterious physical thing in the universe is the human brain. Even more perplexing to them is the interrelationship between mind and body, and they argue it represents the greatest question in modern science. Without the acknowledgment of God, the spiritual realm, and the fact that every human has a spirit intimately connected to both the mind and the body, modern science will continue to be inept at providing a reply to the greatest question contemporary scientists purportedly are asking.

How much clearer can God communicate this reality with us? His creative genius and greatness are unfathomable and beyond human understanding without the help of His Spirit. It is absolutely impossible to perceive the thoughts of God and have a revelation of His creation without His Spirit unveiling it.

> Great is the LORD, and highly to be praised, And His greatness is
> [so vast and profound as to be] unsearchable [incomprehensible
> to man]. (Psalm 145:3 AMP)

> For God has unveiled them and revealed them to us through the
> Holy Spirit; for the Spirit searches all things [diligently], even
> [sounding and measuring] the [profound] depths of God [the
> divine counsels and things far beyond human understanding]. (1
> Corinthians 2:10 MSG)

GOD'S SPIRIT MAKES IT POSSIBLE

Access to God's deepest thoughts and perceptions is made available to
us by His Spirit, who discloses, divulges, and uncovers them. What a
profound privilege! Given that God created our minds and our intellectual
capacity as humans, it's a reasonable possibility that He foresaw we may
have difficulty grasping the magnitude of this reality. He therefore made
it crystal clear in His Word by inspiring the apostle Paul to write that
these things aren't supplied by human wisdom but by His Spirit. The most
intelligent Being and Creator of the universe, God Himself, designed this
amazing capacity. Not only did He create our minds magnificently, but He
fashioned them so they could be integrated with His by those who possess
His Spirit. Ponder that fact for a moment.

God wants us all to share His mind, to tune into His intelligence, and to
appreciate His perceptions and how He thinks. He wants our hearts so
deeply united with His and our minds so connected to His mind that our
thoughts and desires are synced with His perspective and purposes. This
synergy of relationship creates the kind of unity needed for us to truly
share His mind. This amazing part of our inheritance, as is true with
any inheritance, must be claimed, though. In steadily appropriating this
incredible birthright, we all have the privilege and potential to develop
profound spiritual intelligence.

The God of the universe's masterful handiwork and supreme intelligence
are clearly discernable throughout creation. King David described this
truth when he wrote Psalms, and the apostle Paul articulated this in the
book of Romans (I've italicized some words for emphasis).

> The heavens are telling of the *glory* of God;
> And the expanse [of heaven] is *declaring* the work of His hands.
> Day after day pours forth speech,

And night after night *reveals knowledge.*
There is no speech, nor are there [spoken] words [from the stars];
Their voice is not heard. Yet their voice [in quiet evidence] has
gone out through all the earth, Their words to the end of the
world. (Psalm 19:1–4 AMP)

For ever since the creation of the world His invisible nature and
attributes, that is, His eternal power and divinity, have been made
intelligible and *clearly discernible* in and through the things that
have been made (His handiworks). So [men] are *without excuse*
[altogether without any defense or justification]. (Romans 1:20
AMPC)

If scientific discovery and the pursuit of truth are adventurous, how much
more adventurous are the discovery and intimate knowledge we could
have with our Creator? In an era offering more superior speed and more
advanced connectivity strength technologically, why wouldn't we want to
at least attempt to upgrade our spiritual smarts and tap into the profoundly
generous capacity God has made available to us?

Who wouldn't want to seek truth out, get to know God personally, and
marvel at His brilliance? It seems totally and spiritually counterintuitive
not to. Even former atheists who had the guts to do so, like Lee Strobel[5] and
Josh McDowell,[6] eventually did find Him. As the Bible says, "If you seek
Him [inquiring for and of Him, craving Him as your soul's first necessity],
He will be found by you; but if you [become indifferent and] forsake Him,
He will forsake you" (2 Chronicles 15:2 AMPC).

He is the Alpha and Omega, the First and the Last, the Before all and the
End of all (Revelation 22:13). He is the Mastermind and Director behind
all creation (Proverbs 8:30). He is the Way, the Truth, and the Life (John
14:6), He is the Author and Finisher, Leader and Source of our faith
(Hebrews 12:2). He is God, the supremely intelligent One and only God
(Deuteronomy 6:4). He is the Lord of lords and God of gods (Daniel 2:47).
No one is like Him, and nothing compares to knowing Him personally
(Exodus 8:10). He is the greatest. He is love (1 John 4:8).

Before we proceed to the next chapter, which explores what spiritual intelligence is, let's pray.

God, as I read this book, help me to appreciate and understand the importance of loving You and others with more than just compassion and energy but intelligence as well. Revolutionize my thinking and help me to grow in my personal relationship with You so I may access Your mind more readily and radiate Your heart and ingenuity more authentically. Help me to love passionately, prayerfully, and intelligently. Forgive me for spiritual apathy and any spiritual naivety and stupidly. Help me to develop spiritual intelligence and my capacity to source knowledge and information directly from You. Help me to learn how to accurately process and pragmatically deliver that knowledge so I can be helpful to others. Strengthen the intensity of my spiritual connectivity to Your mind and help me to develop my spiritual smarts Your way. I ask these things in the matchless name of Jesus. Amen.

Spiritual Intelligence: Acquisition and Application of Revelation Knowledge

But there is a vital force and a spirit of intelligence in man,
and the breath of the Almighty gives them understanding.

—Job 32:8 (AMP)

This Voice of God is not heard with the ear of
flesh, but by the *spiritual intelligence.*

—Antoinette Bourignon (1616–80), author of *An Abridgment
of the Light of the World* (London, 1786), *A Treatise of Solid
Virtue* (1699), and *The Restoration of the Gospel Spirit* (1707)

DEFINING SPIRITUAL INTELLIGENCE

Spiritual intelligence is the capacity to accurately perceive and process revelation knowledge, to effectively use it to guide one's thinking, and to translate it into productive action. It represents the intersection where the human spirit and mind align and synchronize with God's Spirit and mind. Individuals with high spiritual intelligence are skilled at accurately and speedily processing spiritual data and exhibiting life-enhancing behavior as a result. They are competent at precisely comprehending and translating spiritual information into practical and productive action. While spiritual intelligence has competencies and information-processing capacities comparable to other forms of intelligences, it is distinct from them in that it is eternal, limitless, and unbound by time and space.

The spiritual mind in Scripture is associated with the invisible realm and divine attributes of love, empathy, and relationship. Spiritual intelligence forms the juncture at which rationality and relationality meet, where cognition and the spiritual converge. Genuine spiritual intelligence captures the essence and pinnacle of oneness with God; when our hearts converge with His, our minds are entangled in His, and our actions transfer His glory and goodness to a love-starved world. We essentially think His thoughts, feel what He's feeling, see as He sees, and do what He's doing—becoming increasingly more like Him and imitating Him in every area of our lives. This is what He designed us to do. This is the unity He seeks to establish among us. This is what all creation is waiting to experience—a personal encounter with the living God, which achieves nothing less than spiritual rebirth, mental transformation, and radical expressions of compassion and ingenuity toward humanity.

HOW IT COMPARES WITH OTHER FORMS OF INTELLIGENCE

Spiritual intelligence is the spiritual intelligence quotient that is distinct from academic intelligence quotient (IQ); emotional intelligence (EQ)[7]; cultural intelligence (CQ)[8]; linguistic, logical-mathematical, spatial, musical, bodily-kinesthetic, interpersonal, intrapersonal, or naturalist intelligences.[9] Scholars have offered multiple theories of intelligence over the past few decades that have advanced our understanding of intelligences beyond IQ.[10] All these intelligences, however, are temporal and limited to success in the natural realm. Spiritual intelligence is superlative and relevant to eternal success in both the natural and supernatural realms. It transcends academic intelligence, emotional intelligence, cultural intelligence, and artificial intelligence, which are confined by education, culture, and circumstance. Anyone can develop spiritual intelligence through an intimate relationship with God. Let's take a look at how various intelligence types relate to authentic spiritual intelligence.

Emotional intelligence comprises multiple dimensions, namely self-awareness, self-regulation, motivation, empathy, and social skills.[11] It involves the ability to monitor one's feelings and the feelings of others, to distinguish among them, and the ability to use this information to guide behavior. In the way emotional intelligence spans awareness of feelings, self-regulation of those feelings, and the application of interpersonal skills in light of those feelings, so too spiritual intelligence spans spiritual perceptual awareness, the processing of what has been perceived, and the ability to effectively manage relationships in a contextually appropriate way.

Cultural intelligence comprises multiple dimensions, namely drive, knowledge, strategy, and behavior.[12] Like cultural intelligence, spiritual intelligence is also multidimensional, incorporating both mental processes and practical application. Just as cultural intelligence enables people to swiftly switch cultural contexts and act in a manner appropriate to the new national culture, so too spiritual intelligence enables people to quickly and accurately respond to information that is supernaturally obtained in a manner consistent with the culture of heaven.

Spiritual intelligence comprises spiritual perceptual awareness of oneself and others, the ability to accurately and timeously process what has been perceived, and effectively use this information to guide and manage one's relationships. Spiritual intelligence supersedes every other form of intelligence. It isn't dependent on natural talents, age, personality, demography, or geography. Natural intelligences are temporal, bound by time and space, and confined to this world. Spiritual intelligence is eternal and sourced from another dimension of wisdom and understanding beyond this world.

Figure 1 below illustrates the four key dimensions of spiritual intelligence. Each of these dimensions will be explored in more depth in upcoming chapters.

Figure 1: Dimensions of Spiritual Intelligence

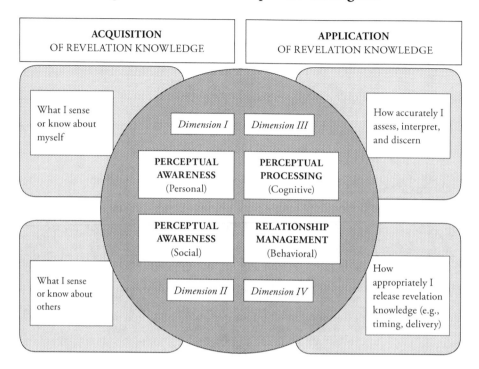

Personal perceptual awareness is the first dimension of spiritual intelligence and is the supernatural ability to employ your spiritual senses to experience the spiritual realm. It involves what you sense or know about yourself. Social perceptual awareness is the second dimension of spiritual intelligence and involves what you spiritually sense and know about others. Perceptual processing is the third dimension of spiritual intelligence and involves the cognitive management of revelation knowledge (for example, assessment, discernment, and interpretation). Relationship management is the fourth dimension of spiritual intelligence and involves what you do behaviorally with revelation knowledge (for example, communication, content, context, timing, and delivery).

SPIRITUAL INTELLIGENCE AND REVELATION KNOWLEDGE

As we saw earlier, all intelligence involves the acquisition and application of knowledge. Natural intelligence involves the application of various types of knowledge, like descriptive knowledge (know what) or operational knowledge (know how). These types of knowledge are acquired through education, training, and experience. Spiritual intelligence, however, goes further and also utilizes revelation knowledge.

Knowledge in Hebrew comes from the root word *yada*, which can be used in a variety of senses, figuratively and literally, and means to acknowledge, be aware, clearly understand, and discern.[13] Two words for "knowledge" in Greek are *gnosis* or *epignosis.* The former refers to "working knowledge."[14] The latter is "contact knowledge."[15]

Revelation knowledge involves experiential knowledge of God revealed to our spirits through a close relationship and personal contact with Him. It allows us to understand Him firsthand without the aid of the natural senses. This kind of knowledge can only be given by the Holy Spirit and doesn't just fill our minds with information delivered through secondhand sources but imparts firsthand insight and personal understanding to us.

As Figure 1 shows, the first and second dimensions involve the acquisition of revelation knowledge, and the third and fourth dimensions involve the application of revelation knowledge. Essentially, the acquisition and application of revelation knowledge will determine the depth and quality of our relationship with God, our understanding of the Bible, our comprehension of spiritual teaching, our discernment of counterfeit spirituality, how we relate to others, and our ultimate spiritual destiny.

Revelation isn't the same as inspiration. Revelation is the supernatural communication of truth to the mind. Inspiration is the capacity to communicate that truth to others with rigor and accuracy. Effective God-ordained teachers and writers do this well. They not only have the capacity to acquire revelation knowledge but also allow revelation knowledge to be accurately understood and applied. People with a high spiritual intelligence will do both; they will obtain clear revelation from God and translate it to others with accuracy. Revelation and inspiration, the accumulation and operationalization of revelation knowledge, are fundamental to spiritual intelligence.

Merriam-Webster's Dictionary defines *revelation* as "something that is revealed by God to humans."[16] Synonyms include *disclosure, divulgence,* and *exposure.* Revelation is associated with a pleasant or enlightening surprise. The Hebrew word for "revelation" is *galah,* which means to uncover. [17] Revelation then is the prerequisite for expression, just as hearing is the prerequisite for faith (Romans 10:17). The Greek word for "revelation" is *apokalupsis,* which means a spiritual manifestation.[18] It denotes a disclosure of things before unknown. The *Jewish Encyclopedia* (Kaufmann Kohler) describes revelation as "a manifestation of God by some wondrous act of His which overawes man and impresses him with what he sees, hears, or otherwise perceives of His glorious presence."[19] It ties in precisely with spiritual intelligence, in that it involves spiritual perception beyond a psychological process, in which the human imagination or mental faculty perceives something. It involves God applying His grace on people and giving them enabling power, which includes His intelligence. The more intelligibly He occupies the human consciousness as an active personality— that is, the more His divine mind is able to be imparted to the human mind, the higher will be the degree of revealed truth and revelation knowledge.

This capacity to share God's mind, to partake of His nature, and to tap into what He's thinking is all part of His divine design. As we grow in spiritual intelligence and intimacy with God, we increasingly learn how to share His mind and receive revelation knowledge directly from Him. Given that this is a process and promise to all God's children, we should endeavor to grow in this capacity and pray enthusiastically for it. While our natural minds may never fully grasp how our minds can be hardwired to God's mind, we know it is truly possible and plainly articulated in the Word of God, as we saw earlier in 1 Corinthians 2:16.

MANIFOLD DIMENSIONS OF THE HOLY SPIRIT

The Source of all revelation knowledge is the Holy Spirit. He is the One who enables us to gain access to God's revealed wisdom and knowledge so we can grasp things beyond mere human understanding (1 Corinthians 2:10). He also gives us access to His divine counsel and courage to make the right choices, exercise sound judgment, and lead with divine intelligence. Read how the Amplified Bible captures His manifold dimensions. "And the Spirit of the Lord shall rest upon Him—the Spirit of wisdom and understanding, the Spirit of counsel and might, the Spirit of knowledge and of the reverential *and* obedient fear of the Lord" (Isaiah 11:2 AMPC).

Take a look at the same verse in the Orthodox Jewish Bible and take a mental note of some key Hebrew words. "And the Ruach [*Hakodesh*] of Hashem shall rest upon Him, the Ruach of Chochmah and Binah, the Ruach of Etzah (Counsel) and Gevurah, the Ruach of Da'as and of the Yir'at Hashem" (Isaiah 11:2 OJB).

The Hebrew word for "Spirit" is *Ruach*, and one of God's names is Hashem. Since God is Spirit, His intelligence is spiritual, and He displays it through seven manifolds of operation (Isaiah 11:2). *Chochmah* is the Hebrew for "wisdom," and *binah* is the Hebrew for "understanding." *Daas* is Hebrew for "knowledge," and *gevurah* denotes "strength" or "courage." *Etzah* is Hebrew for "counsel," and *yir'at Hashem* is Hebrew for the "fear of the Lord." We can see how each of these manifold facets of the Spirit of God relate to spiritual intelligence. All intelligence uses knowledge (awareness and connection), which is then analyzed (comprehended and understood). From that, wisdom and knowledge (*chochmah* and *daat*) take on form and expression. Once the form is analyzed, it generates understanding (*binah*). It's that understanding that then becomes useful to lead and counsel (*etzah*) with courage and fortitude (*gevurah*) to generate solutions and show compassion. We see the cycle of intelligence at work. First, revelation knowledge is acquired, and then it is practically applied.

God's intelligence is perfect. He is the super Intellect with matchless wisdom, superlative knowledge, unrivaled understanding, and unsurpassed counsel. He is the ultimate Genius of geniuses, the Doctor of doctors, the Master of masters, the supremely intelligent One. He is self-existent, self-sufficient, and entirely omniscient. There is no mathematical or statistical problem He is incapable of solving. There is no language He is incapable of understanding or speaking. There is no musical instrument He is unable to play. There is no painting He is incapable of painting or social problem He is unable to resolve. He is the epitome of a genius and the Creator of diverse types of intelligences, mathematics, languages, and music, dance, poetry, artistry, and industry. He doesn't struggle with a left-brain, right-brain, or partial-brain dilemma. He is the personification of a whole-brain thinker. His cultural intelligence is flawless. There isn't a nation, people, or ethnic group or race He is incapable of relating to or communicating with.

His emotional intelligence is impeccable. He is keenly aware of His own feelings and the feelings of every person in heaven and on earth. He is capable of simultaneously feeling the deepest joy associated with one individual while feeling and empathizing with the profoundest pain of another individual anywhere on the earth at any time. His spiritual intelligence is flawless and limitless. He is able to perceive and process natural and supernatural information with speed and precision anywhere, anytime, and throughout eternity. This level of intelligence is unfathomable by our human mental aptitudes. His level of intelligence is unrivaled, whether His general intelligence (for example, His mathematical genius or language acumen), His cultural intelligence (for example, His ability to communicate with any ethnic group from any nation in any language), His emotional intelligence (for example, His profound self-restraint and relational skills), or His spiritual intelligence (for example, His vast perceptual awareness, His limitless knowledge and understanding, and His profound wisdom in action). It is immeasurable, inexhaustible, extravagant, boundless, all encompassing, and absolutely profound. The human mind cannot fathom this level of intelligence, but God possesses it and has always wanted to share some of it with us. His mind in alignment with our minds produces authentic spiritual intelligence.

Access to God's intelligence, divine brilliance, solutions, answers, and perspective—this is what developing and maintaining spiritual intelligence achieve. All spiritual things manifest themselves in the natural realm, and so too genuine spiritual intelligence, which is sourced from the Spirit of God, was designed to be practically realized by anybody. The counterfeit has copied the archetype of true spiritual intelligence, but the inferior fabric of its formulation and forged labeling of its contents will be uncovered as we dare to become personally acquainted with the Original. In the intelligence era and a time in history when knowledge is so widespread, it is vital that we understand what genuine spiritual intelligence is and avoid falling prey to the counterfeit. Join me as we explore it more fully.

DIFFERENT DEGREES OF KNOWING

Knowing information *about* God isn't the same as knowing Him personally. The natural senses or natural mind alone cannot perceive the revealed wisdom or knowledge of God. Only the Holy Spirit knows everything (1 Corinthians 2:10–11). This points to just how imperative it is to develop a close, personal relationship directly with God. If the motive to obtain revelation knowledge is merely for ammunition for religious debate or attention-seeking ministry rather than an authentic relationship with God, it will *not* manifest or take on form. God is the One who chooses to reveal Himself to us. He cannot reveal Himself to those who lack a genuine desire to know Him or to those who choose not to interact with Him. God never forces His will on people. He reveals, He convicts, He pursues, and He imparts; but He never decides to have an intimate relationship with us without our consent. Just like when you want to AirDrop information to a person, they need to have their AirDrop settings open to accept it. So, too, vital, life-transforming information is always present, but we need to acknowledge and be open to receiving it.

Accepting God's "AirDrops" of divine revelation dramatically boosts our levels of wisdom, insight, and understanding of things, both natural and spiritual, thereby developing our spiritual intelligence. This capacity to tap into the mind of an ever-present God is freely available, but people need to be receptive to it. People also need to be aware of the counterfeit. Similar to how people can AirDrop intel one to one, our devices also have the ability to conduct mass image sharing and information exchange up to thirty feet away. Here's the difference from a spiritual standpoint. God always asks permission to dispense. The counterfeit doesn't. Just like when your smartphone's AirDrop capability is enabled, you could inadvertently get caught in AirDrop crossfires and receive information or images you never agreed to receive. So too, from a spiritual perspective, you may inadvertently receive data or information that is counterfeit intel just because of whom you're hanging out with or whom you're in close proximity to. Many people don't have a clue what God is saying or doing in their personal lives or in the world because they fail to accept the "AirDrops" of spiritual intelligence God is constantly trying to share with them. Sometimes this is due to blatant indifference and rebellion, but more often it is due to spiritual ignorance, prayerlessness, carelessness, and busyness.

The Bible is so clear on this. Where revelation knowledge is limited, ignorance establishes deep roots, deception grows, and faith is incapacitated. Without ever-increasing revelation knowledge, spiritual intelligence dwindles and disintegrates.

> My people are destroyed for lack of knowledge. (Hosea 4:6 AMPC)

> For I desire *and* delight in [steadfast] loyalty [faithfulness in the covenant relationship], rather than sacrifice,
> And in the knowledge of God more than burnt offerings. (Hosea 6:6 AMP)

Two things are striking from Hosea 4:6. First, it is referring to God's people, not to anyone who is ignorant of the Word of God or doesn't know about God. Second, it says they are "destroyed." "Why such an austere word associated with God's people?" you may ask. Since the Bible doesn't inflate things, we know it's exactly what God is endeavoring to communicate to us. When God's people lose their revealed knowledge of Him, things in their lives that are of eternal worth begin to self-destruct or terminate.

Without revelation knowledge, even His people experience spiritual downgrades, and eventually things spiritually expire. In other words, the depth and intimacy of our relationship with God cannot be sustained if there is no revealed knowledge of Him. Remember, to know God is eternal life (John 17:3), and the only way to know God is through revelation. It should be our primary ambition in life (Philippians 3:10). It is therefore imperative not only that we get revelation knowledge but that we understand how to manage it to ensure it is accessed, understood, remembered, and accurately applied; this is the crux of spiritual intelligence and why it is so vital.

> And this is eternal life: [it means] to *know* (to perceive, recognize, become acquainted with, and understand) You, the only true and real God, and likewise to know Him, Jesus as the Christ (the Anointed One, the Messiah), Whom You have sent. (John 17:3 AMPC; emphasis mine)

> [For my determined purpose is] that I may *know* Him [that I may progressively become more *deeply* and *intimately* acquainted with Him, perceiving and recognizing and understanding the wonders of His Person more strongly and more clearly]. (Philippians 3:10 AMP; emphasis mine)

Notice how the Bible describes what this knowledge is referring to. The knowledge that helps us perceive, recognize, and become deeply and intimately acquainted with God—this is revelation knowledge. Descriptive knowledge associated with God would include things like knowing Scripture, knowing what God has promised in His Word, and knowing what those promises are predicated on. Operational knowledge associated with God would include things like how to pray most effectively, how to think like God, how to read God's written Word most efficiently, and so forth. While there are numerous other types of knowledge, the point is that revelation knowledge of God is what we really need and is the essence of spiritual intelligence.

Descriptive knowledge and operational knowledge are helpful, but revelation knowledge is essential. Revelation knowledge accessed by faith can be sourced only through intimacy with God. Once accessed, revelation knowledge needs to be applied. Knowledge alone simply puffs up (1 Corinthians 8:11). We will explore the importance of how it's applied and the vital requisites to sustain it later in the book. However, for now it's important that you appreciate that it's revelation knowledge of God that is a vital commodity for genuine spiritual intelligence.

BIBLICAL EXAMPLES OF ACQUIRING AND APPLYING REVELATION KNOWLEDGE

Let's take a look more closely at examples of the acquisition and application of revelation knowledge in the Word of God. A great example is when Jesus, whom the Holy Spirit led into the wilderness, was tempted by the devil during His forty-day fast to command the stones to be turned to loaves of bread. Jesus, using the Word of God as a weapon with which to resist that temptation, answered by saying, "It has been written, Man shall not live *and* be upheld *and* sustained by bread alone, but by every word that comes forth from the mouth of God" (Matthew 4:4 AMPC).

Almost every translation of this verse says either "comes from" or "proceeds from" the mouth of God. This means present tense, not past tense. We cannot just know the Scriptures; we need to actually know the Source of the Scriptures to accurately perceive and know what is coming from His mouth today. Spiritual intelligence gives us the capacity to access what the Holy Spirit is speaking today and to accurately translate and apply it in our relationship with God and others. The Holy Spirit will never speak things that are incongruent with the Scriptures. Rather, He takes it and tailors it to our current situation. Let's not be like the Pharisees, who knew the Scriptures but not the Author of them, who were obsessed with the written word but not *the* Word (1 John 5:7). That's why the Bible says we aren't to be ministers of the letter but of the Spirit. The Word of God, devoid of the Spirit of God, is lifeless (even the devil can quote Scripture). It is the Holy Spirit who quickens our spirits as we read the Scriptures; He guides us into truth and reveals what Jesus is saying to us specifically and directly. Read how the Bible distinguishes between the letter and the Spirit. "He has made us competent as ministers of a new covenant—not of the letter but of the Spirit; for the letter kills, but the Spirit gives life" (2 Corinthians 3:6 NIV).

Things you perceive through your natural senses can provide you with knowledge of natural phenomena, but things you perceive through your spiritual senses from the Holy Spirit develop your revelation knowledge. It is this revelation knowledge that fuels spiritual intelligence and mental renewal necessary to generate genuine and sustained life transformation.

It was revelation knowledge that caused Simeon to recognize Jesus as the Messiah, even though He was yet a child. Simeon didn't get this information from descriptive or operational head knowledge. He received the revelation by the Holy Spirit. There was no way for him to have accurately discerned this information by his natural understanding. It was entirely through spiritual perception and accurate processing of what he perceived that he was then capable of responding appropriately.

The Holy Spirit led Simeon to the temple, and he ran to Mary, Joseph, and Jesus, prophesying about what he perceived. He had perceived by the Spirit who Jesus was. He couldn't delay the response because he might not have seen them again. Nor could he falter in his assessment of what he perceived and deliver an erroneous message to them. He was confident in what he'd heard from the Holy Spirit and was promptly obedient in his response. Simeon clearly had high perceptual awareness and knew what to do with the revelation He had received by responding with a prophetic word of blessing to Mary and Joseph, who marveled at the words spoken of Him (see Luke 2:33). They too were being prepared for things to come and were gaining revelation knowledge of who their Son was. This is an excellent example of high spiritual intelligence in practice.

> Now there was a man in Jerusalem whose name was Simeon, and this man was righteous and devout [cautiously and carefully observing the divine Law], and looking for the Consolation of Israel; and the Holy Spirit was upon him. And it had been divinely revealed (communicated) to him by the Holy Spirit that he would not see death before he had seen the Lord's Christ (the Messiah, the Anointed One). And prompted by the [Holy] Spirit, he came into the temple [enclosure]; and when the parents brought in the little child Jesus to do for Him what was customary according to the Law, [Simeon] took Him up in his arms and praised *and* thanked God and said, And now, Lord, You are releasing Your servant to depart (leave this world) in peace, according to Your word. For with my [own] eyes I have seen Your Salvation. (Luke 2:25–30 AMP)

It was revelation knowledge that caused Peter to know without a doubt that Jesus was the Son of God. When Jesus asked Peter who he thought He was, it was entirely through clear spiritual perceptual awareness that Peter was able to respond honestly and appropriately to Jesus by indicating that He was the Messiah and Son of the living God. Peter received the revelation from Father God through the Holy Spirit, not through presumption or because a human had told him so. Jesus even indicated to him that flesh and blood didn't reveal it but His Father. This is a brilliant example of high spiritual intelligence in operation. Peter wasn't following Jesus because he presumed or simply hoped Jesus was the Son of God. Peter emphatically knew without any doubt that Jesus was the Son of the living God through revelation knowledge.

> Now when Jesus went into the region of Caesarea Philippi, He asked His disciples, "Who do people say that the Son of Man is?" And they answered, "Some say John the Baptist; others, Elijah; and still others, Jeremiah, or [just] one of the prophets." He said to them, "But who do you say that I am?" Simon Peter replied, "You are the Christ (the Messiah, the Anointed), the Son of the living God." Then Jesus answered him, "Blessed [happy, spiritually secure, favored by God] are you, Simon son of Jonah, because flesh and blood (mortal man) did not reveal this to you, but My Father who is in heaven. And I say to you that you are Peter, and on this rock I will build My church; and the gates of Hades (death) will not overpower it [by preventing the resurrection of the Christ]. I will give you the keys (authority) of the kingdom of heaven; and whatever you bind [forbid, declare to be improper and unlawful] on earth will have [already] been bound in heaven, and whatever you loose [permit, declare lawful] on earth will have [already] been loosed in heaven." Then He gave the disciples strict orders to tell no one that He was the Christ (the Messiah, the Anointed). (Matthew 16:13–20 AMP)

ADVANCING FROM SELF-HELP MODALITIES TO UNLIMITED DIVINE CONNECTIVITY

Progress always corresponds with the exponential growth of information-gathering methods that are easily translated into practical, life-enhancing solutions. Similarly, God wants us to make spiritual progress through exponential growth in our capacity to acquire and dispense revelation knowledge from Him so we can optimally resolve everyday problems, whether individual, organizational, national, or global. Every year we observe scores of new accomplishments that attract global attention in medicine, gaming, business, academia and everyday life. We continue to witness dramatic enhancements in computer software, autonomous and semiautonomous vehicle improvements, more e-learning capabilities, developments in medical diagnostic competencies, greater global teleconferencing and social media capabilities, and more advanced smart home technologies.

Everywhere intelligence-related and intelligence-aided devices are having a major impact on our everyday lives. Smartphones, banks, homes, automobiles, and even cities use intelligence on a daily basis. Most of us have at least a passing familiarity with this. We can walk into a room and interact with Alexa or Siri to play our favorite playlist, call a friend, keep track of a to-do list, turn up the air conditioner, or dim the lights through our interaction with a device or entity using intelligence. All the more importantly, God wants us to make similar advancements spiritually. Worldwide, even with our incredible technological advancements, we're simply lagging seriously behind in regard to spiritual advancements and progress. The escalating spiritual ignorance, illiteracy, and gullibility explain why the world is in such a mess.

If mere degrees or fragments of God's intelligence have produced such incredible inventions and innovations, imagine what even small degrees of His intelligence bring to those who possess it and actively develop and share it. Imagine how it could assist people as they navigate their spiritual walk. Consider how people could more accurately discern and process spiritual data. Envision God's people more wisely administering the spiritual gifts and more powerfully setting people free from spiritual bondage and oppression. Visualize a body of believers who clearly hear what the Father is saying, accurately relay and convey what He is saying, and know exactly what to do with that information. Ponder how they could provide practical strategies to a world that desperately needs answers and solutions.

Imagine a place where people stop simply knowing *about* God and all He is, does, and gives but genuinely begin to grow in their personal knowledge of Him. Picture a people who can intelligently dispense what His presence brings. Imagine people around the world, not just emotionally excited or mentally inspired through beautiful-sounding music, poetic words, eloquent preaching, or motivational teaching. Visualize people actually experiencing God, hearing His voice, and responding intelligently and appropriately, no matter their culture, age, education, circumstances, or past. Imagine spiritual leaders able to influence and awaken the spiritual senses of their followers and help them analyze, comprehend, and understand spiritual truths, and respond with profound wisdom in action. This is the intelligence God designed us to acquire and develop, but it is accessed only through closeness to Him.

God wants people to know Him intimately, to comprehend and understand what He is saying, to truly access His mind, and to more accurately discern spiritual data and apply it in a way that is consistent with His nature and will. He wants people to stop misrepresenting Him by offering a fragment of "truth" or a mere "impression" of His person to a world that desperately needs the real Him. He wants His people to grow up and not be spiritually illiterate, naive, or gullible.

> To be perfectly frank, I'm getting exasperated with your infantile thinking. How long before you grow up and use your head—your *adult* head? It's all right to have a childlike unfamiliarity with evil; a simple *no* is all that's needed there. But there's far more to saying *yes* to something. Only mature and well-exercised *intelligence* can save you from falling into gullibility. (1 Corinthians 14:20 MSG; emphasis mine)

In an era marked by self-obsession and counterfeit knowledge, authentic spiritual intelligence is desperately needed. We need revealed knowledge of God's omniscience, revealed knowledge of His profound lordship and majesty, revealed knowledge of His overwhelming might and power, revealed knowledge of His remarkable holiness, revealed knowledge of His extravagant wisdom, and revealed knowledge of His exorbitant love. Just one thought from His mind has transformative power to revive nations.

Just one view from His divine perspective can provide solutions to the most complex social problems. Just one glimpse of His majesty can revolutionize a life. Just one taste of His love can heal the most dejected heart.

In his book *God Secrets*, Shawn Bolz echoes the sentiment of the need for more spiritual intelligence. "Just as we have more emotional intelligence in this generation than any other time in history, we need more spiritual intelligence to help us discern how our models are working or failing."[20] It's a phenomenon that God is illuminating in this hour of history. As predicted by the prophet Daniel (Daniel 12:4), there will be a more intense outpouring of revelation knowledge in the earth. Even the worldwide artificial intelligence community senses a change is coming across every segment of society, and thought leaders and spiritual leaders playing a part in that have a huge responsibility to optimize its potential and shape it for the best. This is the time in history when we need to acquire genuine spiritual intelligence, sourced from the mind of an all-powerful and all-knowing God, and a time when we need to be particularly on guard and on heightened alert against counterfeit versions of it.

PRACTICAL ADVANTAGES OF SPIRITUAL INTELLIGENCE

- It raises spiritual perceptual awareness and makes it easier to discern God's voice, to learn from Him, and to identify the real causes of problems and how to solve them.
- It promotes greater receptivity to the Holy Spirit, including His voice, will, and movements.
- It helps us to remain sharp in the Spirit and anticipate coming challenges and how to deal with them.
- It rewires our minds so we can start living up to what it means to share Messiah's mind.
- It helps us to become more spiritually attuned to God's thoughts, ideas, strategies, and solutions.
- It hones our focus on God, helps us to remain on the spiritual cutting edge, and accelerates the purposes of God.

WHY SPIRITUAL INTELLIGENCE MATTERS

- It solves the problem of spiritual blindness, apathy, and dormancy caused by a lack of a genuine and personal relationship with God.
- It reduces spiritual naivety, gullibility, and irresponsibility leading to deception and misrepresentations of God.
- It replaces spiritual ignorance leading to poor choices, compromised decisions, unhealthy relationships, and hopelessness.
- It exposes and illuminates counterfeit spiritual intelligence.
- It helps people to share revelation knowledge in a way that's plainly understood, compassionately delivered, and aligned with the Word of God.
- It exposes dull discernment, erroneous measurements, poor problem solving, and faulty interpretations caused by a lack of accountability and precise attunement to the mind of God.
- It expands our capacity to radiate and display God's love, gifts, and goodness to others.

As the supreme Intellect has been communicating to humankind throughout the ages, He alone is God, and He only is the Originator of true spiritual intelligence. Let's all endeavor to make progress in acquiring it, and let's be alert to the counterfeit knock-off version of it. Let's reject spiritual naivety and seek to stay on the spiritual cutting edge of what God's Spirit is doing in the earth. Let's be consumers of authentic spiritual intelligence and clothe ourselves with heavenly apparel consistent with the features of the original Designer, God Himself. Let's become people who are conduits of His *real* character and conveyers of His actual glory, not fake spiritual hype. Let's reflect His counsel and manifest His brilliance. Let's all ceaselessly search for true spiritual intelligence as though our eternal destinies depended on it, because they do. Let's dare and endeavor to relentlessly develop our spiritual smarts His way.

Before we move on to the next chapter, which explores spiritual perceptual awareness, let's pray.

God, as I continue to read this book, let my spiritual senses come alive and let me be attentive to keys that will unlock more revelation knowledge of

You. Help me to better understand what it means to have Your mind and its accompanying spiritual intelligence. Expand my capacity to truly know and perceive You as I read this book. Let my spiritual eyes be enlightened and my spiritual ears be open to everything Your Spirit is communicating to me. I want more than just words and information. Give me fresh revelation and divine inspiration. Make known to me the mystery of Your will for my life and show me how I can further develop my spiritual intelligence. Give me a hearing heart and discerning mind that hungers to know You more. Remove the spiritual blind spots from my eyes and rescue me from spiritual ignorance and naivety. I pray that the message of spiritual intelligence will equip me to go deeper in my relationship with You and in my ability to share You with others. I ask all these things in the wonderful name of Jesus. Amen.

CHAPTER 3

Spiritual Perceptual Awareness

> So we look not at the things which are seen, but at the
> things which are *unseen*; for the things which are visible
> are temporal [just brief and fleeting], but the things
> which are *invisible* are everlasting and imperishable.
>
> —2 Corinthians 4:18 (AMP; emphasis mine)

Spiritual perceptual awareness is the supernatural ability to apply your senses to experience the spiritual realm. It is the ability to become aware of things through the spiritual senses and to progressively know things beyond the visible realm. It is a vital dimension of spiritual intelligence necessary to hear from God and perceive what He is saying personally (Dimension I) or socially (Dimension II). It involves the acquisition of revelation knowledge, a first glimpse at wisdom and knowledge but not yet at the stage of grasping the precise meaning of what is perceived.

Merriam-Webster's Dictionary defines *perceive* as "to become aware of through the senses."[21] It defines *awareness* as "the quality or state of being aware: knowledge and understanding that something is happening or exists."[22]

The Greek word for "perception" is *horao,* which means to see, often with metaphorical meaning, to see with the mind, to spiritually see through an inward spiritual perception.[23]

The Hebrew word for "perception" is *taam* and denotes taste, judgment, discretion, or discernment.[24]

If anyone claims to be a person of faith, they must have the ability to supernaturally perceive as fact what cannot be experienced naturally by the physical senses. Without the spiritual currency of faith, it is impossible to please God. If people can't grasp that God is real, if they can't genuinely acknowledge Him, it's impossible for them to access genuine spiritual intelligence.

> Now faith is the assurance (title deed, confirmation) of things hoped for (divinely guaranteed), and the evidence of things not seen [the conviction of their reality—faith *comprehends* as fact what cannot be experienced by the physical *senses*]. (Hebrews 11:1 AMP; emphasis mine)

> But without faith it is impossible to please *and* be satisfactory to Him. For whoever would come near to God must [necessarily] believe that God exists and that He is the rewarder of those who earnestly *and* diligently seek Him [out]. (Hebrews 11:6 AMPC)

Divine perceptual awareness can be operationalized in numerous ways, but it is conditional on faith. In other words, faith is essential to be able to perceive as fact what is impossible for the natural senses to experience. God, in His profound wisdom, chose faith in His Son as the entrance to perceiving and truly knowing Him. He alone is the divine door to true spiritual intelligence. Faith comes first, then spiritual illumination.

> Therefore, [inheriting] the promise *depends entirely on faith* [that is, confident trust in the unseen God], in order that *it may be given* as an act of grace [His unmerited favor and mercy], so that the promise will be [legally] guaranteed to all the descendants [of Abraham]—not only for those [Jewish believers] who keep the Law, but also for those [Gentile believers] who share the faith

of Abraham, who is the [spiritual] father of us all. (Romans 4:16 AMP; emphasis mine)

So faith comes by *hearing* what is told, and what is heard comes by the preaching of the message concerning Christ. (Romans 10:17 AMP; emphasis mine)

I am the *Door*; anyone who enters through Me will be saved (and will live *forever*), and will go in and out [freely], and find pasture (*spiritual security*). (John 10:9 AMP; emphasis mine)

Jesus repeatedly expounded on this priceless commodity—the capacity to perceive as fact by spiritual senses that which is impossible by the natural senses.

He reiterated the profound value of this capacity as a prerequisite to grasping spiritual things and explained how blessed people are when they can spiritually perceive things.

For whoever has [*spiritual knowledge*], to him will more be given *and* he will be furnished richly so that he will have abundance; but from him who has not, even what he has will be taken away. This is the reason that I speak to them in parables: because having the power of seeing, they do not see; and having the power of hearing, they do not hear, nor do they grasp *and* understand. In them indeed is the process of fulfillment of the prophecy of Isaiah, which says: You shall indeed hear *and* hear but never grasp *and* understand; and you shall indeed look *and* look but never *see and perceive*. For this nation's heart has grown gross (fat and dull), and their ears heavy *and* difficult of hearing, and their eyes they have *tightly closed*, lest they *see and perceive* with their eyes, and hear *and* comprehend the *sense* with their ears, and grasp *and* understand with their heart, and turn *and* I should heal them. But blessed (happy, fortunate, and to be envied) are your eyes because they do *see*, and your ears because they do *hear*. (Matthew 13:12–16 AMPC; emphasis mine)

The prophet Isaiah originally expressed these powerful words through the inspiration of the Holy Spirit. They reveal that many will have the power to perceive but will lack the ability to activate this power due to hard-heartedness and eyes that refuse to look to God. It describes people who have personally chosen to tightly close their eyes to God; they won't seek Him, won't read His Word, won't view (read, watch, or look at) anything that may give them a glimpse of His reality. Doesn't this describe so many people in this world who actively resist or avoid reading a book or watching a broadcast of anything that may give them a revelation of God or cause them to personally perceive the One who created them? It seems almost counterintuitive but highlights just how powerful hard-heartedness can be in spiritually blinding people and desensitizing them to the truth.

> Their moral understanding is darkened *and* their reasoning is beclouded. [They are] alienated (estranged, self-banished) from the life of God [with no share in it; this is] because of the *ignorance (the want of knowledge and perception, the willful blindness)* that is deep-seated in them, due to their hardness of heart [to the insensitiveness of their moral nature]. (Ephesians 4:18 AMPC; emphasis mine)

Without this capacity to activate the power to perceive, even someone with the highest measure of general intelligence can be perplexed by God's supernatural spiritual intelligence. Unbelievers are befuddled and confounded by the perceptual awareness of God that people in a relationship with Him can have. The idea that someone can "hear" from God or "feel" His presence is considered to be sheer insanity to the spiritually blind. It is meaningless nonsense to those who have no spiritual intelligence. We shouldn't be surprised by this, since the Bible says it is hidden from the spiritually blind and those alienated from God.

> But even if our gospel is [in some sense] hidden [behind a veil], it is *hidden* [*only*] to those who are perishing. (2 Corinthians 4:3 AMP; emphasis mine)

> But the natural, nonspiritual man does not accept or welcome or admit into his heart the gifts and teachings and revelations of the Spirit of God, for they are folly (*meaningless nonsense*) to him; and he is *incapable of knowing* them [of progressively recognizing, understanding, and becoming better acquainted with them] because they are *spiritually discerned* and estimated and appreciated. (1 Corinthians 2:14 AMPC; emphasis mine)

> At that, Jesus rejoiced, exuberant in the Holy Spirit. I thank you,
> Father, Master of heaven and earth, that you *hid* these things from
> the *know-it-alls* and showed them to these innocent newcomers.
> Yes, Father, it pleased you to do it this way. (Luke 10:21 MSG;
> emphasis mine)

God loves to confound the "wisdom" of the so-called wise. I believe He
regularly laughs at the pomposity and pretentiousness of worldly know-
it-alls. At the grand end-time "graduation ceremony," the highest degree
that will be conferred on the worldly "wise" will be shame, and the truly
wise will be recognized and rewarded.

> The wise shall inherit glory (all honor and good) but shame is the
> highest rank conferred on [self-confident] fools. (Proverbs 3:35
> AMPC)

> For it is written, I will baffle *and* render useless *and* destroy the
> learning of the learned *and* the philosophy of the philosophers and
> the cleverness of the clever *and* the discernment of the discerning;
> I will frustrate *and* nullify [them] *and* bring [them] to nothing.
> Where is the wise man (the philosopher)? Where is the scribe (the
> scholar)? Where is the investigator (the logician, the debater) of
> this present time *and* age? Has not God shown up the nonsense
> *and* the folly of this world's wisdom? For when the world with
> all its earthly wisdom failed to perceive *and* recognize *and* know
> God by means of its own philosophy, God in His wisdom was
> pleased through the foolishness of preaching [salvation, procured
> by Christ and to be had through Him], to save those who believed
> (who clung to and trusted in and relied on Him). (1 Corinthians
> 1:19–21 AMPC)

Can you appreciate the weightiness of these words? God will *baffle* (1
Corinthians 1:19). That means He will totally perplex and bewilder the
"smarts" of this world. Think about this for a moment. God will expose
and display the senselessness of this world's "wisdom." These verses
aren't saying that all philosophers and scholars are fools. Many highly
God-fearing scientists have had deeply intimate relationships with God
including Louis Pasteur (the founder of microbiology and immunology),
Ernest Walton (the first person in history to artificially split the atom),

Robert Boyle (considered to be the founder of modern chemistry), and Sir Isaac Newton (widely regarded as the greatest scientist the world has ever produced). However, what these verses *are* indicating is that God will someday show that any wisdom that fails to perceive and acknowledge the Source of all intelligence is nonsense. Worldly wisdom, innovative solutions, creative designs, and human ingenuity that is devoid of faith in God will be brought to nothing. Faith in God doesn't rest on convincing words or human philosophy but on the Spirit of God inspiring the minds of hearers. How can you spiritually hear if your spiritual ears are deaf?

> And my language and my message were not set forth in persuasive (enticing and plausible) words of wisdom, but they were in demonstration of the [Holy] Spirit and power [a proof by the Spirit and power of God, operating on me and stirring in the minds of my *hearers* the most holy emotions and thus persuading them]. So that your faith might not rest in the wisdom of men (human philosophy), but in the power of God. (1 Corinthians 2:4–5 AMPC; emphasis mine)

It is also impossible to have faith in respect to divine spiritual things if you cannot even believe the work of God's hand in what is seen with the natural eye. "I have spoken to you of earthly things and you do not believe; how then will you believe if I speak of heavenly things?" (John 3:12 NIV).

Just as high general intelligence is associated with sensory perception, so too is high spiritual intelligence associated with the sensory perception of spiritual things. Those with no spiritual intelligence are absolutely incapable of comprehending spiritual truths because these revelations can only be spiritually appraised. The spiritually blind are utterly unqualified to discern spiritual matters. Just as an infant cannot yet solve the simplest mathematical problem, the nonspiritual person cannot even begin to perceive the revelations of the Spirit of God. That is why many cannot even begin to grasp the reality of God, even if they have high academic intelligence.

Those with low spiritual intelligence may perceive things, but the quality of that perception may not always be clear. They know to an extent but not fully, they perceive partially but not entirely, and the underlying truth is somewhat hidden and veiled. However, by training and developing our spiritual perceptual awareness, we can strengthen our spiritual sensory acuity. "But solid food is for the spiritually mature, whose *senses* are *trained* by practice to distinguish between what is morally good and noble and what is evil" (Hebrews 5:14 AMP; emphasis mine).

We see numerous times in the Scriptures where Jesus clearly expressed His disdain for poor perceptual ability. He even rebuked His disciples for poor spiritual perception. "And being aware [of it], Jesus said to them, Why are you reasoning and saying it is because you have no bread? Do you not yet *discern* or understand? Are your hearts in [a settled state of] hardness? Having eyes, do you not see [with them], and having ears, do you not *hear* and *perceive* and understand the sense of what is said? And do you not remember?" (Mark 8:17–18 AMPC; emphasis mine).

To the Pharisees, Jesus said, "You foolish ones [acting without reflection or *intelligence*]! Did not He who made the outside make the inside also?" (Luke 11:40 AMP; emphasis mine).

To His followers, He also pointed out their inability to intelligently interpret. "You hypocrites (play-actors, pretenders)! You know how to analyze *and* intelligently interpret the appearance of the earth and sky [to forecast the weather], but why do you not *intelligently interpret* this present time?" (Luke 12:56 MSG; emphasis mine).

Even when Jesus appeared to two of His disciples after His resurrection, they could not recognize Him, and He described their perceptual ability as dull. "And [Jesus] said to them, O foolish ones [sluggish in mind, *dull of perception*] and slow of heart to believe (adhere to and trust in and rely on) everything that the prophets have spoken!" (Luke 24:25 AMPC; emphasis mine).

In these verses, Jesus pointed out a condition in the people of His day, but it is still applicable today. He exposed their lack of perceptual awareness by highlighting their inability to apply themselves to recognizing things beyond the visible realm. They were unable to perceive what was being said and what was actually occurring in that age. Many were unable to genuinely perceive the goodness of God and recognize who Jesus really was. Notice how Jesus exposed their spiritual blindness and deafness, including the dull spiritual perception of His disciples in Mark 8:17–18 and Luke 24:25 above. Notice His disdain for lack of intelligence. He was clearly referring not to their natural intelligence but to their poor spiritual intelligence.

The heart of God hasn't changed on the matter. He is the same yesterday, today, and forever (Hebrew 13:8). He is still pointing out the spiritual perceptual dullness on the part of His children and the spiritual blindness on the part of those who have yet to know Him intimately. God wants people to sharpen their spiritual perceptual capacity so they can "see" things from His perspective.

Let's take a deeper look at this incredible supernatural capacity that has so generously been given to us, who personally know God. Spiritual perceptual awareness is a perception in our inner being the Holy Spirit reveals by way of an unction. It may come through any of the spiritual senses, whether seeing, hearing, touching, or even smelling. It may also be as simple as an inner knowing, an impression, a hunch, or a gut feeling that cannot be fully articulated pictorially. It may also take the form of a mental impression, an image on the screen of one's mind, a vision, or a notion. Spiritual perception can also be the operation of the spiritual gift of a word of knowledge, a word of wisdom, the gift of prophecy, or the discerning of spirits. The bottom line is that God longs to reveal Himself and offer His solutions to a desperate and dying world, and He needs His children to more accurately perceive what He is communicating and help the world to recognize His existence and goodness.

> See what an incredible quality of love the Father has given (shown, bestowed on) us, that we should be permitted to be named and called and counted the children of God! And so we are! The reason that the world does not know (*recognize*, acknowledge) us is that it does not know (*recognize*, acknowledge) Him. (1 John 3:1 AMPC; emphasis mine)

Jesus had remarkable perceptual awareness, and His spiritual eyes and ears perceived things His natural mind didn't necessarily visualize. He personally perceived exactly who He was (Messiah, Son of God, and High Priest), He perceived His Father (Abba, Adonai, Elohim), and He was able to perceive the heart and innermost thoughts of others.

> Jesus, knowing (*fully aware*) that the Father had put everything into His hands, and that He had come from God and was now returning to God. (John 13:3 AMP; emphasis mine)

> I tell the things that I have seen at My Father's side in His very presence; so you also do the things that you heard from your father. (John 8:38 AMP)

> But Jesus for His part did not trust Himself to them, because He knew all men. (John 2:24 AMP)

Let's take a look at some more examples. Jesus knew by spiritual perceptual awareness, through a word of knowledge, that He would be betrayed and by whom (John 6:64). He knew when His hour had come and that it was time for Him to return to the Father (John 13:1). He was also aware of malicious plots against Him (Matthew 22:18), was perceptually aware of people's thoughts (Luke 6:8) and intentions (Luke 11:17), and even knew what His disciples were wondering (John 16:19).

> But [still] some of you fail to believe and trust and have faith. For Jesus *knew* from the first who did not believe and had no faith and who would betray Him and be false to Him. (John 6:64 AMP; emphasis mine)

> [Now] before the Passover Feast began, Jesus *knew (was fully aware)* that the time had come for Him to leave this world and return to the Father. And as He had loved those who were His own in the world, He loved them to the last and to the highest degree. (John 13:1 AMPC; emphasis mine)

> Jesus *knew* that they wanted to ask Him, so He said to them, Are you wondering and inquiring among yourselves what I meant when I said, In a little while you will no longer see Me, and again

after a short while you will see Me? (John 16:19 AMP; emphasis mine)

Another example, detailed in John 4:7–18, is when Jesus had several words of knowledge about the Samaritan woman at the well. He perceived that she didn't know about God's gift of eternal life (John 4:10). He knew she was living with someone who wasn't her husband and that she had previously had five husbands.

> Then a woman from Samaria came to draw water. Jesus said to her, "Give Me a drink"—For His disciples had gone off into the city to buy food—The Samaritan woman asked Him, "How is it that You, being a Jew, ask me, a Samaritan woman, for a drink?" (For Jews have nothing to do with Samaritans.) Jesus answered her, "If you knew [about] God's gift [of eternal life], and who it is who says, 'Give Me a drink,' you would have asked Him[instead], and He would have given you living water (eternal life)." She said to Him, "Sir, You have nothing to draw with [no bucket and rope] and the well is deep. Where then do You get that living water? Are You greater than our father Jacob, who gave us the well, and who used to drink from it himself, and his sons and his cattle also?" Jesus answered her, "Everyone who drinks this water will be thirsty again. But whoever drinks the water that I give him will never be thirsty again. But the water that I give him will become in him a spring of water [satisfying his thirst for God] welling up [continually flowing, bubbling within him] to eternal life." The woman said to Him, "Sir, give me this water, so that I will not get thirsty nor [have to continually] come all the way here to draw." At this, Jesus said, "Go, call your husband and come back." The woman answered, "I do not have a husband." Jesus said to her, "You have correctly said, 'I do not have a husband'; for you have had five husbands, and the man you are now living with is not your husband. You have said this truthfully." (John 4:7–18 AMP)

Another example is when the prophet Isaiah saw by spiritual perception a vision concerning Judah and Jerusalem. "The vision [*seen by spiritual perception*] of Isaiah son of Amoz, which he saw concerning Judah [the kingdom] and Jerusalem [its capital] in the days of Uzziah, Jotham, Ahaz, and Hezekiah, kings of Judah" (Isaiah 1:1 AMPC; emphasis mine).

Yet another example is when Stephen through an open vision spiritually perceived the glory of God and Jesus standing at His right hand prior to being stoned to death for his faith. Notice how he was *full* of the Holy Spirit and *saw* God's glory. "But he, being *full* of the Holy Spirit and led by Him, gazed into heaven and *saw* the glory [the great splendor and majesty] of God, and Jesus standing at the right hand of God" (Acts 7:55 AMP; emphasis mine).

For those of us who have given our lives to Jesus, we have perceived with our spiritual senses sufficiently to turn from our past to the kingdom of light. The Lord continues to cause our spiritual eyes to be enlightened as we make progress in our walk with Him.

> For I always pray to the God of our Lord Jesus Christ, the Father of glory, that He may grant you a spirit of wisdom and revelation of insight into mysteries and secrets in the deep and intimate knowledge of Him, By having the *eyes* of your heart flooded with light, so that you can *know* and *understand* the hope to which He has called you, and how rich is His glorious inheritance in the saints. (Ephesians 1:17–18 AMPC; emphasis mine)

> To open their *[spiritual]* eyes so that they may turn from darkness to light and from the power of Satan to God, that they may receive forgiveness and release from their sins and an inheritance among those who have been sanctified (set apart, made holy) by faith in Me. (Acts 26:18 AMP; emphasis mine)

Notice in the verses above that it takes the opening of spiritual eyes to turn to God and know the hope to which He's called us. Dr. Dave Williams, globally renowned and bestselling author, says in his book *Skill for Battle: The Art of Spiritual Warfare*, "Spiritual blindness must be combated spiritually. True evangelism is never accomplished through human persuasion."[25] The Bible substantiates his claims.

> The god of this age has blinded the minds of unbelievers, so they cannot see the light of the gospel that displays the glory of Christ, who is the image of God. (2 Corinthians 4:4 NIV)

> For the god of this world has blinded the unbelievers' minds [that they should not discern the truth], preventing them from seeing the illuminating light of the Gospel of the glory of Christ (the Messiah), Who is the Image *and* Likeness of God. (2 Corinthians 4:4 AMPC)

The Message version of 2 Corinthians 4:4 captures this reality even more bluntly. I've italicized several words for emphasis. "If our Message is obscure to anyone, it's not because we're holding back in any way. No, it's because these other people are looking or going the wrong way and refuse to give it serious attention. All they have *eyes* for is the fashionable god of darkness. They think he can give them what they want, and that they won't have to bother believing a Truth they *can't see*. They're *stone-blind* to the dayspring brightness of the Message that shines with Christ, who gives us the best picture of God we'll ever get."

Just as persuasive, eloquent, audible words alone can never persuade someone who is naturally deaf to hear, so too even the most impressive visual displays could never make a blind person see. No amount of gifted preaching alone can cause the blind to see and deaf to hear. Essentially, spiritual conditions need to be dealt with spiritually, not naturally. To illustrate this, Dr. Williams shares that an international evangelist traveled around the world preaching the gospel, but few people ever actually got saved. The Lord informed this missionary that he was losing the battle because people's minds were closed. Only once the evangelist prayed for the spiritual blindness to be broken did hundreds start to receive Jesus.[26]

Dr. David Yonggi Cho, renowned teacher, author, and pastor of one of the largest churches in the world, says in his book *Prayer That Brings Revival: Interceding for God to Move in Your Family, Church, and Community*, "The devil has never been too concerned about church ritual—but he is deathly afraid of genuine prayer."[27] Why? Because prayer causes the spiritually blind to see and spiritually deaf to hear. Prayer takes people from a state of having no spiritual intelligence to a place where they begin to know and sense God for themselves. That is why the subject of prayer will be dealt with more specifically later in this book and why you will find numerous prayers for spiritual intelligence after each chapter and in the appendices.

Take the opportunity to pray some of them aloud each day while you are reading this book.

Dr. Cho says "the Holy Spirit can bless you when you read the Scriptures. The Holy Spirit can direct you as you witness for Christ. The Holy Spirit can anoint you as you preach and teach the word of God. But if you want to have intimate communion with the Holy Spirit you need to pray."[28] Dr. Cho sensed the Lord telling him something he described as totally life changing. "You must get to know and work with the Holy Spirit."[29] Notice the words *know* and *with*. Developing an intimate partnership with the Holy Spirit is vital to sharpening spiritual and perceptual awareness.

The spiritual sense of taste is another pathway to perception. A situation or experience may leave a "bad taste" or "sweet taste" in your mouth. Either way, it is a new insight and revealed knowledge. What and how we deal with that revelation is influenced by our overall spiritual intelligence. Some people have described sensing the presence of the Lord through a sweet taste in their mouths.

Prophet and King David said "taste and see that the Lord our God is good," and the prophet Ezekiel and apostle John described eating supernatural scrolls as tasting as sweet as honey in their mouths.

> O taste and see that the LORD our God is good; How blessed fortunate, prosperous, and favored by God is the man who takes refuge in Him. (Psalm 34:8 AMP)

> How sweet are Your words to my taste, sweeter than honey to my mouth! (Psalm 119:103 AMP)

> He said to me, Son of man, eat what you find in this book; eat this scroll; then go and speak to the house of Israel. So I opened my mouth, and He caused me to eat the scroll. And He said to me, Son of man, eat this scroll that I give you and fill your stomach with it. Then I ate it, and it was as sweet as honey in my mouth. (Ezekiel 3:1–3 AMP)

So I took the little book from the angel's hand and ate and swallowed it; it was as sweet as honey in my mouth, but once I had swallowed it, my stomach was embittered. (Revelation 10:10 AMPC)

Spiritual perception may also involve the spiritual sense of hearing. Seven times the book of Revelation warns all who have spiritual ears to hear and heed what the Spirit says.

> He who has an ear, let him hear and heed what the Spirit says to the churches. To him who overcomes [the world through believing that Jesus is the Son of God], I will grant [the privilege] to eat [the fruit] from the tree of life, which is in the Paradise of God. (Revelation 2:7 AMP)

> He who has an ear, let him hear and heed what the Spirit says to the churches. He who overcomes [the world through believing that Jesus is the Son of God] will not be hurt by the second death (the lake of fire). (Revelation 2:11 AMP)

> He who has an ear, let him hear and heed what the Spirit says to the churches. To him who overcomes [the world through believing that Jesus is the Son of God], to him I will give [the privilege of eating] some of the hidden manna, and I will give him a white stone with a new name engraved on the stone which no one knows except the one who receives it.' (Revelation 2:17 AMP)

> He who has an ear, let him hear and heed what the Spirit says to the churches. (Revelation 2:29 AMP)

> He who has an ear, let him hear and heed what the Spirit says to the churches. (Revelation 3:6 AMP)

> He who has an ear, let him hear and heed what the Spirit says to the churches.
> (Revelation 3:13 AMP)

> He who has an ear, let him hear and heed what the Spirit says to the churches.
> (Revelation 3:22 AMP)

You cannot hear what the Spirit is saying if you are spiritually deaf and lacking the capacity to tune to what God is saying to you. This signifies just how important it is that we train our spiritual senses to function and perform as God originally intended. Perceptual awareness should always draw us toward God and empower us to advance His kingdom. We shouldn't simply be seeking and praying for the ability to perceive but should primarily be seeking God Himself. We should also have the motive of growing in perceptual awareness for His benefit and the welfare of others. Our ultimate ambition should be to develop stronger and more acute perceptual awareness so we become better informed as to who God really is and more knowledgeable of His perceptions.

> For Who has ever intimately known the mind of the Lord Yahweh well enough to become His counselor? *Christ has,* and we possess Christ's *perceptions.* (1 Corinthians 2:16 TPT; emphasis mine).

> If any one of you lacks wisdom, let him *ask* God, who gives it to all without reservation and without finding fault, and it will be given to him. (James 1:5 AMPC; emphasis mine)

Having a perceptive heart and a capacity to understand what God is saying is still available to anyone who will ask God. It is a pleasure for God to grant it to whoever asks Him. Remember how pleased God was when Solomon asked God for a perceptive heart, as we saw earlier (1 Kings 3:9–12).

One thought from God concerning a challenge you're facing can be transformative. One thought from God can offer a solution to a social problem that offers tectonic change for a nation. One thought from Him can revolutionize an industry.

Let's not be people who have capacities to access intelligence but fail to activate them. Let's endeavor to train our spiritual senses so our spiritual intelligence grows exponentially and our spiritual blind spots become obsolete. Let's make it our determined purpose to really perceive God so we can grasp the wonders of His person. Let's strive to attune our spiritual senses to the heart and mind of God so we perceive as He perceives. Let's access His "livestream" of profound wisdom, extraordinary understanding, unlimited knowledge, and trustworthy counsel. He designed us to have this capacity so we can truly know Him. Notice the vital importance of *intimacy* in the next verse. "[For my determined purpose is] that I may *know* Him [that I may progressively become more deeply and *intimately acquainted* with Him, *perceiving* and recognizing and *understanding* the wonders of His Person more *strongly* and more *clearly*]" (Philippians 3:10 AMPC; emphasis mine).

Before we proceed to the next chapter, which explores perceptual processing, let's pray.

God, expand my capacity to perceive You and possess Your perceptions. Reinvigorate my spiritual sensory awareness. Let me supernaturally know and sense things with greater acuteness so I can bring the reality of Your kingdom to earth. Help me to increase my personal and social perceptual awareness so I can know more about how You see me and others. Help me to better understand the mysteries of Your kingdom and Your secret counsels hidden from the ungodly. Remove any remaining blind spots from my spiritual eyes and strengthen my spiritual visual acuity. Lord, share with me specific things yet unknown. Open my spiritual eyes and ears so I may perceive what You're doing. Give me a spirit of wisdom and revelation, of insight into mysteries and secrets, and of a deeper and more intimate revelation of You. Give me a perceiving heart so I can know and understand the hope to which You have called me. Thank you that part of my inheritance as Your child is to have the mind of Jesus and His perceptions. Help me to more diligently claim this birthright and the blessing of spiritual intelligence associated with it. In Jesus' impressive name. Amen

CHAPTER
4

Perceptual Processing

All things have been entrusted and delivered to Me by My
Father; and no one fully knows and accurately understands
the Son except the Father, and no one fully knows and
accurately understands the Father except the Son *and anyone*
to whom the Son deliberately wills to make Him known.

—Matthew 11:27 (AMPC)

This calls for a mind [to consider that is packed] with wisdom
and *intelligence* [it is something for a particular *mode of
thinking* and *judging* of thoughts, feelings, and purposes].

—Revelation 17:9 (AMPC; emphasis mine)

Perceptual processing involves the accurate evaluation, comprehension, and understanding of revealed knowledge; and forms the third major dimension of spiritual intelligence. It encompasses what the Bible refers to as the spirit of our minds having the capacity to comprehend things that cannot be understood through our natural senses. It is associated with the quality and depth of that comprehension and the ability to precisely grasp and efficiently manage that revelation.

It is one thing to perceive and another to precisely know how to analyze and what to do with that revelation. Similar to general intelligence, spiritual intelligence is characterized by the ability to accurately analyze and evaluate new information before acting on that information. The higher the spiritual intelligence, the more precise the analysis, and the more effective the behavioral response to that revelation will be (both personally and socially).

If you research characteristics associated with various types of intelligence, they all have certain variables in common. People with high intelligence can process information faster, more easily retrieve memorized data, and display a stronger ability to accurately differentiate and distinguish between information. People with strong cultural intelligence, for example, are able to swiftly switch cultural contexts and act appropriately in new cultural contexts. Aptitude through knowledge, experience, memory, and practice enhances speed of performance with *all* types of intelligence.

Let's relate this to spiritual intelligence. Knowledge of God and the Bible, and practice using spiritual senses and gifts, will all contribute to the pace and accuracy of perceptual processing. With spiritual maturity, training, and practice, the ability to accurately differentiate between what's moral or immoral and what's of God and what's not of God becomes much easier. "But solid food is for the [*spiritually*] *mature*, whose senses are *trained by practice* to distinguish between what is morally good and *what is* evil" (Hebrews 5:14 AMP; emphasis mine).

Essentially, the perceptual processing dimension of spiritual intelligence will determine the appropriateness and accuracy of the response to the information perceived. If what is perceived is poorly or inaccurately interpreted, the quality of its dispensation will be undermined and even relationally damaging. If the perceptual processing is done correctly, then the relationship management dimension will also be more appropriate in terms of timing, accuracy, and expression, as we will see in the next chapter.

The apostle Paul shed some light on this when he said we need to learn to love appropriately, using our heads, so our love is sincere and intelligent. He stressed we shouldn't succumb to our whims but rather act appropriately, get on with figuring out what pleases God, and then actually do it. I've italicized relevant words for emphasis below.

> So this is my prayer: that your love will flourish and that you will not only love much but well. Learn to love appropriately. You need to use your head and test your feelings so that your love is sincere and *intelligent*, not sentimental gush. Live a lover's life, circumspect and exemplary, a life Jesus will be proud of: bountiful in fruits from the soul, making Jesus Christ attractive to all, getting everyone involved in the glory and praise of God. (Philippians 1:9–11 MSG)

> Just because something is technically legal doesn't mean that it's *spiritually appropriate*. If I went around doing whatever I thought I could get by with, I'd be a slave to my whims. (1 Corinthians 6:12 MSG)

> You groped your way through that murk once, but no longer. You're out in the open now. The bright light of Christ makes your way plain. So no more stumbling around. *Get on with it!* The good, the right, the true—these are the actions *appropriate* for daylight hours. Figure out what will *please* Christ, and then do it. (Ephesians 5:8–10 MSG)

Many get excited when they receive revelation knowledge, but few take the time to pray about it, check with the Holy Spirit, examine its congruency with Scripture, and manage what they discern with pure hearts. Even if the acquisition of revelation knowledge comes through a brilliant mode of thinking, if not examined through the lens of Scripture or discerned with a pure conscience, the delivery will be erroneous. The acquisition of revelation knowledge alone isn't intelligence, just as masterful thinking processes alone don't constitute intelligence. The acquisition of revelation knowledge becomes intelligent only when accurately processed and appropriately *applied*. In other words, whatever is perceived or revelation that's acquired must be carefully analyzed and interpreted *before* it is ready to be dispensed to others. "For our appeal [in preaching] does not [originate] from delusion *or* error or impure purpose *or* motive, nor in fraud *or* deceit" (1 Thessalonians 2:3 AMP).

Jennifer Eivaz, globally renowned author, says in her book *Seeing the Supernatural*, "The mature have learned through practice how to accurately sort out what they are sensing, so they can respond to the information appropriately."[30] I like her emphasis on practice, accuracy, and appropriateness because those are where many believers have fallen short of God's best. People have either listened to someone bring them an inaccurate "word from God" or incorrectly presented an interpretation of what they perceived in the spiritual realm. Both have led to grievous consequences for the recipients.

This is where God wants His people to be, especially wise and on guard. He needs us to be translators of what He is actually saying. He needs us not only to perceive but also to accurately transmit that information in an uncontaminated way. Eivaz also asserts that inaccuracies can occur if a person hasn't studied the Bible well for themselves, has a loveless heart, is inexperienced with the supernatural, or looks only at the outward appearance.[31] While the ability to perceive may occur very quickly for new believers, it takes time and practice to develop the skills to accurately process spiritual information and deliver it in a biblically congruent way. Eivaz stresses that there is a learning curve to it and that it requires community and accountability for a person to grow in accuracy. I couldn't agree more.

God wants to entrust us with secrets, strategies, and solutions. We, however, need to respect the data and honor the people associated with it. When we discern or perceive things that aren't positive, for example, they may be a call to pray and are never an excuse to gossip about or judge others. God wants to help, heal, and restore people, not hurt them. The moment we judge and condemn is the moment our capacity to accurately translate what God is communicating is lost. It's like our spiritual broadband strength is suddenly deactivated, and we no longer have Wi-Fi access. This then would be a good time to get our hearts right with God *before* we proceed with acting on what we have perceived.

Even if what we perceive is clear, if we cannot effectively manage the revelation without becoming proud or judgmental, we forfeit our capacity to honorably and accurately represent God when delivering it.

> Do not judge, and you will not be judged. Do not condemn, and you will not be condemned. Forgive, and you will be forgiven. (Luke 6:37; Matthew 7:1 NIV)

> He who goes about as a gossip reveals secrets, but he who is trustworthy *and* faithful keeps a matter hidden. (Proverbs 11:13 AMP)

THE DANGERS OF ERRONEOUS PERCEPTUAL PROCESSING

Without accurate perceptual processing, prophets won't be able to prophecy with precision, preachers won't be able to preach with rigor, writers won't be able to scribe with exactitude, and publishers won't be able to publish fastidiously. Errors in perceptual processing cause confusion and deception in learners and listeners. This not only nullifies the potential utility of what is being communicated but also undermines the products and services whereby it's being presented. It would be better for people to remain silent than to erroneously present revelation knowledge that has not yet been correctly processed in light of the Scriptures. Those with significant public platforms need to be especially careful not to speak error concerning the Lord or present a version of Him that thereby misrepresents Him. Even publishers of spiritually related books need to be especially cautious not to inadvertently promote inclinations to error through carelessness in the content review of the books they endorse and market.

> A *little* leaven (a *slight inclination to error*, or a few false teachers) leavens the whole lump [it perverts the whole conception of faith or *misleads* the whole church]. (Galatians 5:9 AMPC; emphasis mine)

Notice in Galatians 5:9 that it doesn't take much leaven to spoil the entire batch. A "little" or "slight inclination to error" is all it takes to undermine the entire entity. These subtle errors may be embedded in products or services, whether a podcast, a blog, a survey, a book, or an entire ministry. While the majority of the contents of these products or services may be acceptable, even seemingly trivial errors can pervert the whole conception. God finds this offensive because it misleads people.

False prophets and false teachers love to invent things and then wrap them in truth. Some of them have such dull perceptual awareness that they don't even realize they facilitate the publication of falsehoods about God. Because they may feel the pressure to deliver a message or write, even when they aren't actually receiving clear revelation from God, they begin to present half-truths and craft things from their own imaginations. Often, these are marks of ministers that have lost their capacity to acquire new revelation knowledge and accurately assess it before applying it. Their ministries have become spiritually downgraded due to their lack of accountability and attunement to the mind of God, and the loss of their first love for Him. They have essentially lost their capacity to manage and dispense revelation knowledge with exactitude. Their once "fresh" products and services now display the same characteristics all perishables do over time—they begin to smell, disintegrate, and contaminate things close to them.

> For the fool speaks folly and his mind plans iniquity: practicing profane ungodliness and *speaking error concerning the Lord*, leaving the craving of the hungry unsatisfied and causing the drink of the thirsty to fail. (Isaiah 32:6 AMPC; emphasis mine)

> So then, we may no longer be children, tossed [like ships] to and fro between chance gusts of teaching and wavering with every changing wind of doctrine, [the prey of] the cunning and cleverness of unscrupulous men, [gamblers engaged] in every shifting form of trickery in *inventing errors* to *mislead*. (Ephesians 4:14 AMPC; emphasis mine)

Notice the emphasis on "inventing errors to mislead" in Ephesians 4:14. Sometimes these errors stem from people inventing titles for themselves that, when scrutinized, prove to be lies. Some have entire ministries that rest on a lie about their title and the services they're apparently qualified to offer. Titles can of course be trivial, but if God's people are been misled by them, that's what's extremely offensive to Him. The Bible is riddled with verses pertaining to the importance of accuracy, and the Lord clearly detests misleading measures.

> A false balance and unrighteous dealings are extremely offensive and shamefully sinful to the Lord, but a just weight is His delight. (Proverbs 11:1 AMPC)

> You shall have accurate and just balances, just weights, just ephah and hin measures. I am the Lord your God, Who brought you out of the land of Egypt. (Leviticus 19:36 AMPC)

> [My purpose is] that you may know the *full* truth and understand with certainty and security against *error* the accounts (histories) and doctrines of the faith of which you have been informed and in which you have been orally instructed. (Luke 1:4 AMPC; emphasis mine)

An *ephah* in Hebrew denotes a measure in general, and *hin* is a liquid measure.[32] Any spiritual evaluation of a person that is deceptive or inaccurate is disgusting to God. False assessments, imbalances, and mismeasurements are disgraceful to Him, especially when His name is attached to them. So, for example, bringing a word to someone and saying, "This is what God is saying to you" and then proceeding to say something contrary to what He is actually saying is highly offensive to God. Similarly, compiling a measurement tool that alleges to calculate someone's spirituality but falsely indicates a person's true spiritual condition or actual spiritual gifts is despicable to God, especially when His name is associated with it. This is how some once-anointed spiritual leaders have inadvertently slipped into counterfeit spiritual intelligence, which will be covered later. Some repent and recover, but many do not; and unfortunately neither do many of the people deceived by their products.

MISLEADING SPIRITUALLY RELATED MEASUREMENT TOOLS

Over and over the Word of God demands accuracy of measures, and we are repeatedly warned against deception. We have seen "spiritual gifts" inventories or questionnaires, for example, that aren't entirely accurate when you actually line them up against the Word of God. They purport to measure "spiritual gifts," for example, but in fact measure only self-reported capabilities or interests. These are perhaps useful if trying to assimilate people into organizational positions congruent with their interests. However, where they cross the line is when people think this is their "spiritual gifting" when in fact it is more of a talent or interest and something they had before becoming a believer.

Many spiritual intelligence questionnaires reflect similar errors. They often fail to capture the essence of genuine spiritual intelligence, which is grounded in an intimate relationship with God and a strong connection to His immeasurable omniscience. These subtle deceptions rob God's children of their full inheritance, and people developing and advocating these surveys profit from this misrepresentation. These well-meaning survey developers don't always appreciate the significance of ensuring the validity and reliability of their measurement instruments. This further adds to the erroneous nature of their measurement tools, even if unintentional. People who market measurement instruments allegedly linked with God need to be especially on guard for inadvertent errors and things that can subtly deceive the survey participants. God detests mismeasurements because they are misleading, especially when His name is attached to them. Just as we personally may not enjoy being misquoted or misrepresented, how much more the living God!

With this in mind, let's look at how The Message Bible describes Jesus' warnings about fake Messiahs, false prophets, and lying preachers in the books of Matthew and Mark.

> If anyone tries to flag you down, calling out, "Here's the Messiah!" or points, "There he is!" don't fall for it. Fake Messiahs and lying preachers are going to pop up everywhere. Their impressive credentials and dazzling performances will pull the *wool over the eyes* of even those who *ought to know better*. But I've given you fair warning. (Matthew 24:23–25; Mark 13:21–23 MSG; emphasis mine)

> And many false prophets will rise up and deceive and lead many into error. (Matthew 24:11 AMPC)

> But any prophet who fakes it, who claims to speak in my name
> something I haven't commanded him to say, or speaks in the name
> of other gods, that prophet must die. (Deuteronomy 18:20 MSG)

Notice how the wool can get pulled over the eyes of even those who should know better. Why? Because they assume they know it all and are unaccountable. Unfortunately, these self-proclaimed experts sometimes don't have a clue what they don't know. Almost every industry of society appreciates the importance of external evaluations and audits to check on the accuracy of various calibrations and measurements associated with their products or services. How much more should spiritual leaders, publishers, teachers, and preachers ensure the accuracy of measures before they mass-market products with God's name on them. God is the Mathematician of mathematicians and Statistician of statisticians, and He is offended by erroneous measurement tools that appear to be endorsed by Him but are actually misleading.

We need to be precise mediators of God's wisdom, accurate translators of His wonders, real carriers of His glory, authentic dispensers of His kindness, and genuine conduits of His love. The world is restlessly awaiting the revealing of God's actual children—the living memorials and witnesses to His existence. This unveiling must come through humble vessels, through people united through their attachment to God's heart and possession of His mind. Because His people genuinely know Him, they don't misrepresent Him. Because they actually perceive Him, they can and do imitate Him. Because they are attuned to His perspective, they become powerful problem solvers, strong social reformers, and authentic spiritual revivalists. They're captivated by the God of love, have a sound grasp of His love for them, and accurately transmit it to a world that's desperate for it.

Before we proceed to the next chapter, which investigates the relationship management dimension of spiritual intelligence more specifically, let's pray.

God, thank You for inviting me to have a deep and intimate relationship with You. Help me to be a steward of this opportunity with excellence and teach me to lean on You for everything. Help me to evaluate and comprehend what I perceive from You with speed and accuracy. Let me know the difference between what is divine, demonic, or simply my own imagination. Forgive me for any erroneous perceptual processing due to ignorance or limited accountability. Forgive me for ever misrepresenting You to others by sharing revelation knowledge verbally or in writing that was erroneous. May Your Spirit convict and awaken spiritual leaders who facilitate the marketing of spiritual products that are inaccurate and misleading. Reveal any spiritual blind spots I may have and help me to develop the discernment to recognize phony spiritual products. May I continue to grow in spiritual intelligence and maturity so I more fully embrace the realities You want me to experience. Thank You that, while my mind is constantly being renewed and my life is continuously being transformed by Your Spirit, You remain the same yesterday, today, and forever. Thank You for the constancy of Your love, nature, and Word. In Jesus' beautiful name. Amen.

Relationship Management

God-*friendship* is for God-worshipers;
They are the ones he confides in.

—Psalm 25:14 (MSG; emphasis mine)

Relationship management is the fourth dimension of spiritual intelligence. It includes how we relate to God and others. Like the third dimension of perceptual processing, it involves the application of revelation knowledge. The acuity of our spiritual perceptual awareness and the accuracy of our perceptual processing play a significant role in the quality of how we practically release and share revelation knowledge. Whether we utilize revelation knowledge to problem-solve, pray, teach, or publish, it will always have gone through a process of knowledge acquisition and cognitive analysis.

Intelligence utilizes the thinking processes of observation, analysis, reflection, evaluation, and interpretation. However, it needs to translate these into action. Thinking processes alone don't constitute intelligence, just as simply acquiring revelation knowledge isn't intelligence either. Only once revelation knowledge is accurately processed and appropriately applied does it represent actual intelligence. Similarly, only once thinking processes are translated into productive action do they become useful.

People may have phenomenal thinking capabilities and acquire profound revelation knowledge. However, if they relationally fail to deliver and communicate that revelation in an appropriate and accurate manner, it loses its practical utility. It's the relational delivery that's especially relevant in this dimension of spiritual intelligence. Spiritual intelligence demands both accuracy in perceiving what God's saying *and* practical fulfillment of what He's communicating.

Table 1 below provides a summary of the four dimensions of spiritual intelligence and how each dimension relates to what we sense and know (column 2) and what we do (column 3) personally (row 2) and socially (row 3). Personal and social perceptual awareness involves the acquisition of revelation knowledge. Perceptual processing and relationship management involve the application of revelation knowledge.

Table 1: Four Dimensions of Spiritual Intelligence Relative to Self and Others

	What You Sense and Know *(Acquisition)*	What You Do *(Application)*
About Self	Perceptual Awareness (personal)	Perceptual Processing
About Others	Perceptual Awareness (social)	Relationship Management

People with high spiritual intelligence can acquire revelation, accurately manage that revelation cognitively, and effectively apply it behaviorally. If the delivery is inappropriate at the relationship level, even something that was clearly perceived and accurately interpreted can be rendered unfruitful and unproductive. While the acquisition of revelation is valuable, the accurate analysis and application of that revelation is vital. Things like timing of delivery, audience to whom it is delivered, and the mode of communication are all important components of effective application. If the revelation knowledge is poorly stewarded and not clearly communicated in a way the recipients can understand, it loses its usefulness.

Cultural intelligence with its associated effective cross-cultural communication skills can be helpful here, especially in international contexts. Emotional intelligence with its emphasis on empathy and social skills would also be beneficial. Careful choice of words that aren't mystical, confusing, or religious sounding would be valuable too. The context (public or private) of the delivery (verbal or in writing) would also matter. Having the capacity to communicate with simplicity, clarity, and humility is also important in promoting this dimension of spiritual intelligence. Effective operation of the gifts of the Spirit and the demonstration of all the fruits of the Spirit, especially love, all form part of this dimension of spiritual intelligence as well.

What can also diminish the effectiveness of this dimension of spiritual intelligence is being overly hasty. If revelation knowledge is poorly processed due to a rushed analysis, carelessness, or haphazard commitment, this can have very negative consequences for the relationship management component of spiritual intelligence. People with high spiritual intelligence clearly perceive, carefully process, and compassionately deliver revelation knowledge in a way that honors the recipient(s). Revelation can be delivered through a message, a teaching, a podcast, a prayer, a song, or a book, for example. Even when the revelation pertains to something challenging and difficult like a warning or correction, the recipients should be able to sense the genuine care, humility, and empathy on the part of the deliverer or communicator. Without this, trust may be breached, and respect may be ruptured, thereby undermining the practical worth of what is shared.

The relationship management dimension of spiritual intelligence most importantly involves investing in our relationship with God the Father, Jesus, and the Holy Spirit, paying due attention relationally to each of them. The higher our spiritual intelligence, the healthier, more vibrant, and more fruitful our relationship with God will be. Additionally, as people grow in spiritual intelligence, they will increasingly display the fruits (Galatians 5:22–23) and gifts (1 Corinthians 12) of the Holy Spirit in their relationships with people. We'll investigate the gifts of the Spirit later in this chapter and further explore the fruits of the Spirit in the next chapter.

KNOWING GOD THROUGH FIRSTHAND EXPERIENCE

Let's explore the dimension of relationship management in light of the most profound relationship we can possibly have. That relationship is the relationship we get to develop with God. Without spiritual intelligence and the ability to perceive with our spiritual senses that He is alive, we will struggle to relate to Him. Moreover, without our ability to accurately process and interpret what we perceive in the Word of God or by the Spirit of God, we won't be able to get to know Him for who He *really* is. If you can't know someone for who they really are, it is difficult to rely on that person and tough to develop real trust, right? That's why it's God's desire that all people genuinely come to know Him for themselves and not through secondhand information or religious obligation. He wants to develop a personal and intimate relationship with all of us and designed our hearts and minds in such a way that we could interact and fellowship with Him. It was His motive behind creation. No other relationship will ever be as fulfilling, and nothing else will satisfy our quest for knowledge in the way that truly knowing God does.

This relationship with God is birthed when our spirits are transformed and born again. Jesus said that unless people are born again, they cannot ever see (know, be acquainted with, and experience) the kingdom of God (John 3:3). This spiritual rebirth is essential to beginning a relationship with God, but to develop an *intimate* relationship with Him, we need to be filled *and* remain filled with the Holy Spirit. Jesus is the one who fills us with the Holy Spirit (Matthew 3:11), and the Holy Spirit then empowers us with divine ability, efficiency, and might. "But you shall receive power (ability, efficiency, and might) when the Holy Spirit has come upon you, and you shall be My witnesses in Jerusalem and all Judea and Samaria and to the ends (the very bounds) of the earth" (Acts 1:8 AMPC).

Let's think about the implication of this for a moment. The Father, who already sent His Son to die a brutal death so we could access the free gift of salvation, also wants us to have the gift of His Spirit? His generosity is almost too amazing to fathom. He doesn't just want us spiritually born anew; He wants us empowered with capabilities, proficiencies, and gifts to be His witnesses. The apostle Paul was emphatic. "But ever be filled *and* stimulated with the [Holy] Spirit" (Ephesians 5:18 AMPC).

The verb phrase "be filled" is a causative verb in the active voice and hence literally means to go on being filled with the Spirit. This infilling isn't necessarily confined to a single event, so never feel ashamed of having to get refilled if you didn't genuinely experience the Holy Spirit in a fresh, new way at first or if you don't still enjoy the Holy Spirit's amazing enabling power after years of walking with Jesus. Whether you still need to be filled or perceive that you need to be refilled, be sure to embrace the experience since it's vital for sustaining high spiritual intelligence. A prayer to help you do so is contained in Appendix B.

ADVANCING OUR SPIRITUAL SIGNAL STRENGTH

Let me use an analogy that may illustrate how some of you may feel when it comes to your intimacy with the Holy Spirit. Being filled with the Holy Spirit is like being continuously connected to the internet through a wide-bandwidth transmission that readily transfers data, images, and signals. Knowing Him intimately is like having an advanced spiritual signal booster that facilitates and enhances our spiritual perceptual awareness and the accuracy of our perceptual processing capacity. To access and advance our personal relationship with Him, we all need to ensure we remain strongly connected to Him. Without this link, we miss out on hearing what He is signaling or speaking to us, and we consequently struggle to follow His guidance and direction. It's through the Holy Spirit that we are empowered to do all God has called us to and to faithfully steward what He shares with us. Without a resilient connection to His enabling power, we end up doing things out of presumption or own strength, which is unsustainable and eventually leads to burnout. It's not by our power or strength but by the Spirit of God. "Then he said to me, 'This [continuous supply of oil] is the word of the Lord to Zerubbabel [prince of Judah], saying, "Not by might, nor by power, but by My Spirit [of whom the oil is a symbol]," says the Lord of hosts'" (Zechariah 4:6 AMP).

Knowing the Holy Spirit gives us the capacity to sense and know things through His eyes. He is the Source of revelation knowledge. Since He lives inside us when we turn our lives over to Jesus, this is entirely possible and biblical. The more we get to know Him and the stronger our relationship is with Him, the clearer our spiritual, visual acuity becomes. This is true for all our spiritual senses. The more we interact with Him and follow His guidance, the stronger our connection to Him becomes. We partake of the very activity Jesus employed while on earth. He observed through His spiritual senses what the Father was saying to Him and faithfully obeyed.

All those who endeavor to apply revelation knowledge appropriately must first process that revelation with accuracy. Even Jesus always carefully checked everything He perceived. He recognized and acknowledged that He could do nothing without the help of His Father. Nor would He judge out of His own opinion. He waited for the assessment given by His Father through the Holy Spirit. He accurately perceived what the Father was saying, and He carefully judged based on what He perceived through the Spirit of God. He wasn't perceiving to please Himself; He was seeking only to please the One who had sent Him.

> So Jesus answered them by saying, I assure you, most solemnly I tell you, the Son is able to do *nothing* of Himself (of His own accord); but He is able to do *only* what He sees the *Father* doing, for whatever the Father does is what the Son does in the same way [in His turn]. (John 5:19 AMPC; emphasis mine)

> I am able to do *nothing* from Myself [independently, of My own accord—but only as I am taught by God and as I get His orders]. Even as I hear, I judge [I decide as I am bidden to decide. As the voice comes to Me, so I give a decision], and My judgment is right (just, righteous), because I do not seek *or* consult My own will [I have no desire to do what is pleasing to Myself, My own aim, My own purpose] but *only* the will *and* pleasure of the *Father* Who sent Me. (John 5:30 AMPC; emphasis mine)

Ponder the immensity of Jesus' statements. He said He could do *nothing* on His own, apart from what the Father was communicating to Him through His Spirit. Knowing the Bible never exaggerates; this is quite a strong word. How much more should we acknowledge that we can do nothing of eternal worth without the Holy Spirit guiding and directing us. Apart from our connection to Him, we can do nothing. In today's terms, apart from Him, we remain disconnected and are denied access to the very Source of everything we need to live well. Take a look at some additional verses where Jesus used the definitive word *nothing*.

> So Jesus said, "When you lift up the Son of Man [on the cross], you will know then [without any doubt] that I am *He*, and that I do *nothing* on My own authority, but I say these things just as My Father taught Me."
> (John 8:28 AMP; emphasis mine)

> I am the Vine; you are the branches. The one who remains in Me and I in him bears much fruit, for [otherwise] apart from Me [that is, cut off from vital union with Me] you can do *nothing*.
> (John 15:5 AMP; emphasis mine)

Apart from a close connection to the Father through the Holy Spirit, we simply cannot produce fruit (John 15:4). The Holy Spirit empowers us, fills us with love, gives us spiritual gifts to share, and enables us to produce the kind of spiritual fruit associated with high spiritual intelligence.

SPIRITUAL BLIND SPOTS AND SHORTSIGHTEDNESS

Unfortunately, when people have only low spiritual intelligence, the delivery of revelation knowledge is often poorly applied. They sense and know only partially, have the propensity to make perceptual errors, and struggle to display consistent love toward others. While not spiritually blind like those with no spiritual intelligence, those with low spiritual intelligence are spiritually shortsighted or have spiritual blind spots. It's like an acquaintance who knows about you but not to the extent of a close friend. They presume to know and perhaps talk about you to others as though they "know" you, but they only know very little about you. Just as you may be offended when people misrepresent you, even if inadvertently, so, too, people who present God in a way that's contrary to His nature and personality offend Him. They may say things like, "Thus says the Lord" when the Lord isn't saying that. They may deliver things in a way that makes you think that is the heart of God, when in actual fact it is totally contrary to His heart. They may elevate a person and remark on their legacy, but in reality, that "famous" person is totally the opposite of the kind of person who is popular in heaven.

The Lord has tons of mercy and is slow to anger and easily forgives when people are genuinely repentant, but the personal relationship people have with God will definitely be affected when they misrepresent Him. As we saw in the previous chapter, ministers may still be able to market their misleading products, but their spiritual intelligence will be downgraded. They may be able to profit from their products and grow in earthly popularity and people's praises, but their popularity in heaven and actual spiritual intelligence will decline. Their salvation may still be guaranteed, their calling may still be intact, but their intimacy with God will be affected.

> Woe to (alas for) you when everyone speaks fairly *and* handsomely of you *and* praises you, for even so their forefathers did to the false prophets. (Luke 6:26 AMPC)

> The fear of man brings a snare, but whoever leans on, trusts in, and puts his confidence in the Lord is safe and set on high. (Proverbs 29:25 AMPC)

FRIENDSHIP WITH GOD IS CONDITIONAL

If you really love and fear God, you will get to know Him—His heart, desires, and interests—and quickly rearrange your life to fit in with Him (not the reverse). The fear of the Lord is the beginning of knowledge (Proverbs 1:7), not just the product of knowledge. When you genuinely fear God and love Him with a first love, you will hunger for His counsel, wisdom, thoughts, secrets; and to share His mind—not because of what He will do for you but because of what you can do for Him.

> The *secret* of the sweet, satisfying *companionship* of the Lord have they who fear (revere and worship) Him, and He will show them His covenant and reveal to them its [deep, inner] meaning. (Psalm 25:14 AMPC; emphasis mine)

> You are My *friends if* you do whatever I command you. No longer do I call you servants, for a servant does not know what his master

is doing; but I have called you friends, for all things that I heard from My Father I have made known to you. (John 15:14–15 AMP; emphasis mine)

Notice the words I've highlighted like *secret, companionship, friends,* and *if.* When we are a close friend of God, He reveals secrets to us, and our perceptual awareness is expanded. That close companionship also enhances our capacity to precisely discern things and more accurately demonstrate His nature. Friendship with God, like all deep and intimate relationships, involves trust and time together. It isn't automatic simply because we believe in Him. His love for us is unconditional, but close friendship with Him *is* conditional. We are friends of God if we do whatever He commands us. This is why we pray that God will give us a perceiving heart and insight so we can do whatever He tells us.

> GOD, teach me lessons for living so I can *stay* the course. Give me *insight* so I can *do* what you tell me—my whole life one long, obedient response. Guide me down the road of your commandments; I love traveling this freeway! Give me a bent for your words of wisdom, and not for piling up loot. Divert my *eyes* from toys and trinkets, invigorate me on the pilgrim way. Affirm your promises to me—promises made to all who fear you. Deflect the harsh words of my critics—but what you say is always so good. See how *hungry* I am for your counsel; preserve my life through your righteous ways! (Psalm 119:33–40 MSG; emphasis mine)

HOW WE MANAGE OUR RELATIONSHIP WITH GOD INFLUENCES HOW WE RELATE TO OTHERS

All well-managed relationships are rooted in love. It is the greatest gift, the pinnacle attribute, the culminating feature, and the true litmus test for high spiritual intelligence. Even the supernatural ability to operate in all the spiritual gifts, which we'll explore shortly, and have faith to move mountains pales in comparison to possessing and manifesting God's love in relationships. Not surprisingly, the enemy of our souls has worked overtime to pervert the definition of love and our understanding of it. You may have even heard well-meaning people say, "Love is a decision" as though love were controlled by a mental process we conjure up through our strength because the Bible instructs us to.

If you are a child of God and share in the divine nature and mind of God, then divine love comes easily. Moreover, the closer you get to God and interact with Him, the more you become like Him, and the easier it becomes to love as He loves. This love flows from Him, as we sync our hearts with His, *not* from our own thought-processing or decision-making capacity. That's why God can demand that we love Him with all our passion, prayer, muscle, and intelligence—and love others as ourselves. That's why He can demand that we love Him with a first love above all else because He supplies us with the grace to do so when our minds are connected to His. We are transformed into His likeness by renewing our minds and taking on the mind of the Holy Spirit, who is life and soul peace.

> Now the mind of the flesh [which is sense and reason without the Holy Spirit] is death [death that comprises all the miseries arising from sin, both here and hereafter]. But the *mind of the [Holy] Spirit* is life and [soul] peace [both now and forever]. [That is] because the mind of the flesh [with its carnal thoughts and purposes] is *hostile* to God, for it does not submit itself to God's Law; indeed it cannot. So then those who are living the life of the flesh [catering to the appetites and impulses of their carnal nature] cannot please *or* satisfy God, *or* be acceptable to Him. But you are not living the life of the flesh, you are living the life of the Spirit, if the [Holy] Spirit of God [*really*] dwells within you [directs and controls you]. But if anyone does not possess the [Holy] Spirit of Christ, he is none of His [he does not belong to Christ, is not *truly* a child of God]. (Romans 8:6–9 AMPC; emphasis mine)

Just as our smartphones may have a measure of downloaded information that doesn't require a Wi-Fi connection to access, so too, parabolically speaking, we may have a measure of appreciation for God's love saved on our "hard drive." However, nothing compares to the limitless, real-time flow of God's love "livestreamed" directly from Him, traveling through us, and being dispensed to others. This is what happens in moments of genuine oneness with God when our focus is honed on Him in worship and prayer, and our revelation of His beauty, majesty, brilliance, and eminence is magnified. This is intimacy with God, who is love, which is attainable by His meticulous design. No other love can compare to this. "And so we know and rely on the love God has for us. God is love. Whoever lives in love lives in God, and God in them" (1 John 4:16 NIV).

I like how The Message puts it: "This is how we know we're living *steadily* and *deeply in him*, and *he in us*: He's given us life from his life, from his very own Spirit. Also, we've seen for ourselves and continue to state openly that the Father sent his Son as Savior of the world. Everyone who confesses that Jesus is God's Son participates continuously in an *intimate relationship* with God. We know it so well, we've embraced it heart and soul, this love that comes from God" (1 John 4:16 MSG; emphasis mine).

TRUSTEES OF GOD'S DIVERSE POWERS AND GIFTS

We are living steadily and deeply in Him, and He in us. We are receiving life from His life through an intimate relationship with God. This intimacy with God, since He is spirit, can be achieved only through the Holy Spirit. This deep intimacy involves having access to some of God's innermost thoughts and the feelings of His heart. Relating to Him this way opens up an entirely new dimension of wisdom, counsel, revelation, and insight to us. God wants to be deeply and personally involved in our lives, and one of the many ways He shares His thoughts and purposes is through the gifts of His Spirit.

Everyone filled with the Spirit of God is given spiritual gifts to be used as they relate with others. Spiritual gifts are given as one of the many ways God imparts spiritual intelligence to His people. God also releases revelation through dreams and visions (Job 33:15). While the gift of the Holy Spirit empowers us to develop an intimate relationship with God, the Holy Spirit gives us spiritual gifts to enable us to relate more effectively with people. Those with high spiritual intelligence regularly practice the gifts of the Spirit and dispense them well. Remember that spiritual gifts are only temporal, but spiritual intelligence and the fruits of the Spirit are eternal.

> As *each* of you has received a gift (a particular spiritual talent, a gracious divine endowment), *employ* it for one another as [befits] good *trustees* of God's many-sided grace [faithful *stewards* of the *extremely diverse powers and gifts* granted to Christians by *unmerited* favor]. (1 Peter 4:10 AMPC; emphasis mine)

> Love never fails [never fades out or becomes obsolete or comes to an end]. As for prophecy (the gift of interpreting the divine will and purpose), it will be fulfilled *and* pass away; as for tongues, they will be destroyed *and* cease; as for knowledge, it will pass away [it will lose its value and be superseded by truth]. For our knowledge is fragmentary (incomplete and imperfect), and our prophecy (our teaching) is fragmentary (incomplete and imperfect). (1 Corinthians 13:8–9 AMPC; emphasis mine).

Notice in 1 Peter 4:10 that each believer receives a particular spiritual talent that needs to be employed. In other words, these gifts aren't just for a select few but for *all* God's children. Moreover, the gifts aren't for us but for others. We are merely the conduits for dispensing them. The gifts and callings of God are given by His unmerited favor and are unchangeable (Romans 11:29), meaning, you cannot try to create your own gifts or calling; you can employ only what God has given you and endeavor to be an excellent trustee and faithful steward of those gifts.

Note how the author of Hebrews makes it clear that the gifts of the Holy Spirit are granted to believers according to God's will, not theirs. I've emphasized this truth here. "[And besides this evidence] God also testifying with them [confirming the message of salvation], both by signs and wonders and by various miracles [carried out by Jesus and the apostles] and by [granting to believers the] gifts of the Holy Spirit *according to His own will*" (Hebrews 2:4 AMP).

GENEROUSLY DONATING SPIRITUAL GIFTS

The Latin word for "gift" is *donum*, from which the word *donor* is derived. As we know, a donor is someone who donates and contributes to a good cause. Our spiritual gifts aren't meant to be dormant but donated to God's purposes. The Greek word for "gift" is *dorea* which means "gratuity."[33] A gratuity is "something given voluntarily or beyond obligation," according to *Merriam-Webster's Dictionary*.[34] So we steward these spiritual gratuities, not as a means to gain salvation but beyond that, as a means to relate well with others and to bring God's kingdom to earth. The gifts of the Spirit empower us to continue Jesus' ministry on earth. Read how the apostle Paul associated anointing with the gifts of the Spirit.

> Now it is God who establishes and confirms us [in joint fellowship] with you in Christ, and who has anointed us [empowering us with the gifts of the Spirit]. (2 Corinthians 1:21 AMP)

> That is why I would remind you to stir up (rekindle the embers of, fan the flame of, and keep burning) the [gracious] gift of God, [the inner fire] that is in you by means of the laying on of my hands [with those of the elders at your ordination]. (2 Timothy 1:6 AMP)

The Message Bible says we shouldn't be shy with God's gifts but "bold," "loving," and "sensible" in their dispensation; to keep the gift "ablaze."

> That precious memory triggers another: your honest faith—and what a rich faith it is, handed down from your grandmother Lois to your mother Eunice, and now to you! And the special gift of ministry you received when I laid hands on you and prayed—keep that ablaze! God doesn't want us to be shy with his gifts, but bold and loving and sensible. (2 Timothy 1:6 MSG)

Without using and donating the gifts of the Holy Spirit with boldness, love, and sensibility, we inhibit the power for transformational change God intended for the recipients of the gifts. God's intended change may include the movement from spiritual ignorance to spiritual understanding or a shift from a state of depression and discouragement to a place of encouragement and mental well-being. That's why the apostle Paul was so adamant when he implored the Corinthians not to be misinformed about the spiritual gifts. Other translations of 1 Corinthians 12:1 say not to be ignorant or uninformed or unaware. "Now about the spiritual gifts (the special endowments of supernatural energy), brethren, I do not want you to be misinformed" (1 Corinthians 12:1 AMP).

Spiritual ignorance is the opposite of spiritual intelligence. Being unaware of spiritual gifts or unfit in their dispensation undermines the advancement of God's kingdom and hinders the development of spiritual maturity among believers.

Notice how 1 Corinthians 12 highlights the distinctive varieties and distributions of these gifts. The Holy Spirit is the primary motivator, manufacturer, and distributor of these gifts' and they aren't dependent on title, profession, or age.

> Now about the spiritual gifts (the special endowments of supernatural energy), brethren, I do not want you to be misinformed. You know that when you were heathen, you were led off after idols that could not speak [habitually] as impulse directed *and* whenever the occasion might arise. Therefore I want you to understand that no one speaking under the power *and* influence of the [Holy] Spirit of God can [ever] say, Jesus be cursed! And no one can [really] say, Jesus is [my] Lord, except by *and* under the power *and* influence of the Holy Spirit. Now there are distinctive varieties *and* distributions of endowments (gifts, extraordinary powers distinguishing certain Christians, due to the power of divine grace operating in their souls by the Holy Spirit) and they vary, but the [Holy] Spirit remains the same. And there are distinctive varieties of service *and* ministration, but it is the same Lord [who is served]. And there are distinctive varieties of operation [of working to accomplish things], but it is the same God Who inspires *and* energizes them all in all. But to each one is given the manifestation of the [Holy] Spirit [the evidence, the spiritual illumination of the Spirit] for good *and* profit. (1 Corinthians 12:1–7 AMPC)

The last verse makes it clear, like in 1 Peter 4:10, that each believer is given the "manifestation" of the Holy Spirit for good and profit. Verses 8 through 10 below highlight very specifically the nine key spiritual gifts. These include words of wisdom, words of knowledge, gifts of faith, powers of healing, miracles, prophetic insight, discernment of spirits, tongues, and interpretation of tongues.

> To one is given in *and* through the [Holy] Spirit [the power to speak] a message of wisdom, and to another [the power to express] a word of knowledge *and* understanding according to the same [Holy] Spirit; To another [wonder-working] faith by the same [Holy] Spirit, to another the extraordinary powers of healing by the one Spirit; To another the working of miracles, to another prophetic insight the gift of interpreting the divine will and purpose); to another the ability to discern *and* distinguish between [the utterances of true] spirits [and false ones], to another various kinds of [unknown] tongues, to another the ability to interpret [such] tongues. (1 Corinthians 12:8–10 AMPC)

Verses 11–13 below reiterate that these gifts are inspired and brought to pass by the Holy Spirit, who distributes them to each person as He chooses. Believers, whether Jew or Gentile, are all baptized into one body and made to partake of one Holy Spirit.

> All these [gifts, achievements, abilities] are inspired *and* brought to pass by one and the same [Holy] Spirit, Who apportions to each person individually [exactly] as He chooses. For just as the body is a unity and yet has many parts, and all the parts, though many, form [only] one body, so it is with Christ (the Messiah, the Anointed One). For by [[means of the personal agency of] one [Holy] Spirit we were all, whether Jews or Greeks, slaves or free, baptized [and by baptism united together] into one body, and all made to drink of one [Holy] Spirit. (1 Corinthians 12:11–13 AMPC)

I trust you are noticing the ongoing reference to the Holy Spirit for the inspiration and dispensation of these gifts. Without perceptual awareness and accurate processing of the information derived from these spiritual gifts, our relationship with God and others, and our ability to rightly deliver the gift, is inhibited.

Shawn Bolz, in his book *God Secrets*, offers some excellent tools to help manage relationships when operating in a spiritual gift, particularly words of knowledge. Shawn's book is loaded with stories and practical advice for spiritual growth. Listen to his approach.

In my ministry, I have lowered the stakes by using language and communication in a different way. I ask questions and leverage more of a relational language for communicating words of knowledge or prophecy. The majority of models of prophecy have someone saying a run-on sentence to someone they've just met—a personal message he or she says originates with God. There is little or no interaction, no fact finding, no rapport building, and no feedback. If we want to grow and change the stakes, we have to change this prevailing model. Here's an undeniable truth: If God is the most relational being in the universe, then as people created in His image we're allowed to also be people who relate to others.[35]

While training and practice are essential to improve perceptual awareness and accurate analysis and delivery of spiritual data, every spiritual gift needs to be dispensed appropriately. Some of our traditional modes of delivery need to be reexamined, and better relational strategies need to be employed. While we don't want to compromise or dilute the information we've perceived and processed, we want to be more careful with how, when, and where we relate to people to achieve the optimal results. So, for example, words of knowledge and words of wisdom perceived by the Spirit of God and then delivered to the intended recipients become more like conversations. Prophecy is also inherently relational and therefore highly conducive to a conversation without using hyper-spiritual, religious jargon.

Ultimately, the relationship management dimension of spiritual intelligence, when well executed, gives genuine friends of God the capacity to radiate His love, demonstrate His purposes, and activate His solutions in the natural realm. They become carriers of His glory, image bearers of His goodness, and living testaments to His existence.

HALLMARKS AND HAND BRAKES OF SPIRITUAL INTELLIGENCE

Now that we have covered the main dimensions of spiritual intelligence, Table 2 below provides a summary of the definitions, key hallmarks, and hand brakes associated with each of them. Hallmarks refer to the chief characteristics associated with people who are well developed in each dimension. Hand brakes refer to the main inhibitors that constrain or undermine the development of each of the dimensions. These hallmarks and hand brakes help identify some of the main activities people should be more engaged in to advance and strengthen their overall spiritual intelligence. Practical strategies to develop some of these hallmarks and overcome some of these hand brakes will be covered later in this book.

Table 2: The Dimensions of Spiritual Intelligence: Hallmarks and Hand Brakes

Dimension	Definition	Hallmarks	Hand Brakes
Personal Perceptual Awareness *(Dimension I)*	The supernatural ability to employ your spiritual senses to experience the spiritual realm and acquire revelation knowledge.	• Know who you are in God. • Know the Word of God. • Have strong faith in God and the promises in His Word. • Appreciate divine purpose and identity. • Appreciate divine calling, role, and responsibilities. • Conscious of spiritual gifts, talents, and abilities. • Attentive to personal divine dreams and visions. • Alert to the unseen realm. • Thirst for wisdom. • Practice quick repentance as a lifestyle. • Regularly conduct realistic self-evaluations. • Maintain a clear conscience.	• Loss of first love for God. • Limited prayer life. • Inconsistency in personal study of the Bible. • Inconsistency in personal relationship with God. • Ignorance about spiritual gifts. • Irreverence. • Confusion about divine purpose and identity. • Deception regarding calling, role, and responsibilities. • Denial about actual spiritual condition. • Spiritual apathy. • Perceptual dullness. • Spiritual blind spots. • Seared conscience. • Unforgiveness.

Dimension	Definition	Hallmarks	Hand Brakes
Social Perceptual Awareness *(Dimension II)*	The supernatural ability to apply your spiritual senses to experience the spiritual realm and acquire revelation knowledge.	• Sensitive to the heart and mind of God. • Sensitive to the needs and desires of others. • Attuned to feelings and emotions of others. • Appreciate the thoughts and views of others. • Attentive to divine dreams and visions about others. • Recognize spiritual gifts, talents, and abilities in others.	• Limited prayer life. • Loveless heart. • Judgmental attitude. • Negativism. • Unforgiveness. • Pride. • Criticism. • Self-absorption. • Selfishness. • Ignorance. • Worry. • Spiritual blind spots.
Perceptual Processing *(Dimension III)*	The supernatural ability to effectively process revelation knowledge, accurate discernment, and efficient interpretation of what was perceived.	• Accurately analyze. • Effectively interpret. • Thoroughly evaluate. • Efficiently translate. • Have depth of comprehension. • Effectively manage discernment. • Have extensive knowledge of the Word of God. • Have memory strength and capacity.	• Limited biblical knowledge. • Inadequate biblical meditation. • Unrenewed mind. • Unforgiveness. • Pride. • Lack of accountability. • Poor memory. • Haste. • Lack of discipline in recording or reviewing Scripture. • Inexperience in the supernatural. • Fear of failure. • Limited prayer life. • Personal mental strongholds contrary to the Word of God.
Relationship Management *(Dimension IV)*	The ability to deliver and share revelation knowledge appropriately and pragmatically, demonstrating sensitivity to the following: • Audience • Authority	• Interact with love, kindness, and compassion. • Exercise spiritual gifts with excellence. • Have strength and courage. • Possess discipline, discretion, and restraint. • Have humility and purity.	• Lack of the fear of God. • Limited prayer life. • Pride and judgmental attitude. • Lack of accountability. • Fear of man. • Limited genuine fellowship with other believers. • Easily offended.

Dimension	Definition	Hallmarks	Hand Brakes
	• Recipient • Culture • Context • Content • Communication • Delivery • Timing • Tone	• Be effective in developing others. • Be responsive to the needs of others. • Deliver timeously and clearly. • Appropriately select the mode of communication and audience. • Communicate in a culturally appropriate way. • Demonstrate empathy and care.	• Lack of practicing spiritual gifts. • Discomfort with risk-taking. • Poor social skills. • Limited empathy. • Low cultural intelligence. • Low emotional intelligence.

Before we proceed to the next chapter, which examines the degrees, features, and fruits of spiritual intelligence, let's pray.

God, thank You for our relationship. May it grow in intimacy and strength. Help me to identify my personal spiritual intelligence hallmarks and hand brakes. Show me how to develop each of the dimensions of my spiritual intelligence and free me from the habits and attitudes that constrain their advancement. Help me to perceive and practice the spiritual gifts You impart specifically to me. Expand my capacity to dispense Your gifts in ways that are more relational and conversational. Help me to convey Your love, thoughts, and feelings for people with accuracy, ease, and clarity. Let me be wiser with what, how, and when I relate to people about You. Help me to continue to grow in spiritual intelligence so I can not only acquire revelation from You but also appropriately apply it so it produces transformative results and practical solutions. Help me to help others more fully understand the spiritual wealth You offer. May I be a conduit of Your love, a diligent dispenser of Your kindness, and a clear communicator of Your compassion for humanity. In Jesus' mighty name. Amen.

CHAPTER
6

Degrees, Features, and Fruits of Spiritual Intelligence

> Every tree that does not bear good fruit is cut down
> and cast into the fire. Therefore, you will fully know
> them by their fruits. Not everyone who says to Me,
> Lord, Lord, will enter the kingdom of heaven, but he
> who does the will of My Father Who is in heaven.
>
> —Matthew 7:19–21 (AMPC)

So far, we've explored what spiritual intelligence is, including its hallmarks, potential hand brakes, and each dimension associated with it. In this chapter, we'll examine a spectrum of degrees associated with spiritual intelligence as well as their key features and corresponding fruits. The degrees include high spiritual intelligence, low spiritual intelligence, no spiritual intelligence, and counterfeit spiritual intelligence (illustrated in Figure 2 below).

Figure 2: Degrees of Spiritual Intelligence

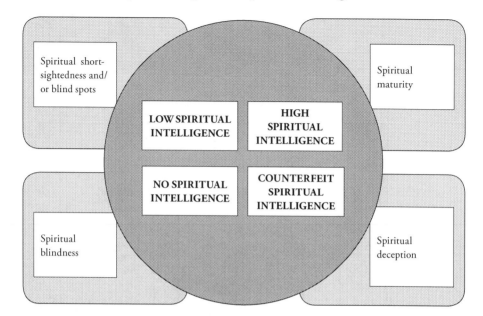

DEGREES, FEATURES, AND FRUITS OF SPIRITUAL INTELLIGENCE

Jesus, speaking parabolically, taught that we would be able to fully know people by examining the fruits associated with their lives. "Thus, by their fruit you will recognize them." (Matthew 7:20 NIV).

We need to heed the words of the One who loves us with the most profound love. We need to be alert and pay attention to the fruits and displays of our genuine spiritual condition. We need to manage personal change in our lives as a consequence of what those fruits are indicating. At times, they serve as a warning of imminent danger and approaching calamity. At other times, they may be indicative that things are in order and progressing healthily. The fruits of high spiritual intelligence are abundant and include things like a potent first love for God, a pure conscience, indescribable joy, peace beyond understanding, phenomenal patience, extreme mercy, genuine kindness, true goodness, amazing faithfulness, authentic humility, and powerful self-restraint.

The diversity, intensity, and quality of these fruits show that even those with significant levels of spiritual intelligence have room to develop and improve. Galatians 5:22–23 highlight the fruits associated with high spiritual intelligence. Conversely, verses 19–21 and 26, to relative degrees, highlight fruits associated with low spiritual intelligence, no spiritual intelligence, or counterfeit intelligence including immorality, impurity, indecency, idolatry, sorcery, enmity, strife, jealousy, ill temper, selfishness, divisions, factions, sects, envy, drunkenness, carousing, vanity, and self-conceit.

> But I say, walk *and* live [habitually] in the [Holy] Spirit [responsive to *and* controlled *and* guided by the Spirit]; then you will certainly not gratify the cravings *and* desires of the flesh (of human nature without God). For the desires of the flesh are opposed to the [Holy] Spirit, and the [desires of the] Spirit are opposed to the flesh (godless human nature); for these are antagonistic to each other [continually withstanding and in conflict with each other], so that you are not free *but* are prevented from doing what you desire to do. But if you are guided (led) by the [Holy] Spirit, you are not subject to the Law. Now the doings (practices) of the flesh are clear (obvious): they are immorality, impurity, indecency, Idolatry, sorcery, enmity, strife, jealousy, anger (ill temper), selfishness, divisions (dissensions), party spirit (factions, sects with peculiar opinions, heresies), Envy, drunkenness, carousing, and the like. I warn you beforehand, just as I did previously, that those who do such things shall not inherit the kingdom of God. But the fruit of the [Holy] Spirit [the work which His presence within accomplishes] is love, joy (gladness), peace, patience (an even temper, forbearance), kindness, goodness (benevolence), faithfulness, Gentleness (meekness, humility), self-control (self-restraint, continence). Against such things there is no law [that can bring a charge]. And those who belong to Christ Jesus (the Messiah) have crucified the flesh (the godless human nature) with its passions and appetites *and* desires. If we live by the [Holy] Spirit, let us also walk by the Spirit. [If by the Holy Spirit we have our life in God, let us go forward walking in line, our conduct controlled by the Spirit.] Let us not become vainglorious *and* self-conceited, competitive *and* challenging *and* provoking *and* irritating to one another, envying *and* being jealous of one another. (Galatians 5:16–26 AMPC)

Everyone longs to satisfy the yearnings of their soul. Galatians 5:16 highlights that only by living habitually in the Holy Spirit is this achievable. *Habitual* denotes serial and deeply entrenched behavior, not an occasional or intermittent responsiveness to the Holy Spirit.

Take a look at how the Bible links intelligence with the fruit of love. As we exercise diligence, faith, and virtue to develop intelligence (which I've highlighted for emphasis), we exhibit the fruits of self-control, patience, and love.

> For this very reason, adding your diligence [to the divine promises], employ every effort in exercising your faith to develop virtue (excellence, resolution, Christian energy), and in [exercising] virtue [develop] knowledge (*intelligence*), And in [exercising] knowledge [develop] self-control, and in [exercising] self-control [develop] steadfastness (patience, endurance), and in [exercising] steadfastness [develop] godliness (piety), And in [exercising] godliness [develop] brotherly affection, and in [exercising] brotherly affection [develop] Christian love. (2 Peter 1:5–7 AMPC)

THE MOST IMPORTANT FRUIT OF SPIRITUAL INTELLIGENCE

Genuine first love toward God, displayed in authentic compassion toward humanity, is at the apex of high spiritual intelligence. When spiritual intelligence is optimal, love isn't something people merely try or pretend to do. It is something that flows from the ultimate Source thereof. It is unconstrained, unconditional, and free of any cognitive dissonance between what people profess and what people actually feel in their hearts. It's only by this authentic love that the world will get real revelation of the fact that we belong to God and that He is indeed love. Those who don't love don't really know God. How can we expect the world to "perceive" Him if we're not reflecting His reality because we don't know Him intimately?

> By this everyone will *know* that you are My disciples, if you have *love and unselfish* concern for one another (John 13:35 AMPC; emphasis mine)

> But if one loves God truly [with affectionate *reverence, prompt obedience*, and grateful recognition of His blessing], he is known by God [recognized as worthy of His *intimacy* and love, and he is owned by Him]. (1 Corinthians 8:3 AMPC; emphasis mine)

> He who does not *love* has not become acquainted with God [does not and never did *know* Him], for God is *love*. (1 John 4:8 AMPC; emphasis mine)

It's this genuine love for God and this type of personal revelation knowledge of Him that is at the core of genuine spiritual intelligence. This love becomes fully apparent when we have a real-time revelation of His person and actually perceive Him for ourselves. We catch a glimpse of His glory and gaze with our spiritual eyes on His beauty and attractiveness. We perceive His presence, and the eyes of our understanding are enlightened. We begin to grasp His magnificence and majesty, and we respond with awe and wonder. From this perspective and vantage point, we can view Him for who He really is and more accurately perceive His countenance. Once we grasp and appreciate His magnificence and get a taste of His goodness, we can't help but respond by worshipping Him. This is an example of spiritual intelligence in action. We perceive His presence with our spiritual senses (perceptual awareness), we accurately comprehend and grasp His love toward us (perceptual processing), and we respond by relating to Him and interacting with Him with praise, prayer, and adoration (relationship management).

Table 3 below highlights some of the key features and fruits associated with each degree of spiritual intelligence. The features underscore the main qualities associated with each degree of spiritual intelligence. The fruits highlight biblical examples of things that may be associated with each degree of spiritual intelligence. Table 3 is intended to integrate and clarify, to serve as a heuristic, and not to be an all-encompassing, exhaustive inclusion of every type of feature and fruit that may be associated with spiritual intelligence.

Table 3: The Degrees, Features, and Fruits of Spiritual Intelligence

Degrees	Description	Features	Fruits
High Spiritual Intelligence	The supernatural ability to acquire and accurately process spiritual information with the appropriate, life-enhancing application.	• Have a strong and intimate relationship with God. • Know God personally and firsthand. • Have wisdom and revelation knowledge of God and His Word. • Possess first love for God. • Fear God. • Have an inclusive love for all people, including enemies. • Possess an extensive prayer life. • Have a good, clear conscience (1 Timothy 1:5). • Diligently study the Bible. • Habitually worship God. • Conduct regular realistic self-examinations and practice quick repentance (2 Corinthians 13:5). • Possess clear appreciation for divine purpose and identity. • Have strong appreciation for divine calling, role, and responsibilities. • Be sensitive to the heart and mind of God. • Be sensitive to the needs and desires of others.	• Love, sound judgment, personal discipline, well-balanced mind and self-control (2 Timothy 1:7). • Wisdom, revelation, and intimate insight; true knowledge of God (Ephesians 1:17). • Wisdom, understanding, counsel, strength, knowledge, and the fear of the Lord (Isaiah 11:2). • Fruits of the Spirit and presence of God (Galatians 5:22–23; Ephesians 4:1–2; Romans 8:23), which includes love, joy, peace, patience, kindness, goodness, faithfulness, gentleness, and self-control for the purpose of holiness and character. • Spiritual gifts (1 Corinthians 12:1–9; 4:8; 14:1, 12; 2 Corinthians 1:21; Hebrews 2:4; 1 Peter 4:10; Ephesians 4:13) for the purpose of power. • Goodness, righteousness, and truth (Ephesians 5:9). • Righteousness (Philippians 1:11). • Knowledge and intelligence in every branch of wisdom, including dreams and visions (Daniel 1:17). • Courtesy and gentleness (2 Timothy 2:25).

Degrees	Description	Features	Fruits
High Spiritual Intelligence (continued)		• Have unobtrusive humility and meekness (unselfishness, gentleness, mildness), with patience, bearing with others, *and* making allowances because you love others (Ephesians 4:2).	• Admirable character, moral courage, personal integrity, bearing fruit in every good work, and steadily growing in the knowledge of God with deeper faith, clearer insight, and fervent love for His precepts (Colossians 1:10). • Grace; peace; perfect well-being; all necessary good; all spiritual prosperity; freedom from fears and agitating passions and moral conflicts; full, personal, precise knowledge of God; godliness; Christian love; glory; excellence; virtue; partakers of the divine nature; Christian energy; knowledge; intelligence; self-control; patience; endurance; piety (2 Peter 1:1–7). • Powerful and answered prayers for self and others (James 5:16). • Grace and spiritual peace (peace with God and harmony, unity, and undisturbedness) (Ephesians 1:2). • Compassionate, kind, humble, having quiet strength, disciplined, even tempered, content with second place, quick to forgive an offense (Colossians 3:12–14).

Degrees	Description	Features	Fruits
Low Spiritual Intelligence	Only partially perceive and often inaccurately process spiritual information with sometimes inappropriate and ill-timed delivery and behavioral responses.	• Know about God but not intimately. • Have mainly descriptive knowledge and operational knowledge of God and the Bible. • Have limited revelation knowledge of God. • Read the Bible but don't diligently study it personally. • Understand God based on what others have said about Him. • Pray but do not have a lifestyle of prayer. • Believe that Jesus is Lord but struggle to put faith into action. • Have limited discipline. • Possess spiritual cognitive dissonance. • Doctrinally inexperienced and unskilled.	• Unanswered worry prayers (James 1:8). • Confusion, jealousy, rivalry, selfish ambition. (James 3:13–16). • Discouraged when disciplined (Hebrews 12:5). • Struggle to forgive (Matthew 6:15). • Backsliding and careless ease (Proverbs 1:32). • Idle and unproductive (2 Peter 1:8). • Prone to gossip (Job 15:1–16). • Double minded, unstable, restless (James 1:8). • Easily misled and unstable (Ephesians 4:14). • Spiritual shortsightedness (2 Peter 1:9).
No Spiritual Intelligence	Inability to perceive the spiritual realm and process spiritual information.	• Unable to grasp the reality of the spiritual realm. • Have spiritual eyes that are blind and ears that are deaf (2 Peter 1:9). • Have limited ability to tell right from wrong. • Remain defiant or ignorant.	• Inflated pride, touchy, fretful, resentful (1 Corinthians 13:5). • Trivialize religion and turn spiritual conversation into gossip (Job 15:1–16). • Habitual blasphemy and irreverent use of God's name (Deuteronomy 5:11). • Mocking and scoffing (Proverbs 1:22). • Ignorance and resisting God's will (Ephesians 4:18). • Envious and self-seeking, boasting, and lie against the truth (James 3:13–16). • Fear (1 John 14:18). • Moral decay, rottenness, corruption, covetousness, lust, greed (2 Peter 1:4).

Degrees	Description	Features	Fruits
			• All-consuming but never satisfied wants (Galatians 5:19–21). • Malice, pretense, envy, and hurtful talk (1 Peter 2:1–3). • Oppression (Proverbs 28:16). • Guilty conscience (Hebrews 10:22).
Counterfeit Spiritual Intelligence	Counterfeit spiritual intelligence involves an erroneous analysis of spiritual information and behavioral responses that are misleading and inherently destructive.	Practice activities such as: • Consult mediums and soothsayers (Isaiah 8:19). • Consult mediums or wizards (Leviticus 19:31). • Practice divination, fortune-telling, witchcraft, interpreting omens, sorcery, charm, or spell casting; being a medium or necromancer (Deuteronomy 18:9–14). • Practice murder and sorcery (Revelation 9:21; Jeremiah 27:9). • Worship handmade gods or idols (Jeremiah 10:11–15; 51:17). • Pay homage to idols (Revelation 9:20; Deuteronomy 4:28). • Trust in pagan lies and counterfeit gods (Jeremiah 13:25; Ezekiel 20:28). • Use occult arts and books (Acts 19:19). • Practice divination (Jeremiah 14:14; 27:9). • Counterfeit meditation (Psalm 38:12). • Use magic, omens, *or* witchcraft (or predict events by horoscope or signs and lucky days) (Leviticus 19:26).	• Distress and anguish (Isaiah 8:22) • No peace (Isaiah 48:22). • Destruction and shame (Philippians 3:19) • Death (Romans 6:23; Leviticus 20:27). • Confusion and destruction (Deuteronomy 28:20). • Separation from God (Romans 5:15–17). • Blasphemer of God and persecutor of His church; outrageous and violent aggressor toward believers (1 Timothy 1:13). • Loveless, joyless, paranoid loneliness, brutal temper, uncontrolled, and uncontrollable addictions (Galatians 5:19–21). • Conditional love and affection (John 15:19). • Obsession with evil, hate for the truth 1 (2 Thessalonians 2:9–12). • Contrived doctrine and self–focus (Matthew 7:16). • Lawlessness, violence, and corrupt wisdom (Ezekiel 28:16–17).

Degrees	Description	Features	Fruits
Counterfeit Spiritual Intelligence (continued)		• Worship nature, the moon, or stars (Deuteronomy 4:15–20). • Counterfeit apostles (2 Corinthians 11:13). • Counterfeit prophets who prophesy lies in God's name (Jeremiah 14:14; 23:15; Ezekiel 13:9; 14:10; Lamentations 4:13). • Counterfeit teaching (Galatians 1:7; 5:9). • False preachers (Matthew 7:15–20) • False leaders, deceivers, seducers, imposters (2 John 1:7).	• Puffed up with pride and stupefied with conceit; woefully ignorant; morbid fondness for controversy and disputes and strife, which result in envy and jealousy, quarrels and dissension, abuse and insults and slander, and base suspicions; perpetual friction (1 Timothy 6:3–5). • Vexation, irritation, exasperation, aggravation, annoyance, anger, sorrow, regret, disappointment, worry, unhappiness (Ecclesiastes 1:18). • Delusion, seduction, lying, hypocrisy, and seared conscience (1 Timothy 4:1–2). • No contrition (Revelation 16:9).

HIGH SPIRITUAL INTELLIGENCE

People with high spiritual intelligence have the supernatural capacity to acquire and appropriately apply revelation knowledge received from God. They can clearly perceive and accurately process revelation knowledge with the appropriate behavioral responses. The key distinguishing feature of people with high spiritual intelligence is that they love God with all their passion, prayer, and intelligence. He is their first and vital need, and they fear Him. They have unconditional and inclusive love for all people, including enemies. These individuals have an extensive prayer life, diligently study and meditate on the Word of God, and habitually worship Him. They have a pure conscience and work diligently to keep it clear through a lifestyle of quick repentance. They have extensive firsthand revelation knowledge of God, not just descriptive and operational knowledge about Him and the Bible. In addition to their spiritual rebirth through faith in Jesus, they are filled with the Holy Spirit, and they habitually practice operating in the gifts of the Spirit. They regularly do realistic self-examinations, are accountable, and possess unobtrusive humility and unselfishness.

The fruits of high spiritual intelligence, summarized in Table 3, reflect the nature of Jesus. He is righteous (Philippians 1:11), courteous, and gentle (2 Timothy 2:25). He ministers deliverance (Matthew 12:28). He has intense love for people (2 Peter 1:1–7) and is full of compassion (James 3:17), just to name a few. People with high spiritual intelligence regularly practice the spiritual gifts highlighted in 1 Corinthians 12:8–10 and habitually display the fruits of the Holy Spirit (Galatians 5:22–23). The fruits of love, faith, and hope are the finest and choicest of these fruits, with the greatest being love (1 Corinthians 13:13). Without love, the nine spiritual gifts simply become annoying distractions (1 Corinthians 13:1–2).

> If I speak with the tongues of men and of angels, but have not love [for others growing out of God's love for me], then I have become only a noisy gong or a clanging cymbal [just an annoying distraction]. And if I have the gift of prophecy [and speak a new message from God to the people], and understand all mysteries, and [possess] all knowledge; and if I have all [sufficient] faith so that I can remove mountains, but do not have love [reaching out to others], I am nothing. (1 Corinthians 13:1–2 AMP)

Additionally, without hope you can't even begin to have faith because faith is being sure of what you hope for (Hebrews 11:1–3). Without faith it's impossible to please God (Hebrews 11:6), and without love we can do nothing, are nothing, and gain nothing (1 Corinthians 13:2–3). *Nothing*, as we've seen earlier, is quite a definitive word denoting "of no interest, value, or consequence," according to *Merriam-Webster's Dictionary*.[36] Essentially, it is saying that without love, the nine vital spiritual gifts, as wonderful as they are, are rendered of no consequence.

God's grace gives us the power to be eternally saved, helps us become one with Jesus, empowers us to have His mind, unites us with His Spirit, and blesses us with every spiritual blessing. "All praise to God, the Father of our Lord Jesus Christ, who has blessed us with *every spiritual blessing* in the heavenly realms because we are *united* with Christ" (Ephesians 1:3 NLT; emphasis mine).

Table 3 highlights all the primary fruits of the Holy Spirit from Galatians 5:22–23 and Ephesians 4:1–2. These are listed below, together with additional fruits and outcomes a person closely connected to the Holy Spirit with high spiritual intelligence will generate.

- Love, sound judgment, personal discipline, well-balanced mind and self-control (2 Timothy 1:7).
- Wisdom, revelation, and intimate insight; true knowledge of God (Ephesians 1:17).
- Wisdom, understanding, counsel, strength, knowledge, and the fear of the Lord (Isaiah 11:2).
- Fruits of the Spirit and presence of God (Galatians 5:22–23; Ephesians 4:1–2; Romans 8:23), which includes love, joy, peace, patience, kindness, goodness, faithfulness, gentleness, and self-control for the purpose of holiness and character.
- Spiritual gifts (1 Corinthians 12:1–9; 4:8; 14:1, 12; 2 Corinthians 1:21; Hebrews 2:4; 1 Peter 4:10; Ephesians 4:13) for the purpose of power.
- Goodness, righteousness, and truth (Ephesians 5:9).
- Righteousness (Philippians 1:11).
- Knowledge and intelligence in every branch of wisdom, including dreams and visions (Daniel 1:17).
- Courtesy and gentleness (2 Timothy 2:25).
- Admirable character, moral courage, personal integrity, bearing fruit in every good work, and steadily growing in the knowledge of God with deeper faith, clearer insight, and fervent love for His precepts (Colossians 1:10).
- Grace; peace; perfect well-being; all necessary good; all spiritual prosperity; freedom from fears and agitating passions and moral conflicts; full, personal, precise knowledge of God; godliness; Christian love; glory; excellence; virtue; partakers of the divine nature; Christian energy; knowledge; intelligence; self-control; patience; endurance; piety (2 Peter 1:1–7).
- Powerful and answered prayers for self and others (James 5:16).

- Grace and spiritual peace (peace with God and harmony, unity, and undisturbedness) (Ephesians 1:2).
- Compassionate, kind, humble, having quiet strength, disciplined, even tempered, content with second place, quick to forgive an offense (Colossians 3:12–14).

BIBLICAL EXAMPLES OF HIGH SPIRITUAL INTELLIGENCE

Let's look at some more biblical examples of high spiritual intelligence and the acquisition and application of revelation knowledge. Remember that all intelligence involves the acquisition and dispensation of some form of knowledge. For example, cultural intelligence involves descriptive knowledge of cultural norms and values, and spiritual intelligence involves revelation knowledge from God—revelation of His goodness, revelation of His reality, revelation of His love. It was Daniel's spiritual intelligence that enabled him to interpret King Nebuchadnezzar's dream with accuracy. Daniel didn't get this information from descriptive knowledge or earn it through formal education. There was no way for him to accurately interpret this dream by his natural understanding. He received the revelation knowledge by the Holy Spirit. It was entirely through clear and accurate perceptual processing of what he had perceived that he was then capable of responding appropriately to the king. This is another stunning example of high spiritual intelligence in practice.

> As for these four youths, God gave them knowledge and *intelligence* in every *branch of* literature and wisdom; Daniel even understood all *kinds of* visions and dreams. Then at the end of the days which the king had specified for presenting them, the commander of the officials presented them before Nebuchadnezzar. The king talked with them, and out of them all not one was found like Daniel, Hananiah, Mishael and Azariah; so they entered the king's personal service. As for every matter of wisdom and understanding about which the king consulted them, he found them ten times better than all the magicians *and* conjurers who *were* in all his realm. (Daniel 1:17–20 NASB; emphasis mine)

Notice that the source of Daniel's knowledge was God (Daniel 1:17), and his intelligence made a way for him and his three friends to stand before the king. Daniel's Babylonian name was Belteshazzar (Daniel 1:7), Hananiah's name was Shadrach, Mishael's name was Meshach, and Azariah's name was Adednego (Daniel 1:19). These four young men possessed divine spiritual intelligence ten times greater than all the learned magicians and enchanters who possessed counterfeit spiritual intelligence.

> Then Daniel went to his house and made the thing known to Hananiah, Mishael, and Azariah, his companions, So that they would desire *and* request mercy of the God of heaven concerning this secret, that Daniel and his companions should not perish with the rest of the wise men of Babylon. Then the secret was revealed to Daniel in a vision of the night, and Daniel blessed the God of heaven. Daniel answered, Blessed be the name of God forever and ever! For wisdom and might are His! He changes the times and the seasons; He removes kings and sets up kings. He gives wisdom to the wise and knowledge to those who have understanding! He reveals the deep and secret things; He knows what is in the darkness, and the light dwells with Him! I thank You and praise You, O God of my fathers, Who has given me wisdom and might and has made known to me now what we desired of You, for You have made known to us the solution to the king's problem. (Daniel 2:17–23 AMPC)

Notice that Daniel sought the Lord for the disclosure of the dream's interpretation, and the Lord answered him through a vision of the night. Pay attention to Daniel's response once he obtained the revelation. He blessed the Lord, acknowledging and proclaiming that wisdom and might belong to God. Daniel also acknowledged that God gives wisdom and knowledge, that God reveals deep and secret things, and that it was God who made the solution to the king's problem known to him and his friends.

Later in Daniel 3:13–30, we see the spiritual intelligence of these youths in action again. When Shadrach, Meshach, and Abednego were summoned to serve Nebuchadnezzar's gods and the golden image of him or face being burned alive, they confidently responded by saying they would not do so and that God would deliver them. If they were simply employing natural intelligence and common sense at this point, they would have come across as stupid fools, since the fire would surely have painfully killed each of them. Merely employing descriptive knowledge about the extreme dangers of fire would've prevented them from entering the furnace. However, their confidence to enter the furnace came from their *revelation* knowledge. They perceived and understood with absolute certainty that God would deliver them, and they even verbalized that to the king. This knowledge was derived not from their natural intelligence but from their spiritual intelligence.

While all the men who handled them were killed, the three youths came out from the midst of the fire, unscathed. The three didn't have the attitude of "Oh well, I guess we're all going to die since we won't worship any false gods." No, they genuinely *knew* they would be delivered and responded with confidence in God. They accurately perceived and managed their revelation well, with the appropriate corresponding behavior and good relationship management. They trusted in God and continued to show respect to the king. All these responses were completely contrary to how someone placed in the same situation would have responded using their natural perceptual ability. Naturally, no one would be dumb enough to willingly enter a furnace nor naive enough to confidently believe they would come out alive. This would be viewed as absolute insanity by those with no spiritual intelligence. The approach of these young men could be achieved only through the Holy Spirit and the spiritual intelligence He grants. The end of the story for Daniel and his three friends was that the king blessed God as well. Did you get that? Their exceptional spiritual intelligence and the subsequent miracle also generated a transformational change in Nebuchadnezzar.

In Daniel 11:32 we see how an angel confirmed that the people who knew their God would prove themselves strong and stand firm and do exploits for God. Moreover, Daniel got revelation that in the end-times knowledge would increase exponentially. We are living in this very time in history— what a privilege!

> The people who know their God shall prove themselves strong and shall stand firm and do exploits [for God]. (Daniel 11:32 AMPC)

But you, O Daniel, shut up the words and seal the Book until the time of the end. Then many shall run to and fro and search anxiously [through the Book], and knowledge [of God's purposes as revealed by His prophets] shall be increased and become great. (Daniel 12:4 AMP)

THE FIVE-FOLD MINISTRY'S ROLE IN HELPING PEOPLE DEVELOP HIGH SPIRITUAL INTELLIGENCE AND MATURITY

The responsibility of the five-fold ministry is to *fully* equip God's people so they grow in spiritual intelligence and maturity. Jesus Himself appoints people to the five-fold ministry to equip His people so they manifest His completeness. Ephesians 4:11–15 highlights that He Himself appoints some as apostles (special messengers, representatives), some as prophets (who speak a new message from God to the people), some as evangelists (who spread the good news of salvation), and some as pastors and teachers (to shepherd and guide and instruct).

And [His gifts to the church were varied and] *He Himself appointed* some as apostles [special messengers, representatives], some as prophets [who speak a new message from God to the people], some as evangelists [who spread the good news of salvation], and some as pastors and teachers [to shepherd and guide and instruct], [and He did this] to *fully equip* and *perfect* the saints (God's people) for works of service, to build up the body of Christ [the church]; until we all reach *oneness* in the faith and in the *knowledge* of the Son of God, [growing spiritually] to become a *mature* believer, reaching to the measure of the *fullness* of Christ [manifesting His *spiritual completeness* and *exercising our spiritual gifts* in unity]. So that we are no longer children [spiritually immature], tossed back and forth [like ships on a stormy sea] and carried about by every wind of [shifting] doctrine, by the cunning and trickery of [unscrupulous] men, by the deceitful scheming of people ready to do anything [for personal profit]. But speaking the truth in love [in all things—both our speech and our lives expressing His truth], let us grow up in all things into Him [following His example] who is the Head—Christ. (Ephesians 4:11–15 AMP; emphasis mine)

Notice that the apostle Paul clarified the goal of reaching to the measure of the fullness of Christ. Why? So we are no longer like spiritual children (spiritually immature and ignorant), unstable or easily deceived by every new doctrinal trend, by counterfeit preachers or phony teachers who are ready to do anything for selfish ambition. By expressing the truth in love, we grow up. What's striking about this passage is that God wants His people not only to exercise their spiritual gifts in unity but also to display the totality of Jesus. The fullness of Jesus means His heart, intellect, and intentions. He wants His people fully equipped so they will grow up to full spiritual maturity and possess high spiritual intelligence so they won't be gullible or easily deceived. Whenever we see ignorance and immaturity in God's people, they are indicative that the five-fold ministry hasn't been functioning as God intended.

Dr. Guillermo Maldonado, Founder of King Jesus International Ministry, one the fastest growing multicultural churches in the USA, says in his book *How to Walk in the Supernatural Power of God:*

> When we reject the pastoral ministry, we fail to care for the sheep, and they are likely to lose their way. If we reject the teacher's mantle, we may perish for lack of knowledge. (See Hosea 4:6). When we reject the evangelistic mantle, many souls are not saved. When we reject the ministry of the prophet, the church lacks important vision and direction concerning the things that God is doing and saying. If we reject the apostolic mantle, the church operates largely without direction, vision, edification, impartation, revelation, advancement of the kingdom, and supernatural power to perform miracles.[37]

Dr. Maldonado insists that simply because certain offices have been taken to the extreme, we cannot allow past sins and errors of a few to cause us to reject a God-given office.

Pastors exercise spiritual intelligence and employ spiritual gifts as they care for their sheep. Teachers utilize spiritual intelligence to accurately perceive and wisely deliver what the Holy Spirit is directing them to emphasize, clarify, articulate, and integrate. Evangelists use spiritual intelligence to know what, where, and how to introduce people to the Lord. Prophets employ spiritual intelligence to accurately perceive and wisely communicate the things God is doing and saying. Apostles engage spiritual intelligence to accurately perceive and convey overall direction, vision, and revelation from God with spiritual gifts typically associated with the working of miracles. When high spiritual intelligence isn't maintained in any of these five-fold ministry roles, the fullness of Jesus isn't on display, and His nature and purposes are misrepresented. The development and maintenance of high spiritual intelligence is absolutely vital for individuals God has called to serve in the five-fold ministry. They need to not only continue to make progress in developing it but also help those they serve develop and maintain it as well.

People with high spiritual intelligence increasingly share more of God's divine nature (2 Peter 1:4) *and* mind (1 Corinthians 2:10–16); they continue to grow in their capacity to truly know Him and to make Him known. People with high spiritual intelligence keep their side of the contract with the Holy Spirit so they can maintain a strong connection to God. They are faithful in partnering and "pairing" their hearts *and* minds with Him. They allow themselves to be led by Him, and they remain "plugged in" so they can constantly receive fresh "downloads" of revelation knowledge. People with high spiritual intelligence continue to make spiritual progress and increasingly reflect God's nature so others can get a glimpse of Him through them. Let's endeavor to be people who pursue and attain high spiritual intelligence so we walk worthy of being counted as God's children. Let's not squander our responsibility to help the world spot Him through us.

> For all who are *allowing themselves to* be led by the Spirit of God are sons of God. (Romans 8:14 AMP; emphasis mine)

> See what great love the Father has lavished on us, that we should be called children of God! And that is what we are! The reason the world does not know us is that it did not know him. (1 John 3:1 NIV)

Before we proceed to the next chapter, which investigates the dangers of low and no spiritual intelligence, let's pray.

God, thank You for the capacity to develop high spiritual intelligence. Help me to make constant spiritual progress and to maintain a close connection to You. May I increasingly share more of Your divine nature and mind, as Your Word promises. Help me to love You with all my passion, prayer, and intelligence. Fill me with Your Spirit and help me to follow You more nearly. May I increasingly perceive Your presence, and let my spiritual eyes be enlightened. Help me to see You for who You really are and more accurately perceive Your perspective on things. Expand my prayer life and help me to diligently study and meditate on Your Word. Help me not only to acquire more revelation but also to learn how to steward and apply it well. May my entire life be an expression of worship to You. Help me to continue to grow in my capacity to truly know You and make You known. May I represent You well as Your child. Help me to always believe the best about people, and may they get a glimpse of You through me. In the majestic name of Jesus. Amen.

Dangers of Low or No
Spiritual Intelligence

To be perfectly frank, I'm getting exasperated with your *infantile thinking*. How long before you grow up and use your head— your *adult head*? It's all right to have a childlike unfamiliarity with evil; a simple no is all that's needed there. But there's far more to saying yes to something. Only *mature* and *well-exercised intelligence* can save you from falling into *gullibility*.

—1 Corinthians 14:20–25 (MSG; emphasis mine)

LOW SPIRITUAL INTELLIGENCE

People with low spiritual intelligence represent spiritual infants (Hebrews 11:8–14) and babies (1 Corinthians 3:1). Hence, while they have experienced a spiritual rebirth, they are only beginning to access and perceive spiritual information and their behavioral responses, like babies or toddlers aren't always appropriate. People with low spiritual intelligence have some spiritual perceptual awareness, but they may not always accurately process that spiritual information and communicate it in a way that provides practical solutions that help people and glorify God. The analysis and interpretation of what they perceive is often erroneous and misrepresented or poorly translated to the people it was actually intended to bless. Let me use an analogy: it is as though their "Wi-Fi connection strength" is limited, their "broadband connection width" is narrow, and they often have low "battery" life and frequent "power" disconnects. They are barely able to communicate spiritually and are often confused. Take a look at how The Message Bible describes them. "So God will start over with the simple basics and address them in baby talk, one syllable at a time—'Da, da, da, da, blah, blah, blah, blah. That's a good little girl, that's a good little boy.' And like toddlers, they will get up and fall down, get bruised and confused and lost" (Isaiah 28:13 MSG).

The key distinguishing feature of people with low spiritual intelligence is that they typically have to be fed and cleansed, and need to be carefully nurtured by others. Like young toddlers, they are still easily stumbling, highly dependent, irresponsible, and spiritually uninformed. They are often vulnerable and easily persuaded, and they cannot yet discern with confidence between right and wrong. Their consciences are unreliable and vulnerable. They can't always protect themselves, and what they are able to spiritually eat isn't much more than spiritual milk. Spiritually and practically speaking, they are at the elementary stages of their spiritual walk and only beginning to grasp some of the basic truths and promises associated with God's written Word. They haven't yet learned how to diligently study and meditate on the Bible for themselves. They may believe Jesus is Lord but struggle to put their faith into action. What they believe mentally doesn't always align with what they believe in their hearts. Whereas they should have matured, their personal desires, thought lives, and ambitions are typically not yet lined up with God's. Like nursing babies, they tend to come across as self-centered and needy, and they are easily upset by the smallest discomfort. They haven't yet learned self-discipline and are doctrinally inexperienced, immature, and gullible.

> I have a lot more to say about this, but it is hard to get it across to you since you've picked up this bad habit of not listening. By this time you ought to be teachers yourselves, yet here I find you need someone to sit down with you and go over the basics on God again, starting from square one—*baby's milk*, when you should have been on solid food long ago! Milk is for *beginners*, *inexperienced* in God's ways; solid food is for the mature, who

have some practice in telling right from wrong. (Hebrews 5:11–14 MSG; emphasis mine)

It's great that those with low spiritual intelligence have been translated from the kingdom of darkness to the kingdom of light and that they have escaped the eternal predicament of those with no spiritual intelligence, but God doesn't want them remaining spiritual babes with infantile thinking. It's too risky, they are too vulnerable, and the chances of them experiencing defeat, if left to fend for themselves without strong spiritual parents, are too great.

Take a look at how the apostle Paul describes the believers in Corinth. He describes them as babes in Christ. Their spirits have been reborn, but their minds are still unrenewed. They have saved hearts but carnal minds.

> But for right now, friends, I'm completely frustrated by your unspiritual dealings with each other and with God. You're acting like *infants* in relation to Christ, capable of nothing much more than nursing at the breast. Well, then, I'll nurse you since you don't seem capable of anything more. (1 Corinthians 3:1–3 MSG; emphasis mine)

> Brothers and sisters, do not be children [immature, childlike] in your thinking; be infants in [matters of] evil [completely innocent and inexperienced], but in your minds be mature [adults]. (1 Corinthians 14:20 AMP)

Some spiritual parents and teachers prefer their spiritual children to be in this condition because it maintains their children's level of dependence on them. The mindset of the parent may be something like this: *If they depend on me, they will need me, and if they need me, they will stay with me, and that will give me a sense of purpose.* Some natural parents struggle to let go of their children because, when they are dependent, this state reinforces the need for the parent. When the child grows up, they may begin asking questions the parent can no longer answer, and the parent may begin to feel a loss of identity as the caregiver. Also, some spiritual and natural parents prefer to hold the monopoly on knowledge as they get a sense of power through it. This is a picture of what many religious leaders did in the past (and some still do) to preserve their positional power. The mindset is the same. They withhold information and keep their followers ignorant to gain power over them. Also, young children make a lot of mistakes that parents are called on to help them out with. This situation again keeps them dependent on the parents and completely reliant on them for discernment.

Note that with low spiritual intelligence, there is perceptual awareness, but it is incomplete and not always accurate, and the appropriate behavioral responses aren't always present. There is often a level of spiritual and emotional cognitive dissonance, in which the way people perceive themselves is incongruent with the way God sees them. Anyone who has made Jesus the Lord of their life would have experienced what it is like to have some (albeit low) spiritual intelligence at the beginning of their spiritual journey. As spiritual babes or toddlers, we may have struggled to read the Bible, for example. We may have relied entirely on others to get our spiritual food, to digest it for us, and to "spoon-feed" us. We may simply have relied on and trusted others with communicating what they had read in the Bible and how they interpreted it. For some of us, these "spiritual" parents, teachers, or preachers were accurate and called of God to do just that. For others of us, we were taught inaccurately, even perhaps by well-intentioned teachers. This meant it took a little longer to make significant progress toward higher spiritual intelligence because we had to unlearn some things before we could proceed.

Another feature of low spiritual intelligence is that prayer may be a practice, but it isn't habitual or a lifestyle activity. When we have low spiritual intelligence, prayer is usually a response to a crisis and reactive in nature. As believers grow in spiritual intelligence, ripen in character, and become spiritually mature, their prayers too become fueled with full assurance that what they're praying for will come to pass because it's willed by God. The Bible exemplifies this truth. "[He is] always striving for you earnestly in his prayers, [pleading] that you may [as persons of ripe character and clear conviction] stand firm *and* mature [in spiritual growth], convinced *and* fully assured in everything willed by God" (Colossians 4:12 AMPC).

Those with low spiritual intelligence (like the believers in Corinth) display fruits such as spiritual shortsightedness (2 Peter 1:9), instability, and gullibility (1 Corinthians 14:20–25). Naturally, the variance across these fruits will be extensive, and the opportunities and grace for development and progress from low to high through the guidance and nurturing of the Holy Spirit are potentially limitless.

Below is a list of some additional fruits associated with low spiritual intelligence. These may also be generated by those with no spiritual intelligence or by people who dabble in counterfeit spiritual intelligence (even if inadvertently).

- Unanswered worry prayers (James 1:8).
- Confusion, jealousy, rivalry, selfish ambition. (James 3:13–16).
- Discouraged when disciplined (Hebrews 12:5).
- Struggle to forgive (Matthew 6:15).
- Backsliding and careless ease (Proverbs 1:32).
- Idle and unproductive (2 Peter 1:8).
- Prone to gossip (Job 15:1–16).
- Double minded, unstable, restless (James 1:8).
- Easily misled and unstable (Ephesians 4:14).
- Spiritual shortsightedness, seeing only what is near (2 Peter 1:9).

For some, they may feel like their lives hover somewhere between low spiritual intelligence and no spiritual intelligence. They may feel no direct, clear, or real-time connection to the mind of God. They acknowledge Him as God but often feel disconnected. They may feel like they're barely breathing, spiritually speaking. They may feel like they have little to no spiritual sensory awareness and no fresh revelation of God. They may even have descriptive knowledge of Him but lack revelation knowledge of Him.

Many believers may go through this, but God doesn't want His people living so close to the edge of low to no spiritual intelligence. He wants us making progress toward high spiritual intelligence, far away from dull perceptual awareness, poor spiritual acuity, and deception. For some hovering between low and no spiritual intelligence is compounded by counterfeit spiritual activities. They aren't just struggling to hear what God is saying to them personally, but they are also experiencing spiritual oppression. The spiritual cognitive dissonance is now amplified, and depression readily sets in. It's like they are not only struggling to keep their heads above water but also finding it difficult to breathe through foam above the water. The "foam" is from the counterfeit spiritual intelligence— spiritual intel that isn't sourced in God and knowledge that isn't edifying or true. Their spiritual visual acuity isn't just weak; they are perceiving things spiritually that aren't associated with God's kingdom.

In nature, sea foam is formed through agitation of higher concentrations of matter like algae. Through churning by breaking waves in the surf zone, surfactants under these turbulent conditions trap air, forming persistent bubbles that stick to each other through surface tension. Let us relate this to spiritual intelligence. People hovering between the realms of light and darkness (even if inadvertently) experience spiritual tension. The effects of these stresses on the mind are then compounded by higher concentrations of deception if they're involved in counterfeit spiritual activities. Spiritual dullness and apathy are now aggravated and exaggerated because of additional spiritual realities. This "foam" of deception is spiritually dangerous and potentially deadly. Naturally speaking, even some of the best swimmers and most resilient surfers may struggle to stay afloat if foam is in the water. So too, the strongholds and seductive power of alternate spiritual realities can spiritually suffocate people who were once strong believers. That's why God warns us so emphatically in His Word not to become entangled in any form of idolatry, sorcery, divination, or counterfeit spiritual activities. Your spiritual senses will become so dull, and your conscience will become so obscured that you will be unable to stay spiritually buoyant.

> So that we are no longer children [spiritually immature], tossed back and forth [like ships on a stormy sea] and carried about by every wind of [shifting] doctrine, by the cunning *and* trickery of [unscrupulous] men, by the deceitful scheming of people ready to do anything [for personal profit]. (Ephesians 4:14 AMP)

> That you may walk (live and conduct yourselves) in a manner worthy of the Lord, fully pleasing to Him *and* desiring to please Him in all things, bearing fruit in every good work and steadily growing *and* increasing in *and* by the knowledge of God [with fuller, deeper, and clearer insight, acquaintance, and recognition]. (Colossians 1:10 AMPC)

No wonder the apostle Paul pleaded with the Ephesians and Colossians to grow up and walk worthy of their divine calling, not in their own strength but through the profuse empowering grace of God. Not only does this maturity generate behavior that gives credit to God, but it pleases Him. "I therefore, the prisoner for the Lord, appeal to *and* beg you to walk (lead a life) worthy of the [divine] calling to which you have been called [with behavior that is a credit to the summons to God's service]" (Ephesians 4:1 AMPC).

NO SPIRITUAL INTELLIGENCE

The key distinguishing feature of people with no spiritual intelligence is that they are unable to perceive the spiritual realm and process spiritual information. They are what the Bible describes as spiritually blind and deaf. They may have natural eyes and ears, but their spiritual eyes and ears are inactive (2 Peter 1:9). The concept of a spiritual realm and a spiritual God is difficult for them to grasp and comprehend. They tend to trivialize religion and turn spiritual conversation into gossip (Job 15:1–16). They struggle to fathom how people can possibly believe in and devote their lives to an "unseen" God. Their very attitude blinds and deafens them, and their spiritual senses are desensitized. Similar to spiritual babes, they are often vulnerable and cannot discern between right and wrong, and they struggle to perceive the truth. Their consciences are also often injured due to traumatic or abusive life circumstances. Spiritually and practically speaking, they have yet to grasp God's love for them and appreciate other basic truths and promises contained in the Bible.

> For whoever lacks these qualities is blind, [spiritually] shortsighted, seeing only what is near to him, and has become oblivious [to the fact] that he was cleansed from his old sins. (2 Peter 1:9 AMPC)

A scoffer seeks Wisdom in vain [for his very attitude blinds and deafens him to it], but knowledge is easy to him who [being teachable] understands. (Proverbs 14:6 AMPC)

Table 3 highlights some of the fruits associated with no spiritual intelligence, which those with counterfeit spiritual intelligence may also yield. These are listed below.

- Inflated pride, touchy, fretful, resentful (1 Corinthians 13:5).
- Trivialize religion and turn spiritual conversation into gossip (Job 15:1–16).
- Habitual blasphemy and irreverent use of God's name (Deuteronomy 5:11).
- Mocking and scoffing (Proverbs 1:22).
- Ignorance and resisting God's will (Ephesians 4:18).
- Confusion (James 3:13–16).
- Fear (1 John 14:18).
- Moral decay, rottenness, corruption, covetousness, lust, greed (2 Peter 1:4).
- All-consuming but never satisfied wants (Galatians 5:19–21).
- Malice, pretense, envy, and hurtful talk (1 Peter 2:1–3).
- Oppression (Proverbs 28:16).
- Guilty conscience (Hebrews 10:22).

People with no spiritual intelligence may have descriptive knowledge of God and know about Jesus, but they have yet to experience and have an encounter with Him firsthand. They may have heard or read verses in the Bible, but the words merely seemed to represent letters on the page of a historical book. Some may even have gone as far as studying the Word but have never actually developed a real relationship with the Word (John 1:1). Some may even believe Jesus is Lord but may not yet have made Him their personal Lord. Others may once have known Him, but due to carelessness, prayerlessness, or busyness, they have drifted from a place of low spiritual intelligence into a place of no spiritual intelligence. They are incapable of hearing God and therefore are unable to listen to what He is directing them to do. Because they can't perceive what He's saying, they cannot heed His counsel. Their spiritual senses aren't functioning as they were designed to due to a disconnect with God. Look how the Bible magnifies this truth. "Whoever is of God listens to God. [Those who belong to God hear the words of God.] This is the reason that you do not listen [to those words, to Me]: because you do not belong to God *and* are not of God *or* in harmony with Him" (John 8:47 AMPC).

GOD WISHES ALL TO BE SAVED AND INCREASINGLY PERCEIVE AND KNOW THE TRUTH

You can appreciate why God has so much compassion for this group of people and why when Jesus was on earth He spent so much time setting these kinds of people free and granting them spiritual sight and spiritual hearing. God wishes all to be saved and increasingly and precisely perceive the truth. He wants them progressively transitioning from no spiritual intelligence to high spiritual intelligence and remaining there.

> Jesus said, "You're absolutely right. Take it from me: Unless a person is born from above, it's not possible to *see* what I'm pointing to—to God's kingdom." (John 3:3 MSG; emphasis mine)

> Who wishes *all* men to be saved and [increasingly] to *perceive* and *recognize* and *discern* and *know precisely* and correctly the [divine] Truth. (1 Timothy 2:4 AMPC; emphasis mine)

If really knowing God (not just about Him) and doing His will (not just generally but specifically) are absolutely vital to eternal life (John 17), it is essential that people get spiritual intelligence and develop it. No other type of intelligence, although well recognized and useful for success in the natural realm and this life, will secure our access to God's kingdom or a personal, firsthand knowledge of God. General intelligence and language ability may enhance our capacity to read Scripture, memorize it, and appreciate every detail of history associated with the Bible. However, it won't ensure that we develop a personal relationship with God or guarantee our eternal life. We are reborn and develop this personal relationship with God by the Holy Spirit, not by the written letter of the Word. It takes a spiritual awakening to hear His voice speak to our hearts and obtain spiritual intelligence. The gateway to the supernatural is a genuine relationship with Jesus, and the Holy Spirit is the One who empowers us to do so. Being spiritually reborn is what moves us from no spiritual intelligence or counterfeit spiritual intelligence to genuine spiritual intelligence.

> This is how much God loved the world: He gave his Son, his one and only Son. And this is why: so that no one need be destroyed; by believing in him, anyone can have a whole and lasting life. God didn't go to all the trouble of sending his Son merely to point an accusing finger, telling the world how bad it was. He came to help, to put the world right again. Anyone who trusts in him is acquitted; anyone who refuses to trust him has long since been under the death sentence without knowing it. And why? Because of that person's failure to believe in the one-of-a-kind Son of God when introduced to him. (John 3:16–18 MSG)

God wants every one of His children to grow in spiritual intelligence and never to regress. Being totally on fire for God, all in for Him, and totally devoted to Him is the ultimate place to live. God wants all people to possess high spiritual intelligence. He wants everyone to have a strong perceptual awareness of Him, a deep appreciation for who they are in Him, an accurate interpretation of what He is saying to them, and the power to do His will. His divine enabling power has given us absolutely everything necessary for a dynamic spiritual life and godliness through a genuine and personal relationship with Him. As sharers of His divine nature, we are empowered to develop moral excellence, knowledge, self-control, steadfastness, godliness, and love. It also enables us to bear fruit and steadily increase in *and* by the knowledge of God, with a more complete, deeper, and clearer acquaintance with Him. All these qualities are ours and are increasing in us as we grow in spiritual maturity from low to high spiritual intelligence.

BARRIERS TO SUSTAINING A SPIRITUALLY INTELLIGENT LIFESTYLE

The first hurdle to any genuine change is acknowledgment of the need to change. The second is acting on what you know to be true. The third is maintaining that action long term. We've learned that the acquisition and application of knowledge are fundamental to intelligence and that true spiritual intelligence isn't just *knowing* God's will but *acting* on it. Acknowledging something is one thing, but action is what is necessary to generate productive results. Similarly, positive action is great, but if it isn't sustained, long-term results won't be forthcoming. It's like knowing you need to eat nutritious food for physical health, but it may take you a while to put that wisdom into practical action. Doing that once, however, won't be sufficient for sustained change either.

Learning and action generate intelligent behavior, but learning and *sustained* action generate an intelligent lifestyle. Likewise, with spiritual intelligence, simply obtaining revelation knowledge and putting it into effective action once isn't sufficient for a lifetime of progress. To have a spiritually intelligent lifestyle demands ongoing translation of revelation knowledge from God into appropriate, biblically congruent action. It takes the maintenance of a focused spiritual journey and a *continuation* on that path, not just a single event or a once-off encounter with God.

> Time is just about up. Let evildoers do their worst and the dirty-minded go all out in pollution, but let the righteous *maintain* a straight course and the holy continue on in holiness. (Revelation 22:10–11 MSG; emphasis mine)

> He who *perseveres and endures to the end* will be saved [from spiritual disease and death in the world to come]. (Matthew 10:22 AMPC; emphasis mine)

> He who patiently *perseveres and endures to the end* will be saved (made a partaker of the salvation by Christ, and delivered from spiritual death). (Mark 13:13 AMPC; emphasis mine)

The development and maintenance of high spiritual intelligence aren't intended so you alone benefit. It isn't a selfish endeavor to enhance your own self-actualization. That is often the intent of people seeking counterfeit spiritual intelligence, as we will see. Authentic spiritual intelligence helps both the beneficiary *and* those they lead to develop a more intimate relationship with God and to guard that relationship. This is another distinguishing feature of people who have high spiritual intelligence. It isn't competitive or self-seeking. Genuine spiritual intelligence raises all

God's people to become spiritually mature and advances God's kingdom and His agenda. It ensures His will gets done on the earth and that people genuinely know Him (not a minister or ministry) so they can manifest His goodness, nature, and glory to a world that so desperately needs Him.

> All around us we observe a pregnant creation. The difficult times of pain throughout the world are simply birth pangs. But it's not only around us; it's *within* us. The Spirit of God is arousing us within. We're also feeling the birth pangs. These sterile and barren bodies of ours are yearning for full deliverance. That is why waiting does not diminish us, any more than waiting diminishes a pregnant mother. We are enlarged in the waiting. We, of course, don't see what is enlarging us. But the longer we wait, the larger we become, and the more joyful our expectancy. (Romans 8:22–25 MSG)

In this chapter, we've explored low and no degrees of spiritual intelligence overall, and provided more specific examples of the key features and fruits associated with them. The next chapter will focus more specifically on counterfeit spiritual intelligence.

Before we proceed to the next chapter, let's pray.

God, help me to make progress toward high spiritual intelligence far away from dull perceptual awareness and deception. Free me from spiritual naivety and gullibility. Open the eyes of my heart and give me a discerning mind. Forgive me for carelessness, prayerlessness, and ignorance, which cause my spiritual intelligence to dwindle. Help me to acknowledge where I need to change and to swiftly act on what I know is true. Let me maintain a spiritually intelligent lifestyle and keep me far from spiritual dormancy and demise. Give me strong spiritual parents and help me to learn how to study Your Word for myself so that I too may become a good spiritual parent. Give me insight, hindsight, and foresight so I can grow in understanding and increasingly grasp what You are communicating to me. As I advance to spiritual maturity, let me maintain a humble and teachable heart. Help me to continue to make spiritual progress and sustain high spiritual intelligence. I love You deeply and long to know You more intimately. In Jesus' awesome name. Amen.

CHAPTER
8

Counterfeit Spiritual Intelligence: The Copy

Examine and test and evaluate your own selves to see whether
you are holding to your faith and showing the proper
fruits of it. Test and prove yourselves [not Christ]. Do you
not yourselves realize and know [thoroughly by an ever-
increasing experience] that Jesus Christ is in you—unless
you are [*counterfeits*] disapproved on trial and rejected?

—2 Corinthians 13:5 (AMPC; emphasis mine)

So far in this book, we've explored the dimensions of spiritual intelligence and their associated hallmarks and hand brakes. We've also looked at various degrees of spiritual intelligence and their associated features and fruits. In this chapter we'll focus more specifically on the copy.

COUNTERFEIT SPIRITUAL INTELLIGENCE

Counterfeit means spurious, made in exact semblance of an original with the intention to defraud. It denotes something fake, forged, phony—a fraudulent imitation of something valuable.[38] *Merriam-Webster's Dictionary* defines it as "made in imitation of something else with the intent to deceive."[39] Counterfeit spiritual intelligence does precisely that. It is a copy of the original spiritual intelligence and is designed to deceive.

In the military, counterintelligence is the act of preventing an enemy from obtaining secret information. Counterfeit spiritual intelligence pretends to be enlightening, freeing, and uplifting. It imitates the components of true spiritual intelligence and even attempts to steal the techniques to achieve it. One of the key distinguishing features associated with counterfeit spiritual intelligence is its distorted view of who God is and an alteration, dilution, or outright rejection of the Bible as the Word of God. The fruits associated with counterfeit spiritual intelligence ultimately result in spiritual death. "For the wages of sin is death, but the gift of God is eternal life in Christ Jesus our Lord" (Romans 6:23 NIV).

The enemy, the devil, works overtime to try to prevent people from coming into or maintaining a relationship with God. His mission is to steal, kill, and destroy any knowledge of God and prevent people from obtaining or preserving it. Part of the enemy's strategy is to deceive, bolster ignorance, and blind people so they are unable to perceive the truth. Jesus died and paid a hefty price so we could perceive and know God for ourselves and enjoy eternal life and a life of astounding well-being on earth. "The thief comes only in order to steal and kill and destroy. I came that they may have and enjoy life, and have it in abundance (to the full, till it overflows)" (John 10:10 AMPC).

The counterfeit god of this world is obsessed with trying to imitate and copy what God does. He is bent on robbing people from the full and abundant life God intended for them. He copies the original intent of life, which is to know the one true God intimately, and attempts to counter simulate it by spiritually blinding the minds of people. Read how the Amplified Bible magnifies this reality. "For the *god* of this world has *blinded* the unbelievers' *minds* [that they should not discern the truth], preventing them from seeing the illuminating light of the Gospel of the glory of Christ (the Messiah), Who is the Image *and* Likeness of God" (2 Corinthians 4:4 AMP; emphasis mine).

The enemy even had the audacity to think he could get Jesus to worship him. The spiritual naivety and outrageous presumption that counterfeit intelligence manifests are clearly demonstrated here. "And he said to Him, these things, all taken together, I will give You, if You will prostrate Yourself before me and do homage *and* worship me. Then Jesus said to him, Begone, Satan! For it has been written, you shall worship the Lord your God, and Him alone shall you serve. Then the devil departed from Him, and behold, angels came and ministered to Him" (Matthew 4:9–11 AMPC).

The old Latin phrase "caveat emptor," meaning "buyer beware," captures the need to be careful about what we buy into. Counterfeit products and counterfeit intelligence copy something of real value and are shrewdly designed to appear authentic when they are in fact fake. So many have been caught by the lure of bogus spiritual intelligence and, in so doing, have been defrauded and constrained from accessing the original.

Unlike authentic spiritual intelligence characterized by a first love for God, His Word, and all people, counterfeit intelligence involves erroneous analysis of spiritual information, amplified focus on self, and behavioral responses that are contrary and sometimes hostile to God and His followers. Counterfeit spiritual intelligence poses as the real thing and always promotes and markets itself as "good." Its bogus benefits and enticing lure catch people with low or no spiritual intelligence unawares. Its sometimes-enchanting value traps the spiritually naive off guard. Its "low cost" attractiveness catches the ignorant "buyer." Using deceptive manipulation, it wraps itself in lies, like pretty packaging, which makes an inferior product appear valuable.

SIMILARITIES BETWEEN HOSTILE AMBIENT INTELLIGENCE AND COUNTERFEIT SPIRITUAL INTELLIGENCE

Let's use the analogy of ambient intelligence to drive home the importance of avoiding counterfeit spiritual intel. Whenever intelligence is demonstrated by electronic devices in the surrounding environment, it is referred to as "ambient intelligence." With all our technological advances, we're learning that ambient intelligence is an electronic environment that is sensitive and responsive to the presence of people. In an ambient intelligence world, devices work in accordance with people to help support and improve the quality of their everyday lives. Our smartphones, for example, can identify our current locations and provide us with the precise location of desired destinations, with ongoing real-time instruction and assistance. We've also come to depend on our devices and applications so extensively that we get frustrated when they sometimes appear to miscalculate or miscommunicate the information, right? In an ambient intelligence environment, everyday tasks and habits become easier to execute.

We're also realizing, however, that though ambient intelligence can help promote the quality of our everyday lives, it can also cause us inconveniences when erroneous. Moreover, when artificial intelligence and ambient intelligence are exploited or abused, the repercussions aren't just inconvenient; they can become grievous. Let's apply this to spiritual intelligence. Many of us can appreciate how traveling to a novel destination without ambient intelligence (through a map application) can lead to unnecessary detours, excessive cul-de-sacs, and endless erroneous directions. These simply lead to wasted time and inconveniences, correct? However, when ambient intelligence is hostile and intelligence is being used against us for exploitative purposes, the ramifications ramp up quite significantly. This is similar to how hostile artificial intelligence isn't always immediately detected; so too counterfeit spiritual intelligence can, unbeknownst to us, be used against us and eventually lead to disastrous outcomes.

Maybe like many, you're seeking answers to *precise* evaluations of the state of your actual spiritual well-being, for example. Or perhaps you need more accurate predictive assessments of potential future outcomes based on spiritual choices and decisions you're making today. It's going to take spiritual intelligence to answer these questions, right? Why then would we be so careless as to make such critical life assessments using potentially erroneous or hostile intel as our guide?

When embarking on a spiritual journey through life, why wouldn't we seek to tap into the *original* intelligence capabilities offered to us by our Creator. The ultimate, super Intellect, God Himself, in His genius and brilliance designed our minds to have the capacity to sync with His. Of all the intelligence capabilities He designed us to experience, the most vital is spiritual intelligence—where our intelligence harmonizes with His. If you think ambient intelligence, which helps us with everyday activities and choices, is helpful, how much more spiritual intelligence, which is designed to be advantageous for life on earth and in the life to come.

Just as our smartphones will instruct us to reroute if we're erroneously going off course, for example, so, too, spiritual intelligence will instruct us to reset our spiritual courses if it detects deceptive and erroneous paths, which will prevent us from reaching our optimal destination. It may sound like common sense, but it is astounding how few people really tap into God's intelligence this way and choose rather to access spiritual intel from counterfeit sources. Some of the reasons why people get entangled in counterfeit spiritual activities isn't always because of intentionality. People don't intentionally get engaged in hostile artificial intelligence; likewise, they may simply be ignorant or indifferent to it.

In the section that follows, I further explain this by identifying three groups of people who may be guided by counterfeit spiritual intelligence: the ignorant, the indifferent, and the intentional. The ignorant people represent people who inadvertently and unintentionally get involved in counterfeit intelligence activities. The indifferent people are those who are somewhat aware but don't really care. God's heart is especially broken for the ignorant and the indifferent, since many of His children are members of these groups. The third group represents those who are intentionally engaged in counterfeit spiritual activities and openly admit their allegiance to counterfeit gods. Parabolically, in the artificial intelligence world, these are people who knowingly engage in hostile intelligence activities.

THE IGNORANT

The ignorant are unaware that they are participating in spiritual activities incongruent with the will of God. These individuals may be spiritual babes who are excited about learning more about the supernatural but begin to get involved in counterfeit spiritual activities. They are new to the faith and therefore are unfamiliar with the Bible for themselves. They are dependent on others to digest the Word for them and rely on spiritual parents to feed them. Like natural babes, they are vulnerable to danger and need to be closely nurtured and protected.

The ignorant could also represent people who once had high spiritual intelligence but lost their first love for God (Revelation 2:1). They may have started off strong, in the fear of the Lord, but due to busyness, carelessness, and the pressures of ministry or enticements toward fame and fortune, they lost their anointing. They maintained their descriptive knowledge of God and His Word but lost their capacity to access revelation knowledge due to a lack of intimacy with Him. Just as perishable food eventually deteriorates, they failed to maintain a strong connection to the Source of revelation knowledge, and their supply dwindled (see Hosea 4:6).

For some, their consciences may have become calloused due to delusions about their superiority and the denial of their need to live a repentant lifestyle. Parabolically, their Wi-Fi connection to God became weakened. For others, due to the pressures of their positions, they started to craft their own messages, full of the letters of the Word and yet devoid of *the* Word. They became modern-day Pharisees without knowing it. They fell in love with the letter of the Word more than God Himself. They became more passionate about ministry than the Master. Their initial prayerfulness turned to prayerlessness. They once personally prayed for hours but eventually delegated that responsibility to others. They once had a strong connection to the mind of Christ (1 Corinthians 2:16), but over time they became more "in tune" with their own imaginations and ideas. Basically, they got to a place where they were no longer living a life of obedience to the *original* Shepherd. They no longer loved Him with *all* their passion, prayer, and intelligence—and others as themselves.

Whether ignorance due to spiritual immaturity or ignorance due to diminishing connectivity to the mind of God, these individuals are unintentionally getting involved in counterfeit activities. The apostle Paul highlighted this condition in Ephesians 4:18, 1 Corinthians 9:27, and 2 Corinthians 13:5. He emphasized that these people risk being found to be unfit counterfeits due to ignorance and perceptual blindness. This further reinforces the criticality of maintaining a clear conscience, self-evaluation, and regular testing of the fruits in your life. I've italicized some key words for emphasis.

> Their moral understanding is darkened and their *reasoning* is *beclouded*. They are alienated (estranged, self-banished) from the life of God with no share in it; this is because of the *ignorance* (the want of *knowledge* and *perception*, the willful blindness) that is deep-seated in them, due to their *hardness* of heart [to the insensitiveness of their moral nature]. (Ephesians 4:18 AMPC)

> But like a boxer I buffet my body [handle it roughly, discipline it by hardships] and subdue it, for fear that after proclaiming to others the Gospel and things pertaining to it, I myself should become *unfit* [not stand the test, be unapproved and rejected as a counterfeit]. (1 Corinthians 9:27 AMPC)

For the ignorant, their perceptual awareness and capacity to process spiritual information are cloudy or full of static. They cannot fully perceive or grasp what God is trying to communicate to them. Notice that the apostle Paul clarified that this is due to a hardness of heart (Ephesians 4:18). This could be a heart that once was enlightened and pliable in the hands of God. It may also represent someone who is young in their faith, still recovering from past heartaches and working through unforgiveness. Either way, the person's ignorance causes static in their capacity to perceive what God is communicating, and their spiritual intelligence is compromised as a result.

THE INDIFFERENT

This second group is involved in counterfeit activities, but they don't recognize the implications of those activities and don't really care either way. They may have experienced spiritual rebirth but have developed a self-confidence in spiritual matters instead of maintaining humility, selflessness, and the fear of God. Some may even be more mature believers who have developed spiritual blind spots, and instead of growing in intimacy with God, they've gotten more familiar with Him. Unbeknownst to them, their perceptual awareness is progressively becoming downgraded, since they've failed to maintain a healthy reverence for Him. Some may have unknowingly hardened their hearts to God and the things of God due to hurt, rebellion, or spiritual pride. Due to things like gossiping about other believers or defaming and demonizing God's children, they cause a veil of deception to cover their consciences. With their consciences seared, their capacity to perceive what God is saying is compromised and deactivated. Their consciences lose their capacity to accurately discern between right and wrong, and they no longer feel convicted when they sin. Some may have become so spiritually proud that they don't even believe they are capable of being convicted of sin. In this context, deception continues to thrive, and delusion intensifies due to mounting unconfessed sin and growing self-righteousness.

People in this group may even be people who once had significant ministries but succumbed to the lure and seduction of fame and fortune and prefer the praises of humans than living for an audience of One. They may have started strong and humbly, but they have become self-absorbed and blinded by their own self-importance. Revelation 3:16, Job 33:10, and Psalm 125:5 highlight and exemplify the traits associated with this group. These people suffer from lukewarmness and subsequently risk being alienated from God due to indifference. Again, I've italicized certain words for emphasis and clarity.

> But behold, God finds occasions against me and causes of alienation and *indifference*; He counts me as His enemy. (Job 33:10 AMPC)

> So, because you are *lukewarm* and neither cold nor hot, I will spew you out of My mouth! (Revelation 3:16 AMPC)

> As for such as turn aside to their crooked ways [of *indifference* to God], the Lord will lead them forth with the workers of iniquity. Peace be upon Israel! (Psalm 125:5 AMPC)

Notice that indifference, which I highlighted, is associated with alienation from God. These could well be people who know the truth but no longer practice it. They may believe God, but since they don't act on that faith, they render it inoperative (James 2:17). They have a form of godliness, but it's become destitute of God's power. They may have descriptive knowledge of God but progressively spend less time in His manifest presence. They may once have been popular in heaven but now prefer popularity on earth. Their faith has lost its power, because it's no longer activated and displayed through acts of obedience and a genuine first love.

> As the body without the spirit is dead, so faith without deeds is dead. (James 2:26 NIV)

> So also faith, if it does not have works (deeds and actions of obedience to back it up), by itself is destitute of power (inoperative, dead). (James 2:17 AMPC)

THE INTENTIONAL

This third group is intentionally involved in counterfeit spiritual activities and fully embracing it. They aren't oblivious to the fact that there is a spiritual realm, but they enter that realm through a portal other than the only safe Door.

> So Jesus said again, I assure you, most solemnly I tell you, that I Myself am the Door for the sheep. (John 10:7 AMPC)

People in this group explicitly and openly engage in counterfeit spiritual activities and experience very real encounters with spiritual forces, which are at odds with the kingdom of God. The Scriptures are very explicit in condemning involvements in these activities. As reflected in Table 3, here are just some of the biblical examples of counterfeit practices or roles.

- Consult mediums and soothsayers (Isaiah 8:19).
- Consult mediums or wizards (Leviticus 19:31).
- Practice divination, fortune-telling, witchcraft, interpreting omens, sorcery, charm, or spell casting; being a medium or necromancer (Deuteronomy 18:9–14).
- Practice murder and sorcery (Revelation 9:21; Jeremiah 27:9).
- Worship handmade gods or idols (Jeremiah 10:11–15; 51:17).
- Pay homage to idols (Revelation 9:20; Deuteronomy 4:28).
- Trust in pagan lies and counterfeit gods (Jeremiah 13:25; Ezekiel 20:28).
- Use occult arts and books (Acts 19:19).

- Practice divination (Jeremiah 14:14; 27:9).
- Counterfeit meditation (Psalm 38:12).
- Use magic, omens, *or* witchcraft (or predict events by horoscope or signs and lucky days) (Leviticus 19:26).
- Worship nature, the moon, or stars (Deuteronomy 4:15–20).
- Counterfeit apostles (2 Corinthians 11:13).
- Counterfeit prophets who prophesy lies in God's name (Jeremiah 14:14; 23:15; Ezekiel 13:9; 14:10; Lamentations 4:13).
- Counterfeit teaching (Galatians 1:7; 5:9).
- False preachers (Matthew 7:15–20)
- False leaders, deceivers, seducers, imposters (2 John 1:7).

The Bible overtly condemns the practice of consulting with mediums and soothsayers (Isaiah 8:19–22), and consulting with mediums or wizards (Leviticus 19:31), divination, fortune-telling, witchcraft, sorcery, and spell casting (Deuteronomy 18:9–14), to name just a few. Divination is mentioned again in Jeremiah 14:14 and Jeremiah 27:9. Sorcery is again emphasized in Revelation 9:21 and Jeremiah 27:9. Counterfeit activities involving the worship of idols, nature, and counterfeit gods are highlighted in Jeremiah 10:11–15; 13:25; 51:17; Deuteronomy 4:15–28; Ezekiel 20:28; and Revelation 9:20. Counterfeit apostles, prophets, teachers, preachers, and leaders are highlighted in 2 Corinthians 11:13; Jeremiah 14:14; 23:15; Ezekiel 13:9; 14:10; Lamentations 4:13; Galatians 1:7; 5:9; Matthew 7:15–20; and 2 John 1:7.

SHIFTING FROM COUNTERFEIT SPIRITUAL INTELLIGENCE TO AUTHENTIC SPIRITUAL INTELLIGENCE

Interestingly, some of the people who demonstrate high spiritual intelligence today (even some well-known ministers) once fell into one of the three categories of people described above. They once had counterfeit spiritual intelligence and openly talk about how deceived they were and how oppressive it was. Their affinity for things to do with the spiritual realm helped them quickly accelerate through the degrees of spiritual intelligence, and today they represent some of the most well-respected spiritual leaders. Sid Roth, world-renowned author and host of *It's Supernatural*, and many of his guests exemplify how people can transition from counterfeit spiritual intelligence to high spiritual intelligence.[40]

The apostle Paul, who wrote most of the New Testament, is another example of someone who shifted from counterfeit intelligence to high spiritual intelligence. He was someone who demonstrated strong counterfeit spiritual intelligence before his spiritual encounter with Jesus. Interestingly, he was quickly responsive to Jesus when He appeared to him in a vision. In that moment, Paul could perceive God; he could see with his spiritual eyes and knew without question whom he was communicating with. He also accurately assessed and discerned what he was perceiving and responded wisely by promptly obeying the instructions Jesus gave. This is yet another example of spiritual intelligence, quick and accurate processing of spiritual input, and appropriate relationship management with the Son of God, in this case. In Paul's Damascus moment, when he perceived Jesus for the first time, he speedily responded with repentance and swiftly shifted his attitude and prior mindset toward God's will. This is also a great example of quick repentance, which is so vital for advancing to spiritual maturity. Paul displayed phenomenal features and fruits associated with high spiritual intelligence, clear perceptual awareness, a quick mindset shift, prompt obedience, and the fear of God. Interestingly, his natural sight was temporarily removed upon obtaining his spiritual sight.

Before acquiring his revelation of Jesus, Paul regularly assaulted, imprisoned, and murdered believers, pursuing them as a violent antagonist. He understood there was a God but was inadvertently waging war against His people. Like most modern-day versions of counterfeits, he hated anyone who didn't agree with him. After receiving revelation knowledge from Jesus and quickly repenting, however, he went on to experience incredible levels of spiritual intelligence and enjoyed many more of the fruits associated with it.

The following verses paint a picture of Paul when he had counterfeit spiritual intelligence:

But Saul began ravaging the church [and assaulting believers]; entering house after house and dragging off men and women, putting them in prison. (Acts 8:3 AMP)

Even though I was formerly a blasphemer of our Lord and a persecutor [of His church] and a shameful and outrageous and violent aggressor [toward believers]. Yet I was shown mercy because I acted out of ignorance in unbelief. (1 Timothy 1:13 AMP)

Notice in the verses below the dramatic change in Paul's life when he developed high spiritual intelligence. Paul not only perceived God clearly and processed with precision what God was saying, but his message was followed by dramatic signs, wonders, and miracles. He not only perceived accurately, but he responded appropriately with behavior that was highly congruent with the culture of heaven. His spiritual intelligence was spectacular.

Now in Iconium Paul and Barnabas went into the Jewish synagogue together and spoke in such a way [with such power and boldness] that a large number of Jews as well as Greeks believed [and confidently accepted Jesus as Savior]. (Acts 14:1 AMP)

So Paul and Barnabas stayed for a long time, speaking boldly *and* confidently for the Lord, who continued to testify to the word of His grace, granting that signs and wonders (attesting miracles) be done by them. (Acts 14:3 AMP)

God was doing extraordinary *and* unusual miracles by the hands of Paul. (Acts 19:11 AMP)

THE COUNTERFEIT COPIES THE AUTHENTIC

Let's think this through more thoroughly. If spiritual intelligence grows through the renewing of your mind with truth and thoughts that align with God's Word, then counterfeit intelligence deviously copies the same mental processes but uses lies and destructive thoughts that are contrary to the knowledge of God. We need to pay attention to our thought lives, focus on what's excellent, meditate on the Word of God, imagine Him, and replace toxic thoughts with God's truth (Philippians 4:8).

> For though we walk (live) in the flesh, we are not carrying on our warfare according to the flesh and using mere human weapons. For the weapons of our warfare are not physical [weapons of flesh and blood], but they are mighty before God for the overthrow and destruction of strongholds, [Inasmuch as we] refute *arguments* and *theories* and *reasonings* and every proud and lofty thing that sets itself up against the [true] knowledge of God; and we lead every thought and purpose away captive into the obedience of Christ (the Messiah, the Anointed One). (2 Corinthians 10:3–5 AMPC; emphasis mine)

Look carefully at the words *arguments*, *theories*, and *reasonings*, which I italicized in the verses above. These are all intellectual mental processes. There is nothing wrong with them per se, but what makes them counterfeit in this example is that they are setting themselves up against the true knowledge of God. Remember that eternal life is to know God, and many will be denied access into heaven because they didn't truly know God (John 17). That is one of the highest revelations the enemy wants to deprive all people of. He doesn't seem to care if people *believe* in a version of God or the things of God, just as long as they don't get to genuinely *know* God.

A key difference across the various degrees of spiritual intelligence is the manifest fruits they generate in a person's life. Unlike the rich, vitality offered by the life-giving fruits associated with high spiritual intelligence, counterfeit spiritual intelligence manifests vastly different fruits. Some of these are reflected below and in Table 3. Even if counterfeit spiritual activities may be appealing and seem "innocent" at first, the eventual outcomes and fruits are revealing. Counterfeit spiritual activities eventually generate fruits associated with darkness, destruction, depression, paranoid loneliness, extreme pride, and deep-seated hate. Take a closer look at some additional fruits associated with it.

- Distress and anguish (Isaiah 8:22)
- No peace (Isaiah 48:22).
- Destruction and shame (Philippians 3:19)
- Death (Romans 6:23; Leviticus 20:27).
- Confusion and destruction (Deuteronomy 28:20).
- Separation from God (Romans 5:15–17).

- Blasphemer of God and persecutor of His church; outrageous and violent aggressor toward believers (1 Timothy 1:13).
- Loveless, joyless, paranoid loneliness, brutal temper, uncontrolled, and uncontrollable addictions (Galatians 5:19–21).
- Conditional love and affection (John 15:19).
- Obsession with evil, hate for the truth l (2 Thessalonians 2:9–12).
- Contrived doctrine and self–focus (Matthew 7:16).
- Lawlessness, violence, and corrupt wisdom (Ezekiel 28:16–17).
- Puffed up with pride and stupefied with conceit; woefully ignorant; morbid fondness for controversy and disputes and strife, which result in envy and jealousy, quarrels and dissension, abuse and insults and slander, and base suspicions; perpetual friction (1 Timothy 6:3–5).
- Vexation, irritation, exasperation, aggravation, annoyance, anger, sorrow, regret, disappointment, worry, unhappiness (Ecclesiastes 1:18).
- Delusion, seduction, lying, hypocrisy, and seared conscience (1 Timothy 4:1–2).
- No contrition (Revelation 16:9).

LOVE IS OUR GREATEST SPIRITUAL WEAPON

God didn't leave us helpless, though. He made it possible for us to really know Him and gain complete victory over the schemes of the enemy. Through our union with Jesus, we possess weapons of warfare and strategies powerful enough to overthrow and destroy all the enemy's strongholds. God also gave us His love, authority, and power over all the power the enemy possesses.

> Behold! I have given you authority and power to trample upon serpents and scorpions, and [physical and mental strength and ability] over *all* the power that the enemy [possesses]; and *nothing* shall in any way harm you. (Luke 10:19 AMPC; emphasis mine)

> In conclusion, be strong in the Lord [be empowered through your union with Him]; draw your strength from Him [that strength which His boundless might provides]. Put on God's whole armor [the armor of a heavy-armed soldier which God supplies], that you

may be able successfully to stand up against [all] the strategies and the deceits of the devil. For we are not wrestling with flesh and blood [contending only with physical opponents], but against *the despotisms, against the powers, against [the master spirits who are] the world rulers of this present darkness,* against the spirit forces of wickedness in the heavenly (*supernatural*) sphere. Therefore put on God's complete armor, that you may be able to resist and stand your ground on the evil day [of danger], and, having done all [the crisis demands], to stand [firmly in your place]. Stand therefore [hold your ground], having tightened the belt of truth around your loins and having put on the breastplate of integrity and of moral rectitude and right standing with God, And having shod your feet in preparation [to face the enemy with the firm-footed stability, the promptness, and the readiness produced by the good news] of the Gospel of peace. Lift up over all the [covering] shield of saving faith, upon which you can quench all the flaming missiles of the wicked [one]. And take the helmet of salvation and the sword that the Spirit wields, which is the Word of God. Pray at all times (on every occasion, in every season) in the Spirit, with all [manner of] prayer and entreaty. To that end keep alert and watch with strong purpose and perseverance, interceding in behalf of all the saints (God's consecrated people). (Ephesians 6:10–18 AMPC; emphasis mine)

Notice, as God's family, our spiritual challenge is against the despotisms, powers, and the master spirits who are the world rulers of this present darkness in the supernatural sphere. We must stay alert and watch with a strong purpose, not just for ourselves but for those who inadvertently engage in counterfeit spiritual intelligence activities. We were born to counter the darkness and display God's love despite it. We were called to love all humans, even the unlovable and those who hate us. God has empowered us to do so; it's our greatest weapon, and it works without fail every time.

Before we proceed with the next chapter, which explores some of the contemporary versions of counterfeit spiritual intelligence, let's pray.

God, forgive me for any ignorance and indifference associated with spiritual things. I renounce any involvement in counterfeit spiritual activity (consciously, subconsciously, knowingly, or unknowingly) at any time in my life. Forgive me, God, and cleanse me of all unrighteousness associated with those activities. Forgive me for any of the things I have done and said because of my involvement in those activities. I apologize for offending You and breaking Your heart. Please free me from any bondage and strongholds I may have developed because of my involvement. Illuminate and expose any counterfeit spiritual activity I may currently be ignorantly involved in, and free me from any spiritual blind spots I may have. Let every stronghold in my mind associated with these activities be eradicated from my subconscious and conscious mind. Thank You for Your endless mercy, profound forgiveness, and unconditional love for me. In Jesus' precious name. Amen.

CHAPTER
9

Contemporary Versions of Counterfeit Spiritual Intelligence

Your coins are all counterfeits.
Your wine is watered down.
Your leaders are turncoats
who keep company with crooks.
They sell themselves to the highest bidder
and grab anything not nailed down.
They never stand up for the homeless,
never stick up for the defenseless.

—Isaiah 1:21–23 (MSG)

In this chapter, we will examine some modern-day manifestations of counterfeit spiritual intelligence. We'll also explore the major distinctions between genuine and counterfeit spiritual intelligence.

THE RISE OF CHRISTIANS INVOLVED IN NEW AGE PRACTICES

Research shows that 62 percent of Americans who self-identify as Christian hold some kind of New Age belief, including almost 50 percent of evangelical Protestants.[41] Just as the New Age movement has attempted to adopt quantum physics as their mantra, New Age scholars have crafted counterfeit versions of spiritual intelligence using an approach devoid of God and disguised under a shroud of quantum physics theory and idealism. Current scientific research, however, is demonstrating a remarkable convergence of quantum physics and biblical theology. Quantum physics actually substantiates the existence of the spiritual realm. New Agers focus on cultivating a sense of universal oneness and the belief that all is god and all is one. By contrast, those with genuine faith in the God of the Bible believe passionately in the existence of God as a *personal* being who is clearly set apart from His creation.

God wants everyone to move into the realm of knowing Him through firsthand experience, not secondhand theological dogma, blind adherence, wishful thinking, or religious obligation. New Age pantheism teaches that you are god and that your consciousness is divine consciousness. Scripture, however, teaches us that there is only one true God, and only through a spiritual rebirth experience through His Son can people have access to His mind. Biblical teaching makes it very explicit that while we are to imitate God (Ephesians 5:1–2), partake of His divine nature (2 Peter 1:4), and share His mind (1 Corinthians 2:16), we aren't God and will never be. Moreover, knowing God intimately and personally through genuine revelation knowledge of Him is completely different from merely "believing" through secondhand descriptive knowledge of a distant entity or a New Age idea that you are god and everything is one.

The biblical worldview makes it very clear that the supernatural should be a natural part of every believer's life experience, and their faith is based on God and His Word, not on some positive energy, self-elevation, or vibration. The common thread in most New Age thought, however, is the idea of oneself changing self. The irony is that this line of thinking is nothing new. The age-old temptation of the false promise of godhood or divinity continues to try to reinvent itself, even audaciously referring to itself as "new." Counterfeit intelligence, remember, is the copy of something of significant value and is cunningly designed to appear legitimate. Since genuine spiritual intelligence is such a valuable commodity for success in this life and the life to come, and is derived only from an authentic relationship with the living God, it's no wonder the enemy has attempted to copy it.

THE RISE OF COUNTERFEIT PRODUCTS AND SERVICES

Interestingly, results of a 2016 study by the Organization for Economic Co-operation and Development (OECD) revealed that trade in counterfeit goods was increasing at an alarming rate and amounted to as much as 3.3 percent of world trade.[42] Consumers who confuse fake products for the real thing can experience dangerous side effects. Moreover, organizations whose products are counterfeited also potentially suffer devastating results due to false products disguised as the real thing and getting negative or false reviews. Unsuspecting customers who have inadvertently been ripped off become despondent and leery of even previously reputable products. Honest manufacturers and sellers suffer losses directly in diminished profits and indirectly through downgraded reputations and poor public perception. Counterfeit goods get fake positive reviews, and genuine products get poor reviews because of the inferior quality of products posing in their place. The ramifications of this problem in the global economy are huge.

This growing surge of fake products, lookalike merchandise, and misrepresentations of authentic products is also a reflection of what is taking place spiritually. Many people are being ripped off by phony prophets. They are being lied to by popularity-seeking plastic pastors, who are no longer shepherds with hearts after the one true Shepherd (see Zechariah 10:3). They're been presented with a false gospel by counterfeit evangelists and being fed false promises by bogus teachers. These pulpit profiteers and manipulative ministry marketers are the modern-day versions of the temple traders in Jesus' day. While counterfeit traders on earth may get away with their deceptive schemes, Jesus is coming to turn the "tables" and expose the modern-day ministry masqueraders around the temple who market to His people.

False preachers are saturated with practiced sincerity and have the appearance of promoting the Word. Instead of staying true to the original call of God on their lives, they exploit people's emotions and peddle their overhyped products for their own purposes. People with low spiritual intelligence are often duped into following their farces and don't discern the deception behind their brands. They tend to talk the world's language, and their unsuspecting followers buy their lies, believing everything they say.

> Be wary of false preachers who smile a lot, dripping with practiced sincerity. Chances are they are out to rip you off some way or other. Don't be impressed with charisma; look for character. Who preachers *are* is the main thing, not what they say. A genuine leader will never exploit your emotions or your pocketbook. These diseased trees with their bad apples are going to be chopped down and burned. (Matthew 7:15–20 MSG)

> My dear children, you come from God and belong to God. You have already won a big victory over those false teachers, for the Spirit in you is far stronger than anything in the world. These people belong to the Christ-denying world. They talk the world's language and the world eats it up. But we come from God and belong to God. Anyone who knows God understands us and listens. The person who has nothing to do with God will, of course, not listen to us. This is another test for telling the Spirit of Truth from the spirit of deception. (1 John 4:4–6 MSG)

THE RISE OF SELF-OBSESSION AND FALSE CREDIBILITY

The Bible warns us that in the end-times people will be lovers of themselves, self-centered, and lovers of vain amusements rather than lovers of God. It makes sense then that books, ideologies, and worldviews that focus on oneself changing self, the attainment of personal perfection, or the elevation of self to the level of divinity will become increasingly popular in these latter days. Sustained regeneration and genuine personal transformational change don't come through our personal power but by the Spirit of God (see Zechariah 4:6).

There is a plethora of information on the internet that uses quantum jargon to create an appearance of scientific credibility. Don't be duped into thinking that the proliferation of books linking New Age beliefs and quantum physics means that quantum physics is New Age or that New

Age beliefs are new. By appearing knowledgeable about quantum physics, many New Age authors or "Christians" who dabble in New Age practices have gained credibility by association. New Age pantheism is a type of theology that believes there is no transcendent, personal deity outside of time and space. Rather, it insists that God is the substance and innermost essence of each individual thing in the universe. New Agers assert that consciousness isn't a by-product of brain activity but the building block of the universe itself and that reality is ultimately reduceable to it.[43]

Former New Agers Steven Bancarz and Josh Peck wrote *The Second Coming of the New Age: The Hidden Dangers of Alternative Spirituality in Contemporary America and Its Churches*. In their book, they say "mediation and yoga, for example, are both predicated on the assumption that there is a fundamental field of consciousness (God) that lies at the foundation of the natural world. The word "yoga" literally means "union" and refers to the unification of the personal self with the universal self. Yoga cannot exist definitionally or in practice with its commitments to pantheism, and meditation loses spiritual context if there is ultimate reality available in nature that one can access."[44] *Merriam-Webster's Dictionary* defines *yoga* as "a Hindu theistic philosophy teaching the suppression of all activity of body, mind, and will in order that the self may realize its distinction from them and attain liberation."[45] Most people who practice yoga and are professing followers of Jesus are simply looking to stretch and enhance their physical well-being. Stretching is something we should all do, but posturing through the practice of yoga involves spiritual activity beyond physicality.

Counterfeit intelligence will always disguise itself as something beneficial to the recipient, but while the intentions may be "innocent," the outcomes can be costly. While there are numerous levels of spiritual techniques employed in different types of yoga, at its root, the practice is Hindu and one of self-transcendence, which is incompatible with monotheism. It's like trying to force competing smartphones to sync or like trying to mix oil and water. Just like the structure of an oil molecule is nonpolar and more attracted to other oil molecules, so too water molecules are more attracted to each other. Spiritually this same pattern occurs. Pantheism is attracted to itself, and monotheism is attracted to itself; the two are spiritually incompatible and irreconcilable.

If your ultimate ambition is to genuinely know God and connect with His heart and mind in the most personal and intimate way, why would you risk compromising that relationship by dabbling in anything that has its roots in pantheism? The shocking reality, however, is that there is a movement that seeks to retool yoga to fit the teachings of Jesus, and entire Christian yoga ministries and businesses are being formed as a result.[46] The Bible warns us *not* to pay homage to idols (Revelation 9:20; Deuteronomy 4:28; Acts 15:29), which include things like postures named after Hindu gods (even if unintentionally). Scripture strictly forbids practicing idolatry in any form and trusting in pagan lies and counterfeit gods (Jeremiah 13:25; Ezekiel 20:28). They are forbidden not just because God is a jealous God (Exodus 20:5) but because the consequences of these activities can have negative immediate and eternal ramifications.

THE RISE OF COUNTERFEIT CHRISTIANITY

Counterfeit Christianity often disguises itself as something extraordinary but incorporates things like quantum physics or neuroscience to enhance its credibility by association. Quantum physics and neuroscience are both clear expressions of God's brilliance, but don't be so gullible as to believe everything someone says simply because they incorporate these concepts into their works. Research on the topic of spiritual intelligence illustrates this very point. While popular authors on the subject present some insightful scientific points of view, they unfortunately wander into New Age thought and quantum mysticism. These pseudoscientists present quantum phenomena as substantiation for their pantheistic beliefs. The reality, however, is that quantum physics actually *further* endorses the biblical worldview and existence of a personal God, who is the intelligent Designer behind the entire quantum world.

Quantum mysticism essentially tries to relate quantum mechanics to things like intelligence, spirituality, and consciousness. That's why so many books written on spiritual intelligence usually incorporate quantum mysticism to create an illusion of legitimacy through association. Buyer, beware! New

Age quantum mystics are lured into the seductive fantasy that all is God and all is one. They try to infer that everything that exists has a form of consciousness, but this is inconsistent with the real science of quantum physics and the Word of God. Be wary of self-proclaimed scientists, who set themselves up as Christian experts and yet personally align themselves with New Age practice. Be watchful of professional Christians offering spiritual products and services that are wrapped in biblical terminology and Christian jargon but are rooted in New Age philosophy.

> The whole point of what we're urging is simply *love*—love uncontaminated by self-interest and counterfeit faith, a life open to God. Those who fail to keep to this point soon wander off into cul-de-sacs of gossip. They set themselves up as experts on religious issues, but haven't the remotest idea of what they're holding forth with such imposing eloquence. (1 Timothy 1:5–7 MSG)

Quantum physics is different from quantum mysticism. Quantum physics emphasizes the observer's effect on the behavior of a subatomic particle. Quantum mysticism stretches this to imply that the thoughts and intentions of the observer influence the behavior of a subatomic particle. The only One who has the authority and power to alter reality at the quantum level is God. The problem is when Christians who aren't actually qualified scientists draw incorrect conclusions and develop new "Christian" teachings around these interpretations. These teachings influence people to believe that even protons have consciousness. This view is neither biblical nor scientific. Humans have minds, but subatomic particles don't. Be careful of being deceived into thinking it's up to you to alter reality at the quantum level so you can create whatever you want in your world through your spiritual intelligence. True spiritual intelligence is accessed only from the Source thereof, God Himself.

Even Jesus said He couldn't do anything without the help of the Holy Spirit (John 5:19; 8:28). He performed miracles and displayed profound intelligence, not because he had mastered a mystical thinking technique but because of His connection to the heart and mind of His Father through the Holy Spirit. Likewise, we can do nothing truly spiritually intelligent without accessing the mind of God through His Spirit. Counterfeit spiritual intelligence poses as the real thing and places the focus of creative power on the created rather than the Creator, on human effort rather than on the Holy Spirit.

Former New Ager Phil Mason says in his book *Quantum Glory: The Science of Heaven Invading Earth,* "It is my personal conviction that the science of quantum physics has been hijacked by New Age teachers ... God is the supreme Quantum Physicist, the world of the quantum has been beautifully and intentionally crafted by a personal God to respond to His voice, and that God alone has the power to alter reality at a quantum level for His glorious redemptive purposes."[47] He asserts, "The rejection of the personal Creator has left them in a twilight zone where they have a consciousness of the mystery without an understanding of the cause or the means through which the mystery came into being"[48]

People who dabble in New Age practices, even if inadvertently out of ignorance or carelessness, inevitably open themselves to the spiritual realm and spiritual forces that are counterfeit. These experiences and encounters are real and constitute a knock-off spiritual reality pervading much of contemporary America and the church. Human effort rather than a firsthand relationship with the Holy Spirit tends to be at the root of New Age thinking. Be very cautious and discerning of New Age practices disguised as "Christian" but involve spiritism and divination. Also be watchful when you see the Holy Spirit presented as a "spirit" with a lowercase *s.* Remember the words of Jesus when He warned that many will come professing to be "The Christ." The Scriptures explicitly condemn these practices, which are actually disguised forms of divination (Deuteronomy 18:9–14; Jeremiah 14:14; 27:9). Apparently some New Agers will even quote Scripture to give the appearance of being "Christian" but are merely masquerading to lure their unsuspecting followers. Pay attention to Jesus' forewarnings. "For false messiahs and false prophets will appear and perform great signs and wonders to deceive, if possible, even the elect" (Matthew 24:24 NIV).

Because we are three-part beings (body, mind, and spirit), we seek meaning and well-being in all three areas. It is therefore not surprising that many get involved in spiritual activities with the intention of enjoying a vibrant life. The unfortunate thing, though, is when so many well-intentioned Christians initiate their spiritual experiences through involvement in New Age practices instead of through Jesus. They inadvertently open themselves up to the spiritual realm through portals other than the only safe Door (John 10:7). Do not be duped into believing you can increase your spiritual intelligence by engaging in mental or spiritual activities rooted in New Age philosophy. Neither be so gullible as to believe you can instantaneously develop authentic spiritual intelligence without an intimate relationship with God.

THE RISE OF CHARISMATIC WITCHCRAFT AND DIVINATION IN THE CHURCH

Charismatic witchcraft, with its associated intimidation and control, is nothing new. Witchcraft is like rebellion (1 Samuel 15:23) and has seductive, manipulative power. It seeks to dominate, intimidate, and control believers to shift their will toward the manipulator's own viewpoint. Some may see this as effective marketing or promotion, but the sad truth is that the church isn't a business and that these activities shouldn't be part of its mode of operation. Ways this can manifest is when initially sincere leaders begin to build their own churches instead of building God's church. They begin to try to intimidate people for their own purposes and manipulate them into making sacrifices they would otherwise not make. This manipulation through fear, eventually affects the minds and spiritual well-being of the members. Spiritual intelligence is vital not only to perceive what is taking place but also to accurately discern the difference between the original and the counterfeit, and what to do if entangled in the latter.

In her book *Discerning Prophetic Witchcraft: Exposing the Supernatural Divination That Is Deceiving Spiritually Hungry Believers*, Jennifer LeClaire warns of the rise of "prophetic cults," "prophetic con artists," "charismatic witchcraft," and "Christian" witches and psychics.[49] Like her, I believe a dramatic showdown is coming to the body of Christ where false prophets, bogus teachers, and plastic pastors are going to be exposed. She defines charismatic witchcraft as "exerting ungodly influence through carnal powers of charisma to seduce someone to think or act according to your will."[50]

The Discipleship Movement or Shepherding Movement, which began in the 1970s, was one such example of charismatic witchcraft. Like so many ministries and ministers, it may have started with fair motives but eventually it became a cultlike movement. People were to check with their pastor for permission before they made any life choices. It got so manipulative that pastors sometimes made those life choices for them. This was extreme manipulation, but it can still be seen in small ways in some of our charismatic churches. This often stems from churches that become more like business organizations. In these once-vibrant organizations, marketing now becomes more important than the Master, meetings are more focused on promoting products than on people, and profitability is given a higher priority than prayer. Since so many of these nonprofit organizations depend on the generosity and volunteering of their members, if they aren't achieving their "business goals," manipulation tends to ensue. *Merriam-Webster's Dictionary* defines *manipulation* as "to control or play upon by artful, unfair, or insidious means especially to one's advantage."[51]

So whether it involves subtle forms of control or extreme versions of domination, it is still counterfeit and contrary to God's heart. Counterfeit preachers, teachers, and prophets will manipulate spiritual data for their advantage to gain power or give themselves a sense of superiority over their followers. They'll exaggerate or lie about what the Lord has said, who they are, and what they can do, for their personal advantage.

Charismatic witchcraft is also evident when ministers seek to build their personal ministry empires at the expense of meeting the genuine needs of their followers and the community in which they're located. In these ministries Jezebel-inspired leaders attempt to abuse, control, and manipulate their flock to gain power. They seek to control and extort unsuspecting followers by manipulating them to offer up their time, talent, and finances to serve the leaders' needs and aspirations. We see this when, for example, finances are subtly redirected to support the pastor's prominence rather than the needs of the people. Where the ministry previously had biblical vision statements, words are tweaked to deceptively justify the diversion of resources. Once-anointed preaching and teaching consequently becomes diluted and watered down. Ministry meetings once focused on Jesus eventually become business meetings focused on marketing and promotion. These "ministers" are often operating out of a Jezebel spirit, which despises the true prophets, teachers, and apostles. The Jezebel spirit always seeks to control and is bent on destroying anything truly prophetic. Jezebel spirits love to maneuver their way into positions of power, insisting on recognition and thriving on discouraging true men and women of God.[52]

Divination is another counterfeit spiritual practice. *Merriam-Webster's Dictionary* defines it as "the art or practice that seeks to foresee or foretell events or discover hidden knowledge usually by the interpretation of omens or by the aid of supernatural powers."[53] The practice of divination and trust in counterfeit gods is explicitly counterfeit and forbidden by Scripture (Jeremiah 14:14; 27:9; Ezekiel 20:28).

Remember, the counterfeit poses as the genuine. Not surprisingly then, spirits of divination masquerade as the Holy Spirit. Idolizing people operating in spiritual gifts or hero-worshipping people with secret "arts" to hearing from God are red-flag warnings of the counterfeit.

In the New Testament, we see an example of a slave girl possessed by a spirit of divination, who was highly profitable for her slave owners. She was foretelling the future and sharing hidden knowledge through the supernatural power of a demon. This a clear example of counterfeit spiritual intelligence. Read how the Bible describes her. "As we were on our way to the place of prayer, we were met by a slave girl who was possessed by a spirit of divination [claiming to foretell future events and to discover hidden knowledge], and she brought her owners much gain by her fortunetelling" (Acts 16:16 AMPC).

The beauty of having authentic spiritual intelligence is that we go to God and seek Him *directly*. Jesus taught us to pray to the Father directly (Matthew 6:9–13), and all examples of godly characters in the Bible modeled how to communicate directly with their Maker. The Lord has expressly told us to ask Him for wisdom (James 1:5). This is another reason why leaders (and followers) must work to maintain a clear conscience through regular spiritual checkups and a lifestyle of quick repentance. To guard against the counterfeit, we need to stay alert, discern the spirits, and walk in the Holy Spirit and Him alone (Romans 8:14; Galatians 5:16).

Reading cards in an attempt to foretell the future or contact a spiritual entity is divination and the converse of genuine spiritual intelligence. Things like tarot cards, pendulums, runes, or any other types of readings that depend on communicating with "spirit" or spirits to obtain information represent counterfeit spiritual intelligence. Enhancing our spiritual connection to God to obtain His spiritual intelligence never involves intuitive card readings of any kind. Nowhere in the Bible does it say to draw near to God using cards. Unfortunately, many who engage in these activities are ignorant of the fact that delving into counterfeit spirituality actually undermines their capacity to hear from God. Remember an analogy we looked at earlier; these individuals are beginning to drift from the dangerous currents of low spiritual intelligence to the tumultuous, foamy waves of counterfeit spiritual intelligence. As we saw earlier, foam makes it difficult to breathe, and even gifted swimmers, if caught in foamy waters, can eventually succumb to its perils.

Beware of counterfeit gifts of prophecy that may be disguised as "Christian" but actually are just another form of divination. An example of this is a New Age practice called "angel boards." These are offshoots of Ouija boards but essentially still represent an attempt to contact spirits. The only spirit we should be inquiring of and communicating with is the Holy Spirit. Any form of "talking boards" or "spirit boards," even if disguised under biblical terminology, remains a form of counterfeit spirituality leading to counterfeit intelligence. Be careful of collecting or inadvertently purchasing objects or receiving gifts associated with paganism, witchcraft, idolatry, palm reading, horoscopes, sorcery, astrology, magic, or anything that seeks to normalize spiritualism without the Holy Spirit. These objects don't have the power to separate you from the love of God, but they can hinder you from walking in spiritual freedom and peace. They can open you to spiritual "AirDrop" downloads you never requested simply because of your proximity to them. Remember, the counterfeit poses as the authentic. Look at how the Bible links rebellion to the sin of witchcraft. "For rebellion is like the sin of divination, and arrogance like the evil of idolatry" (1 Samuel 15:23 NIV).

THE ORIGINAL WILL EXPOSE THE COUNTERFEIT

As people better understand true spiritual intelligence and more easily apply it in their everyday lives, the transformative fruits will become evident. Those who possess it and preserve it will progressively grow more personally acquainted with God and increasingly alert to the bogus version of it. As we make progress in developing authentic spiritual intelligence, the forged version will become more easily detectable. Remember, the only safe portal into the spiritual realm is Jesus, and spiritually intelligent declarations about the future are always and only done through an intimate connection with the Holy Spirit. The Bible instructs us to test the spirits. "Dear friends, do not believe every spirit, but test the spirits to see whether they are from God, because many false prophets have gone out into the world" (1 John 4:1 NIV).

Table 4 below highlights some of the key differentiators between authentic and counterfeit spiritual intelligence. The counterfeit version hasn't enhanced our wisdom nor satisfied our spiritual appetites. The knock-off brand hasn't answered our questions or kept its fake promises of enhanced "peace," "love" and "enlightenment." Only sanctified spiritual intelligence—the original, sourced from God Himself—can accomplish such a feat.

Table 4: Comparisons between Authentic Spiritual Intelligence and the Counterfeit

Spiritual Intelligence	Authentic	Counterfeit
	• Original	• Copy
	• Biblical	• Extra-biblical
	• Eternal	• Temporal
	• Created by God	• Reinvented
	• Involves an invitation	• Involves subtle manipulation
	• Demands a lifelong process of sanctification	• Offers false promise of instantaneous "transformation"
	• Involves self-sacrifice	• Involves self-actualization
	• Generates God-confidence	• Generates pride
	• God conscious	• Self-conscious
	• Friendship with God	• Familiarity and irreverence
	• Popular in heaven	• Popular on earth
	• Relies on the Holy Spirit	• Relies on human effort
	• Involves humility and selflessness	• Involves arrogance and self-centeredness
	• Righteousness through God	• Self-righteousness

The counterfeit poses as the real thing. It often copies the name of the original or uses a mock version of it. The knock-off brands have labels with names like "spirit," "messiah," or "Christ." The Scriptures warn us this situation will be commonplace in the end-times. Just as identity theft has become rampant globally, so too the fake brands of spirituality will attempt to steal the identity of the actual Spirit of God. If we were shopping for an original designer brand, we would make a concerted effort to check the label, right? If we're in a wholesale store or purchasing a product through a third-party seller, we're particularly on guard, right? Why would we then so gullibly purchase and consume counterfeit spirituality without paying close attention to the label?

Missing labels or labels including alternate places are all telltale signs of a counterfeit product, right? How much more should we be on guard for counterfeit versions of the "truth" that comes from a place other than heaven. Why are we so naive as to settle for reinvented versions of the real thing? Counterfeit merchandizers are masters at forgery and all that's fake and faux. Many of us have probably bought inexpensive faux leather, knowing it wasn't real. However, purchasing and consuming a deceptively counterfeit, spiritually related product that, unbeknownst to us, was fake is *never* appreciated.

Before we proceed to the next chapter on modern-day Pharisees and Gnostics, let's pray.

God, thank You for showing me the difference between bogus spiritual intelligence and the real thing. Help me to be especially on guard against any counterfeit versions of it. Forgive me for having any ignorance and for inadvertently getting involved in charismatic witchcraft or divination of any kind. Forgive me for participating in any so-called ministry that manipulates the will of its congregants and uses deception to lure people into doing things they would otherwise not do. Help me to assist others in recognizing the difference between the original and the copy. Free Your people around the world from manipulative "ministries" and pulpit profiteers. Expose the false prophets of our day as well as the plastic pastors, bogus teachers, and self-appointed apostles. Help us to truly appreciate and honor Your real prophets, Your appointed pastors, and Your anointed teachers. Free the global church from the fear of man and help us to fear You alone. Illuminate and expose all counterfeit spiritual activity Your churches may be inadvertently affiliated with. Help us to make the necessary shifts so our ministries become more spiritually intelligent. Thank You for forgiving us and for cleansing us from any contamination by the counterfeit. In Jesus' healing name. Amen.

Modern-Day Pharisees and Gnostics: Masters of the Art of Counterfeit Spiritual Intelligence

> Don't be lured away from him by the latest speculations
> about him. The grace of Christ is the only good
> ground for life. Products named after Christ don't
> seem to do much for those who buy them.
>
> —Hebrews 13:9 (MSG)

> So don't let anyone lead you astray with all
> sorts of novel and exotic teachings.
>
> —Hebrews 13:9 (TPT)

Counterfeit spiritual intelligence may be readily identifiable when we observe people practicing or embracing pantheism, divination, witchcraft, sorcery, or incantations. However, when professing Christian leaders teach falsehoods or peddle God's Word, we observe another unfortunate and deceptive form of counterfeit spiritual intel as well. Read how the New International Version Bible highlights this peddling for profit. "Unlike so many, we do not *peddle the word of God for profit*. On the contrary, in Christ we speak before God with sincerity, as those sent from God." (2 Corinthians 2:17 NIV; emphasis mine).

The Message Bible puts it more bluntly. "This is a terrific responsibility. Is anyone competent to take it on? No—but at least we don't take God's Word, *water it down*, and then take it to the streets to *sell it cheap*. We stand in Christ's presence when we speak; God looks us in the face. We get what we say straight from God and say it as honestly as we can" (2 Corinthians 2:16–17 MSG; emphasis mine).

Notice the emphasis on "peddling God's Word," "water[ing] it down," and "sell[ing] it cheap" in the verses above. These peddlers and pulpit profiteers shortchange the written Word of God by watering it down and selling it cheap. They masquerade as ministers but are actually counterfeits. The counterfeit may even come as a form of Christ but is a twisted or diluted version of Him. The counterfeit entices the "buyer" with captivating terms, but the truth is compromised. If you want to avoid purchasing a counterfeit product, you'd purchase it from the original company, right? If a product is inexpensive and marketed through a supplier or source other than the original, you would be especially skeptical, right? If something seems too cheap to be the real thing, caveat emptor. Notice how the Bible warns us of masquerading counterfeits. "For such people are false apostles, deceitful workers, masquerading as apostles of Christ" (2 Corinthians 11:13 NIV).

The "caveat emptor" always possesses a caveat to the empty promises. Caveats serve as warnings concerning the validity of something. Caveats caution against potential misinterpretation or unfairness. Sometimes these consumer warnings reveal themselves only once the "buyer" is overly committed to the seller or supplier. The "buyer" eventually feels trapped by the ongoing "subscription" to a product that doesn't allow them to cancel or opt out. These are simply analogies, but they help conceptually to capture the bondage these counterfeit spiritual products and services can and do generate. The empty sales promises and the inferior product quality are usually revealed only much later once the purchase commitment has been made. For those of us who have purchased knock-off brands, we recognize that while they may be significantly less expensive, they quickly lose their luster due to their inferior quality. The same is true for counterfeit spiritual products, services, and activities. They are inexpensive and full of hollow promises. Genuine spiritual intelligence is costly but worth the investment.

Counterfeit spiritual products will always seek to elevate "you." They will place all the buyer's attention on themselves. Over time, the focus will become increasingly more on the "self," further enticing the "buyer" into follow-up purchases. False promises about experiencing things like more peace and personal perfection will probably be near the top of the list of promised returns. Because the bogus brand doesn't deliver on its promises, though, the "buyer" will remain unfulfilled and have a perpetual sense of emptiness inside. This ever-increasing counterfeit consumption ironically leads to even further hollowness, an ever-increasing sense of not having enough and never achieving self-actualization.

One of the most deceptive versions of counterfeit spiritual intelligence is when spiritual products or services have God's "signature" forged on the cover, in the contents, or in the packaging. We also addressed this in the chapter on perceptual processing when we explored the importance of ensuring the accuracy of measures, especially when God's associated with them. Clues to the counterfeits who appear to be godly or use His name to help promote the products include the following:

- They're cheap and easily accessible (they don't require people to truly surrender to God).
- There's usually a sales hype attached to them (they exaggerate and overemphasize the features and benefits instead of acknowledging the high price of following God).
- The Word of God is watered down or diluted to make it more marketable to the masses.
- They make promises about how to become a "perfect" version of "self."
- They include extra-biblical "revelation."

- They appeal to the buyer's "selfish" ambitions (rather than the virtue of selflessness).
- And they use enticing words that appear biblical but are actually bogus (they include lots of motivational talk and attach Scripture to them to make them appear godly).

COUNTERFEIT SPIRITUAL MERCHANDISE VERSUS GENUINE SPIRITUAL INTELLIGENCE

In his book *The End of the American Gospel Enterprise*, Dr. Michael Brown, world-renowned and bestselling author, captures counterfeit Christianity succinctly. "We have sold the Son of God for profit and marketed the Holy Spirit for gain. We have merchandized the Word for money and turned the anointing into a commodity. Preaching the gospel is now big business—our spiritual executives grow fat while the hungry sheep go unfed. What will our God do? We have made the ministry into an industry and the church into a corporate name. Instead of revival we have revenue. Big profits are up; true prophets are down."[54] He continues, "We have exchanged soul-winning for showmanship and passed up travail for talent. Once we had powerful ministries, challenging us with the Word. Now we have multi-media extravaganzas, and even sinners find them fun. Salesmanship is at an all time high, salvation at a relative low."[55]

People with high spiritual intelligence know God intimately, not through a familiarity with doctrine but despite it. They have an overwhelming revelation of the majesty and awesomeness of God, and passionately pursue His presence. They regularly engage the mind of Christ and know Him well. They aren't self-righteous or self-centered, and they remove themselves from stardom. They appreciate the importance of renewing their minds and bringing every thought captive. They understand that God is pouring out His Spirit in these last days and that many will be able to prophesy in His name. They also know counterfeit prophetic witchcraft is on the rise in an attempt to counter what God is doing. They aren't confused. They know God firsthand and deeply. They adore Him, not ministry; they embrace their relationship with Him, not a religious system. They have a lifestyle of prayer and diligently study the Scriptures for themselves. They love God with a first love and care deeply about others. They have a distinct revelation of the high stakes and high price of discipleship, and they clearly discern the counterfeit.

Too many churches have fallen for the counterfeit. They have become experts at acquiring the praises of people but are novices in radiating the power of the High Priest. People employing counterfeit intelligence have a deluded sense of self-righteousness. They are religious gamers, who rely on their own human effort and personal creative power, not on the Holy Spirit.

Take a look at how The Message Bible rebukes these religious gamers.

> Quit your worship charades.
> I can't stand your trivial religious games:
> Monthly conferences, weekly Sabbaths, special meetings—
> meetings, meetings, meetings—I can't stand one more!
> Meetings for this, meetings for that. I hate them!
> You've worn me out!
> I'm sick of your religion, religion, religion,
> while you go right on sinning.
> When you put on your next prayer-performance,
> I'll be looking the other way.
> No matter how long or loud or often you pray,
> I'll not be listening.
> And do you know why? Because you've been tearing
> people to pieces, and your hands are bloody.
> Go home and wash up.
> Clean up your act.
> Sweep your lives clean of your evildoings
> so I don't have to look at them any longer.
> Say no to wrong.
> Learn to do good.
> Work for justice.
> Help the down-and-out.
> Stand up for the homeless.
> Go to bat for the defenseless. (Isaiah 1:13–17 MSG)

In his book *Breaking Intimidation*, John Bevere, globally renowned and bestselling author, makes a sobering point: "Could it be that we have done with the New Testament what the Pharisees did with the Old? Have we limited our knowledge of God to our doctrine and our knowledge of the Scriptures, even in evangelical churches? Doctrine does not establish a relationship with God; it only defines it!"[56]

COUNTERFEIT SPIRITUAL INTELLIGENCE THROUGH MODERN-DAY GNOSTICS

Another form of counterfeit spiritual intelligence is evident in Gnosticism. In his book *The New Gnostics: Discerning Extra-Biblical Revelation in the Contemporary Charismatic Movement*, Phil Mason describes Gnosticism as "a false revelatory movement claiming higher spiritual revelation than the rest of the church."[57] Gnosticism places emphasis on direct prophetic revelation that is extra-biblical. The key to detecting it is that the divine revelations aren't in alignment with Scripture. Gnostics seek spiritual knowledge and mysteries beyond the scope of the Bible. Clearly reflected here once again is the attempt to take something as important as gaining revelation knowledge and perverting it. Mason correctly asserts, "I have observed that Christians who have had a degree of 'word of faith' influence in their spiritual background are particularly susceptible to this kind of teaching. The usual profile is a Christian from the Pentecostal tradition who has some measure of exposure to a brand of theology that focuses upon quantum leap transformational theology and there are plenty of Word of Faith teachers in the body of Christ who propose this 'one step freedom' paradigm."[58]

These teachings and extra-biblical beliefs deny the sometimes-lengthy process of spiritual sanctification and physical healing believers need to go through as they move from spiritual infancy to maturity. The teachings foster ideas of instantaneous restoration and healing from all previous sin the moment people surrender to Jesus. This line of thinking deceives spiritual babes into thinking they've attained the fullness of Christ simply because they said a prayer. These beliefs often negate or ignore the need for new believers to work through their brokenness until genuine freedom is attained. These pastors and teachers, due to ignorance, impatience, or exaggerated self-importance, twist the Scriptures and teach their followers to deny the symptoms of their illnesses and confess whatever they want.

This is when believers get confused between hope and faith. They confess that they're "believing" when in fact they're only hoping.

Hope isn't faith. Hope deferred makes the heart sick (Proverbs 13:12). No wonder so many babes in Christ are heartsick as they've been told to simply confess things and claim things they need. This line of thinking is unscriptural, since the Word says to work out your salvation (Philippians 2:12) and asserts that faith without acts of obedience is dead (James 2:17). The biblical pattern presented by Jesus, the Old Testament Patriarchs, and the New Testament apostles involves genuine remorse for past sins before authentic reconciliation can take place. This is why we see so many people in the church, who are still radically bound, experiencing traumatic mental illness and suffering serious relational problems of every imaginable kind. They have been lied to by modern-day Gnostics, who tell them to simply "confess" they are healed and whole. This robs people with low spiritual intelligence of the genuine life transformation process that is part of their actual inheritance in Christ. Maturity is never something achievable overnight. Even Jesus learned obedience through suffering.

> While he lived on earth, anticipating death, Jesus cried out in pain and wept in sorrow as he offered up priestly prayers to God. Because he honored God, God answered him. Though he was God's Son, he learned trusting-obedience by what he suffered, just as we do. Then, having arrived at the full stature of his maturity and having been announced by God as high priest in the order of Melchizedek, he became the source of eternal salvation to all who believingly obey him. (Hebrews 5:7–10 MSG)

Pastors and spiritual leaders with Gnostic tendencies fail to acknowledge the genuine brokenness of the human condition. This stems from the false belief that people simply need to say a quick prayer and keep confessing whatever they need until it manifests. Examples of this belief would be people with life-threatening conditions being taught to simply confess they are already healed. In "word of faith" circles, this same logic is also often applied to heart conditions and things pertaining to the conscience and confession. Another sign of Gnosticism is the denial of sin and an overemphasis on having already become the righteousness of God in Christ

Jesus. Can you detect the pattern? People are already "healed" and already "righteous." Notice that this robs people of the truth and actual instruction given by the Bible to confess our sins and practice a lifestyle of quick repentance. Can you see the craftiness of the enemy of our soul in all this? Get people to deny they're sick, and they won't actually get healed. Get people to deny they are sinners, and they won't overcome their addictions. If they don't repent, they won't experience restoration. You see the pattern, right?

The denial of the spiritual journey from a babe to maturity through a process of sanctification is what lies at the root of Gnosticism. The idea that you need to grow in spiritual intelligence would also be incompatible with Gnostic logic. The notion that you can drift from high to counterfeit spiritual intelligence would also be incongruent with Gnostic logic. Gnostic logic assumes you are a new creation and that everything that comprised your previous life no longer even exists. This line of thinking assumes that the brokenness and bondage people may have experienced will simply go away by itself. The gospel truth is profoundly simple to grasp. People, however, are extremely complex and need to practically be ministered to and loved. That takes time, tears, and tenacity.

No wonder so many "word of faith" leaders have themselves drifted from high spiritual intelligence to low or counterfeit spiritual intelligence. They dabble in dubious doctrine, and their dilution of the truth confuses vulnerable spiritual babes. Whereas they should be serving as shepherds after God's heart (Jeremiah 3:15), they exchange their responsibilities to genuinely care for people for personal prominence.

COUNTERFEIT SPIRITUAL INTELLIGENCE THROUGH HYPER GRACE AND OTHER FALSE TEACHINGS

In his book *Hyper-Grace: Exposing the Dangers of the Modern Grace Message*, Dr. Michael Brown says, "Within the hyper-grace movement there are some especially dangerous seeds that resemble the ancient Gnostic heresy."[59] Gnostics believe we're incapable of committing real sins, even if our bodies are engaging in them. Extreme hyper-grace teachers emphasize we no longer have a sinful nature, based on verses such as Romans 6:6 and

Romans 7:17, and they believe this means repentance of sin is no longer needed. Hyper-grace teachers misapply Scripture and don't believe sin can separate them from God because it's confined to the flesh; and when they sin, it's not really them.

Can you see the similarity in their logic with Gnostics? They're essentially deceiving people into thinking that after their initial rebirth experience, they don't need to repent of sin again. Can you see how this belief would rob someone from being able to maintain a clear conscience before God and prevent them from establishing and maintaining a close relationship with a holy God? Without a lifestyle of quick repentance and actual remorse for sin, genuine restoration and revival won't be forthcoming. Can you see why the enemy of our souls would want to craft such a heresy? By no actual remorse for sin, genuine connectivity with God is undermined, and the development of spiritual intelligence is seriously impeded.

> We know that our old (unrenewed) self was nailed to the cross with Him in order that [our] body [which is the instrument] of sin might be made ineffective *and* inactive for evil, that we might no longer be the slaves of sin. (Romans 6:6 AMPC)

> However, it is no longer I who do the deed, but the sin [principle] which is at home in me *and* has possession of me. (Romans 7:17 AMPC)

Beware of counterfeit pastors, teachers, preachers, and prophets who expound on the grace of God to the exclusion of teachings on repentance and the confession of sin. The basic tenet of hyper grace teaching is that believers don't need to confess their sins, since all their past, present, and future sins have been forgiven. Be on guard against counterfeit preachers who no longer preach repentance. These are the same people who would tell you that people don't need to renew their minds because they have already attained the fullness of the mind of Christ. What an insult to the brilliance of God's mind! The Bible teaches us that, although we're justified by our faith in Jesus, the process of sanctification takes time. Without repentance there can be no reconciliation, and without restoration there can be no revival—not individually, corporately, locally, or globally.

They seem to ignore one of the most important prayers in the Bible, the Lord's Prayer, which explicitly teaches us to ask for forgiveness of our sins. Jesus' blood on the cross certainly paid the price for all our past, present, and future sins, but we still need to maintain a lifestyle of quick repentance. That's why the word is clear on the importance of confessing our sins so we can pray with power and maintain a clear conscience.

> *Confess* to one another therefore your faults (your slips, your false steps, your offenses, your sins) and *pray* [also] for one another, that you may be healed *and* restored [to a spiritual tone of *mind* and heart]. The earnest (*heartfelt, continued*) prayer of a righteous man makes tremendous *power* available [dynamic in its working]. (James 5:16 AMPC; emphasis mine)

> 'And forgive us our debts, as we also have forgiven our debtors. And lead us not into temptation, but deliver us from the evil one.' For if you forgive other people when they sin against you, your heavenly Father will also forgive you. But if you do not forgive others their sins, your Father will not forgive your sins. (Matthew 6:12–15 NIV)

Beware of false teachers who preach a cheap gospel suggesting that once you get saved, you'll always be saved. The Bible explicitly emphasizes the importance of working out our salvation with the tenderness of conscience and serious caution (Philippians 2:12), and stresses that only those who endure to the end will be saved (Mark 13:13).

> Therefore, my dear ones, as you have always obeyed [my suggestions], so now, not only [with the enthusiasm you would show] in my presence but much more because I am absent, work out (cultivate, carry out to the goal, and fully complete) your own salvation with reverence *and* awe and trembling (self-distrust, with *serious caution, tenderness of conscience*, watchfulness against temptation, timidly shrinking from whatever might offend God and discredit the name of Christ). (Philippians 2:12 AMPC; emphasis mine)

Look at how the Word describes false prophets, false teachers, and backsliders.

> But also [in those days] there arose false prophets among the
> people, just as there will be false teachers among yourselves, who
> will *subtly* and *stealthily* introduce heretical doctrines (destructive
> heresies), even denying and disowning the Master Who bought
> them, bringing upon themselves swift destruction. And many
> will follow their immoral ways and lascivious doings; because
> of them the true Way will be maligned and defamed. And in
> their covetousness (lust, *greed*) they will exploit you with false
> (*cunning*) arguments ... Forsaking the straight road they have
> gone astray; they have followed the way of Balaam [the son] of
> Beor, who loved the reward of wickedness. They promise them
> liberty, when they themselves are the slaves of depravity and
> defilement—for by whatever anyone is made inferior or worse or
> is overcome, to that [person or thing] he is enslaved. For if, after
> they have escaped the pollutions of the world through [the *full,
> personal*] *knowledge* of our Lord and Savior Jesus Christ, they again
> become entangled in them and are overcome, their last condition
> is worse [for them] than the first. For never to have obtained a
> [*full, personal*] *knowledge* of the way of righteousness would have
> been better for them than, having obtained [such knowledge],
> to turn back from the holy commandment which was [verbally]
> delivered to them. There has befallen them the thing spoken of in
> the true proverb, The dog turns back to his own vomit, and, The
> sow is washed only to wallow again in the mire. (2 Peter 2:1–3,
> 15, 19–22 AMPC; emphasis mine)

Notice that I've italicized words like *subtly*, *stealthily*, *greed*, and *cunning*
to describe their actions. They once had a *full, personal knowledge* of the
Lord but backslid. As 2 Peter 2 shows, be especially on guard for pastors
or prophets who once had a full personal knowledge of the Lord but have
backslidden. Those are some of the most dangerous, because the babes in
Christ cannot always discern that these previously committed believers are
now backslidden, and they continue to take direction from them.

Also, I don't think preachers who teach falsehoods started in ministry
with the ambition of becoming a "false" pastor or phony prophet. They
may have started out strong and may even have possessed high spiritual
intelligence, but over time, with the pressures of ministry and their lack
of maintaining intimacy with the Holy Spirit and first love for God, their

spiritual intelligence shifted from high to low or from high to counterfeit. That's why Jesus was (and still is) so adamant that we deny ourselves and pick up our crosses daily if we want to follow Him (see Mark 8:34). Counterfeit spiritual intelligence is the converse: it's all about elevating yourself and living for yourself. True spiritual intelligence leads to fullness of life, and the converse ironically leads to death.

Deception is one of the primary elements of counterfeit spiritual intelligence. Ignorance is therefore very dangerous and never an excuse for involvement in these activities. The Bible repeatedly admonishes us to get knowledge and wisdom, and not to be deceived. As we've seen, Hosea 4:6 highlights the reason why God's people can perish spiritually due to lack of revealed knowledge. Let us become alert and on guard against all counterfeit and false teaching that is extra-biblical or hyper grace.

Jesus is the same yesterday, today, and forever. Any teaching that represents Him in a form other than how He is presented in Scripture is counterfeit. Be on guard for "new," innovative methods for hearing from God that are incongruent with the written Word of God and circumvent the cross. Be watchful for false teachers and deceitful pastors, who subtly embrace replacement theologies that diminish the importance of the Old Testament or Israel. Even if the "new" or "revitalized" revelation is disguised under a shroud of quantum physics or neuroscientific jargon, don't be duped into thinking it's from God unless it lines up with His written Word. Shedding new light on old biblically congruent revelation is good, but creating "new" revelation that contradicts the Scriptures is counterfeit.

> You shall not add to the word which I command you, neither shall you diminish it, that you may keep the commandments of the Lord your God which I command you. (Deuteronomy 4:2 AMPC)

Before we proceed to the next chapter on the importance of a clear conscience and a lifestyle of quick repentance, let's pray.

God, thank You for making me aware of how modern-day Pharisees and Gnostics may masquerade in our midst. Thank You for giving me keys to detect them and their deceitful tactics. Expose the Gnostics and Pharisees of this day; where places of worship have been turned into venues to showcase humans, deliver us. Where once-anointed pastors and teachers have elevated their personal ambitions above Yours, rescue us. Where once-humble and contrite spiritual leaders have grown spiritually arrogant and sought fortune and fame more than You, free us from their products and services. Where self-appointed scientists have masqueraded as ministers, deliver us from their lures and lies. Give us courage to conquer and strength to confront the counterfeit with truth. May genuine spiritual intelligence be clearly understood among Your people, and may it protect us from falling for the bogus brand. In Jesus' brilliant name. Amen.

CHAPTER
11

Clear Conscience and Quick Repentance: Requisites for High Spiritual Intelligence

Whereas the object *and* purpose of our instruction *and*
charge is love, which springs from a pure heart and a
good (clear) conscience and sincere (unfeigned) faith.

—1 Timothy 1:5 (AMPC)

Whatever weakens your reason, impairs the tenderness
of your conscience, obscures your sense of God, takes
off your relish for spiritual things, whatever increases
the authority of the body over the mind, that thing is
sin to you, however innocent it may seem in itself.

—Susana Wesley (John Wesley's mother)[60]

THE IMPORTANCE OF KEEPING A CLEAR CONSCIENCE

Merriam-Webster's Dictionary defines *conscience* as "the sense of consciousness of the moral goodness or blameworthiness of one's conduct, intentions, or character together with a feeling of obligation to do right or be good."[61] In Greek, "conscience" is *suneidesis*, which is one's "moral and spiritual consciousness."[62] The conscience of a person is an inner voice that guides us and confirms that we have conducted ourselves with pure motives and sincerity. All people have this innate capacity to sense and discern between right and wrong.

> Therefore, since we know the fear of the Lord [and understand the importance of obedience and worship], we persuade people [to be reconciled to Him]. But we are plainly known to God [He knows everything about us]; and I hope that we are plainly known also in your *consciences* [*your God-given discernment*]. 2 Corinthians 5:11 AMP; emphasis mine)

Conscience comes from the Latin word *conscientia*, meaning "being privy to" or "with knowledge."[63] God is omniscient, "all knowing," and we all have a conscience "with knowledge." This is much like the difference between having a limited measure of downloaded content on our smartphones compared to the seemingly limitless content available to us if we're livestreaming something from the internet through a service provider. So too, when our limited knowledge ("with knowledge" or conscience) connects with the omniscient God ("all knowing"), we can have access to His limitless knowledge.

So if knowledge is a fundamental component of intelligence, since all intelligence involves the acquisition and application of knowledge, then our consciences will naturally and supernaturally play a significant role in our ability not only to develop but also to maintain high spiritual intelligence.

When we align our minds with God's mind (1 Corinthians 2:16), our limited consciences ("with knowledge") begin to have access to His limitless omniscience ("all knowledge"), and we begin to perceive what He's thinking and sense what He's feeling with the aid of the Holy Spirit. In these moments, when our minds connect with His mind, we can begin to tap into thoughts and ideas that can offer solutions to complex societal problems. One thought from God concerning a challenge you're facing can be revolutionary. One thought concerning an algorithmic, mathematical, or mechanical problem can revolutionize an industry. One thought from God concerning a solution to a social problem can offer tectonic change to a region. Emotions, too, are seated in the mind, so one feeling from

God's heart can heal a community. One emotion of God's can radically change a city.

Most genuine believers have only scraped the surface of this accessibility. It's like we've heard about the capability but have resisted it unintentionally because of ignorance or fear of being too "intellectual." It's amazing how so many believers tend to use the word *intellect* to describe the carnal mind. Intellect is far more multidimensional. *Merriam-Webster's Dictionary* defines *intellect* as "the power of knowing and the capacity for knowledge."[64] For some, it's like "intellect" or "intelligence" triggers thoughts of worldly wisdom so they avoid anything associated with it, including praying for it. God wants us to expand our capacity for knowledge and to live intelligently, pray intelligently, and lead intelligently. He wants us to connect with His intellect and in that way enhance our own.

We can also see how vital a clear conscience is to tap into God's omniscience. Simply having some things downloaded and saved on our desktop ("with knowledge") isn't the same as having nonstop, continuous access to "all knowledge" through the omniscient One. Spiritual intelligence involves acquiring and dispensing that "all-knowing revelation." It is exhaustive, broad, and transferable to any area of life, society, nation, industry, or ministry. It is when our "with knowledge" is in alignment with "*all* knowledge" that we are then able to access revelation knowledge from God with accuracy and clarity, and then dispense it appropriately to a world that is crying out for it.

A conscience is our God-given discernment and ability to sense between right and wrong. Repeated ignorance, indifference, or intentional rejection of what the Spirit of God is communicating with us leads to conscience complexes. These may vary from a major feeling of guilt to absolute heartlessness. People who commit horrendous crimes or abuse people or animals with no remorse would be examples of individuals who have become conscienceless. The Scriptures are clear that there are various contrasting conditions associated with the human conscience. It describes these diverse conditions as follows:

- A good conscience (Acts 23:1)
- A sound conscience (Luke 11:34)
- A clear conscience (1 Timothy 1:5)
- A good, clear conscience (1 Timothy 1:19)
- An enlightened and prompted conscience (Romans 9:1)
- A clear, unshaken, blameless conscience (Acts 24:16)
- A tender conscience (Philippians 2:12)
- An uneasy conscience (Romans 14:23)
- A guilty conscience (Proverbs 28:17)
- A stricken conscience (John 8:9)
- A painful conscience (1 Samuel 25:31)
- A conscience that has been overcome (Proverbs 7:21)
- A hurt conscience (Romans 14:20–21)
- A weak, defiled, injured conscience (1 Corinthians 8:7)
- A seared or cauterized conscience (1 Timothy 4:2)
- A darkened conscience (Matthew 6:23)
- Without understanding, conscienceless, faithless, heartless, loveless, and merciless (Romans 1:31)

The conscience is like a barometer, in which God can instantaneously gauge our deepest thoughts and motives. Just as our automobile fuel gauge reveals when our gas tanks are depleted or how our oil gauges indicate when we need to replenish the oil in our engines, so, too, our consciences provide a snapshot of the genuine condition of our hearts. Maintaining a clear conscience toward God strengthens the intensity of our perceptual awareness of His presence and understanding of His will. A pure conscience helps us to more accurately and effectively manage the revelation knowledge we receive from Him and our relationships in general. The Bible exemplifies this reality. "The spirit (conscience) of man is the lamp of the Lord, searching *and* examining all the innermost parts of his being" (Proverbs 20:27 AMP).

The searing of a conscience comes when we repeatedly ignore the internal warning signals and resist the guidance of the Holy Spirit. This can also cause people to develop spiritual cognitive dissonance, in which they display inconsistencies between what they say they believe and what their hearts actually believe. Whatever is the dissonance between what people believe in their minds and what is really in their hearts generates this misalignment. This could also be when people preach on the importance of the great commandment to love yet selectively and inwardly hate people who offend or disagree with them. These motives, thoughts, and feelings may all be entirely hidden to humans, but God sees them. These misalignments have the potential to constrain our spiritual perceptual awareness, downgrade our discernment, disable our moral compass, and deactivate our connection to the mind of God. That is why we have seen many churches crumble and once spiritually intelligent leaders fall into serious sin.

> Holding fast to faith (that leaning of the entire human personality on God in absolute trust and confidence) and having a *good (clear) conscience.* By rejecting and thrusting from them [their conscience], some individuals have made shipwreck of their faith. (1 Timothy 1:19 AMPC; emphasis mine)

> [Misled] by the hypocrisy of liars whose *consciences are seared* as with a branding iron [leaving them incapable of ethical functioning], (1 Timothy 4:2 AMP; emphasis mine)

Faith can be shipwrecked through a seared conscience. That's why you can observe ministers who once had significant ministries shipwreck their faith, because their consciences became injured.

Notice that Jesus warns us about the dangers of spiritual blindness (lack of visual sense) and how terrible it is when one's conscience is devoid of clarity and illumination. "But if your eye is bad [*spiritually blind*], your whole body will be full of darkness [devoid of God's precepts]. So if the [very] light inside you [your inner self, your heart, your *conscience*] is darkness, how great *and* terrible is that darkness!" (Matthew 6:23 AMP; emphasis mine).

Our aim should be to live a life with a good, clear conscience. It strengthens the alignment between our hearts, minds, and actions; and positions us to function more freely on the frequency of the supernatural. It also serves as a tool to intensify the quality of the connection strength we have with

God. Let's ponder how this may look like using the analogy of a Wi-Fi symbol. That is when our smartphones have a strong service connection displayed in the form of four or five curved lines. When, however, the service connection strength is limited or disabled, fewer or no bars will be visible. Similarly, with a clear conscience, our perceptual awareness will be enhanced, and the speed and accuracy with which we process revelation knowledge will be promoted. Just like our devices may have issues we need to rectify through reactivation or repositioning ourselves to receive, so, too, clearing our consciences, rebooting our minds, and repositioning ourselves to receive from God are absolutely vital.

> In view of this, I also do my best and strive always to have a *clear conscience* before God and before men. (Acts 24:16 AMP; emphasis mine)

> Whereas the object and purpose of our instruction and charge is love, which springs from a pure heart and a *good (clear) conscience* and sincere (unfeigned) faith. (1 Timothy 1:5 AMPC; emphasis mine)

We will all make mistakes and have days or seasons when things are challenging and our relationships with others aren't optimal. However, through the highs and lows of our lives, we should always seek to maintain a pure heart and clear conscience. It's a good idea to pray for this as well. People may misinterpret our motives and falsely accuse us, but if our consciences are blameless, we can maintain a strong connection to God. This is something we can and should examine and pray about every day.

> Create in me a *clean* heart, O God,
> And renew a right *and* steadfast spirit within me. (Psalm 51:10 AMP; emphasis mine)

> This is our [reason for] proud confidence: our *conscience* testifies that we have conducted ourselves in the world [in general], and especially toward you, with pure motives and godly sincerity, not in human wisdom, but in the grace of God [that is, His gracious lovingkindness that leads people to Christ and spiritual maturity]. (2 Corinthians 1:12 AMP; emphasis mine)

> I have lived my life before God with a perfectly *good conscience*
> until this very day. (Acts 23:1 AMP; emphasis mine)

Keeping a clear conscience will protect you from slipping from high to low spiritual intelligence or counterfeit spiritual intelligence. Much like when we have a strong broadband signal on our smartphones and can easily access helpful information and answers, a clear conscience enhances our connections to the heart and mind of God. Conversely, when our consciences become guilty and lose their purity, the connectivity is diminished or disabled. I once asked the Lord how some believers could get away with gossiping (an activity that aggravates a person's conscience). He made it clear that they wouldn't lose their salvation over it, but they would lose their intimacy with Him. Maintaining a tender conscience will protect you from offending God and discrediting His name. Understanding the value of it will make you think twice before you're tempted to engage in any kind of activity that will offend Him and place a veil of obscurity over your conscience.

> Work out (cultivate, carry out to the goal, and fully complete)
> your own salvation with reverence and awe and trembling (self-
> distrust, with serious caution, *tenderness of conscience, watchfulness
> against temptation*, timidly shrinking from whatever might offend
> God and discredit the name of Christ). (Philippians 2:12 AMP;
> emphasis mine)

REGULAR SPIRITUAL EXAMINATIONS TO MAINTAIN A CLEAR CONSCIENCE

God wants us all to do regular "spiritual examinations" of ourselves to keep our consciences clear. Tests and exams can generate anxiety, and people like to avoid them, since they may reveal weaknesses or conditions that they would rather be ignorant of. However, tests ensure we are genuinely making progress toward our goals. Tests bring to light areas of vulnerability and provide evidence of our real progress.

> I tested everything in my search for wisdom. I set out to be wise,
> but it was beyond me, far beyond me, and deep—oh so deep! Does
> anyone ever find it? I concentrated with all my might, studying

and exploring and seeking wisdom—the meaning of life. I also
wanted to identify evil and stupidity, foolishness and craziness.
(Ecclesiastes 7:23–25 MSG)

Test yourselves to make sure you are solid in the faith. (2 Corinthians
13:5 MSG; emphasis mine)

I've italicized the apostle Paul's words "test yourselves," and here's why:
because not only are we to be subject to a test, but we need to do it
ourselves. For example, we can check that we love God with all our passion
and intelligence and with a first love intensity, and others as ourselves. We
can examine whom we focus on and worship. We can check whom we're
following on social media and what sights we habitually or repeatedly
return to. We can examine who and what inspires and motivates us.
We can test ourselves and check who we get ideas from and what we are
devoting our time, treasures, and talents to. We can examine what we
meditate and dwell on, whom and what we consistently think about, and
who and what moves us. Are we getting glimpses of God's thoughts? Are
we perceiving things as He does? Are we getting ideas from Him? Do we
have His mindset and His perceptions on matters we're facing and projects
we're working on, whether we're in the business world, education, or simply
seeking solutions to personal challenges?

In addition to regular self-examinations, let us allow the Lord to cross-
examine us. Let us be sensitive to how we fare on His test and ask Him to
highlight whatever is out of line or needs to change. Just as a college class
may have several examinations, each one helping the student to do better
in the next with the ultimate goal of helping them pass the class well, so,
too, multiple spiritual examinations as we spiritually develop are essential.
Receiving performance evaluations and feedback on examinations allows
us to improve in the future and get through our final exams. If we don't
examine ourselves regularly, we take the risk of forfeiting our ability to
connect with God, potentially downgrading our spiritual intelligence and
even our capacity to fulfill our divine callings.

In his book *Driven by Eternity,* John Bevere makes it clear that "in regard
to your calling; you'll not be judged according to what you did, but rather

according to what you were called to do!"[65] He warns, "We pull Scriptures out such as, 'Believe on the Lord Jesus Christ, and you will be saved' (Acts 16:31). If just believing in His existence and that He's the Son of God is all that's required to be saved, then James shows the demons will be saved because they believe. That is ludicrous! To even drive home the point further, James points out that the demons shudder. In other words, the demons fear God more than some who say they have faith but lack corresponding actions of obedience."[66] "Why have we not proclaimed the entire Gospel, just half the story? Yes, salvation is a gift—it cannot be purchased, and it cannot be earned. This is all true. However, we forgot to tell people that the only way to obtain it is to forsake all. Lay down our lives confessing His lordship, and in doing this we will be empowered to live in accordance with His nature."[67]

DEVELOPING A PERSONAL AND
PRECISE KNOWLEDGE OF GOD

God's empowering grace is free but is conferred on us through the personal knowledge of Him. In other words, we don't simply take the grace and neglect the relationship. Grace comes through that relationship. God's grace enables us to live a life of obedience. It isn't an excuse to do our own thing; it actually makes the expectation and standards higher. Look at how the apostle Peter links the grace of God to a full, personal, and precise knowledge of Him.

> May *grace* (God's favor) and peace (which is perfect well-being, all necessary good, all spiritual prosperity, and freedom from fears and agitating passions and moral conflicts) be multiplied to you in [the full, personal, precise, and correct] *knowledge of God and of Jesus our Lord*. For His *divine power* has bestowed upon us all things that [are requisite and suited] to life and godliness, *through the [full, personal] knowledge of Him* Who called us by *and* to His own glory and excellence (virtue). (2 Peter 1:2–3 AMPC; emphasis mine)

If we *truly* feared God, as the Bible says (at least 167 times), and really understood that God won't and cannot make any exceptions to His Word, we would more carefully scrutinize how we're doing long before the "final exam" of life. The salvation prayer that includes faith and acts of obedience (laying down your life for God) is the first step on your journey in your relationship with God. If you simply believe but don't have accompanying acts of obedience, don't be misled into thinking your place in heaven is secured. A letter grade of C on God's final exam won't secure a pass. Nor will early letter grades of A in former stages of your walk with God secure a pass, if you fall short in the later tests. Just because you got an A on the midterm exam doesn't secure an overall letter grade of an A. Don't let anyone deceive you into thinking discipleship is an "easy A." Salvation may be free, but discipleship is extremely costly. Only those who persevere to the end will be saved. Look at how the Bible reiterates these truths.

> And Jesus called [to Him] the throng with His disciples and said to them, If anyone intends to come after Me, let him *deny* himself [*forget, ignore, disown, and lose sight of himself and his own interests*] and take up his cross, and [joining Me as a disciple and siding with My party] follow with Me [continually, cleaving steadfastly to Me]. (Mark 8:34 AMPC; emphasis mine)

> You will be hated by everyone because of your association with My name, but the one who patiently perseveres empowered by the Holy Spirit and endures to the end, he will be saved. (Mark 13:13 AMP)

Notice above how Jesus makes it very clear; *if* others intend to come after Him, they must deny themselves—forget, ignore, disown, and lose sight of their own interests. This is a huge decision. Let no one reading this book underestimate the cost. Let's not be like people who form a long-term contract with a service provider but eventually stop paying the price and end up breaking the contract with the excuse that we didn't realize how expensive it would be. Let's intelligently count the cost and diligently honor our commitment. Grace is free, but ongoing access to it comes at a significant price.

> So then, any of you who does not forsake (renounce, surrender claim to, give up, say good-bye to) all that he has cannot be My disciple. (Luke 14:33 AMPC)

Take note of the high standard of discipleship—the importance of calculating the cost, of persevering and forsaking all. Let us ask our Father to examine and investigate us to make sure we are healthy inside and out; then we will one day pass the ultimate test well, not taking anything for granted. I've italicized certain words in the verses below for emphasis.

> *Examine me*, GOD, from head to foot, order your battery of tests. *Make sure* I'm fit inside and out. (Psalm 26:2 MSG)

> *Investigate* my life, O God, find out everything about me; *Cross-examine and test* me, get a clear picture of what I'm about; See for yourself whether I've done anything wrong—then *guide me* on the road *to eternal life*. (Psalm 139:23–24 MSG)

> Go ahead, *examine me* from inside out, surprise me in the middle of the night—You'll find I'm just what I say I am. My words don't run loose. (Psalm 17:3 MSG)

THE VALUE OF CONSTANTLY KEEPING A CLEAR CONSCIENCE

We need to continually examine our consciences so we don't take anything for granted and undermine or mismanage what we discern or perceive. Our ambition should be to maintain a clear conscience at all times, knowing that it significantly affects the speed and accuracy with which we process revelation knowledge as well as the intensity of our spiritual connection to the heart and mind of God. The Message Bible magnifies this truth. "On a good day, enjoy yourself; On a bad day, *examine your conscience*. God arranges for both kinds of days so that *we won't take anything for granted*" (Ecclesiastes 7:14 MSG; emphasis mine).

Jesus provides a wakeup call in the parable He gives about ten virgins, describing how a few gained access and others, because of their lack of a personal relationship with Him and their careless approach to eternal life, were denied access.

> Then the kingdom of heaven will be like ten virgins, who took their lamps and went to meet the bridegroom. Five of them were foolish [*thoughtless, silly, and careless*], and five were wise

[*far-sighted, practical, and sensible*]. For when the foolish took
their lamps, they did not take any [extra] oil with them, but the
wise took flasks of oil along with their lamps. Now while the
bridegroom was delayed, they all began to nod off, and they fell
asleep. But at midnight there was a shout, "Look! The bridegroom
[is coming]! Go out to meet him." Then all those virgins got up
and put their own lamps in order [trimmed the wicks and added
oil and lit them]. But the foolish virgins said to the wise, "Give us
some of your oil, because our lamps are going out." But the wise
replied, "No, otherwise there will not be enough for us and for
you, too; go instead to the dealers and buy oil for yourselves." But
while they were going away to buy oil, the bridegroom came, and
those who were ready went in with him to the wedding feast; and
the door was shut and locked. Later the others also came, and
said, "Lord, Lord, open the door for us." But He replied, "I assure
you and most solemnly say to you, *I do not know you [we have no
relationship]*." Therefore, be on the alert [be prepared and ready],
for you do not know the day nor the hour [when the Son of Man
will come]. (Matthew 25:1–13 AMP; emphasis mine)

Notice toward the end how the bridegroom (symbolic of the Lord) denied
access to the five virgins who were thoughtless, telling them He didn't
know them. If God is omniscient (all knowing), what type of knowledge
was He actually referring to? He was saying that we have no relationship.
He didn't know them personally and intimately up until the end of
their lives. Carelessness and the lack of a sustained investment in their
relationship with God cost them everything. My prayer is that no one
reading this book will be denied access because they were spiritually
negligent or focused on religious activities, ministry, or humanitarian
service activities; and neglected the development of a genuine and intimate
relationship with God. Don't let apathy, busyness, or ignorance rob you of
this vital relationship. Take a look at how the apostle John clearly shows
the essential connection between knowing Jesus by experience and keeping
His teachings. Notice the pattern: knowing God and obeying His will.
The evidence of *truly* knowing Him is that we *do* what He says.

We know that we have come to know him if we keep his
commands. Whoever says, "I know him," but does not do what
he commands is a liar, and the truth is not in that person. But if

anyone obeys his word, love for God is truly made complete in
them. (1 John 2:3–5 NIV)

THE IMPORTANCE OF MAINTAINING A
LIFESTYLE OF QUICK REPENTANCE

Just as quick response (QR) codes allow users to rapidly access data to
make choices and apply knowledge, quick repentance helps us to swiftly
change our minds to align with God's will. When we're genuinely sorry
for our actions and motives outside of God's will, and we quickly repent,
that's the moment we gain access to the power to overcome whatever it
was that caused us to sin. Genuine remorse and penitence for sin are what
activate the Holy Spirit's power in us to *do* His will. Through this genuine
sorrow for sin, we reset our minds to know and search out true wisdom.
In so doing, we're not just saying sorry, but we're genuinely apologizing for
our missteps, thereby clearing our consciences and repositioning ourselves
to access and apply true spiritual intelligence.

> I turned about [penitent] and my heart was set to know and to
> search out and to seek [true] wisdom and the reason of things, and
> to know that wickedness is folly and that foolishness is madness
> [and what had led me into such wickedness and madness].
> (Ecclesiastes 7:25 AMPC)

While it is simply an analogy, a QR code, without an alignment with an
imaging device, is simply a square grid of black squares and rectangles on
a white background. Only through the correct placement and alignment
of the two can the patterns be appropriately interpreted. Misalignments
and erroneous positioning of the two, much like false contrition and half-
hearted apologies, won't suffice. Similarly, it takes a genuinely contrite
heart that's fully submitted to God to access the strength and power
necessary to overcome sin. We may get away with insincere verbal apologies
with humans, but God looks at our hearts to assess whether there's real
regret.

> Distress that drives us to God does that. It turns us around. It
> gets us back in the way of salvation. We never regret that kind of
> pain. But those who let distress drive them away from God are

full of regrets, end up on a deathbed of regrets. And now, isn't it wonderful all the ways in which this distress has goaded you closer to God? You're more alive, more concerned, more sensitive, more reverent, more human, more passionate, more responsible. Looked at from any angle, you've come out of this with purity of heart. And that is what I was hoping for in the first place when I wrote the letter. My primary concern was not for the one who did the wrong or even the one wronged, but for you—that you would realize and act upon the deep, deep ties between us before God. That's what happened—and we felt just great. (2 Corinthians 7:10–13 MSG)

My sacrifice [the sacrifice acceptable] to God is a broken spirit; a broken and a *contrite heart* [broken down with sorrow for sin and humbly and thoroughly penitent], such, O God, You will not despise. (Psalm 51:17 AMPC; emphasis mine)

The Lord is close to those who are of a *broken heart* and saves such as are crushed with *sorrow for sin and* are humbly *and* thoroughly *penitent.* (Psalm 34:18 AMPC; emphasis mine)

Authentic repentance generates genuine reconciliation and restoration. It makes us more alive, sensitive, and compassionate. It is this level of repentance that's necessary for real healing in individual hearts and nations alike. Reconciliation and revival don't come without real repentance.

Genuine remorse isn't just associated with obvious and "visible" sins like adultery, theft, or murder. It also involves real regret for covert sins associated with desires, motives, thoughts, and feelings. These are things that may not necessarily be apparent in behavior but are the ones God clearly views. These are sins like unbelief, selfishness, pride, hate, and greed. If they're not dealt with quickly, the consequences can lead to spiritual blindness, seared consciences, and spiritual fatalities. God is no respecter of persons, so no one is exempt from the consequences (Acts 10:34).

Anyone who claims to live in God's light and hates a brother or sister is still in the dark. It's the person who loves brother and sister who dwells in God's light and doesn't block the light from others. But whoever hates is still in the dark, stumbles around in the dark, doesn't know which end is up, blinded by the darkness. (1 John 2:9–11 MSG)

The way we know we've been transferred from death to life is that we love our brothers and sisters. Anyone who doesn't love is as good as dead. Anyone who hates a brother or sister is a murderer, and you know very well that *eternal life and murder don't go together.* (1 John 3:14–15 MSG; emphasis mine)

And even if he sins against you seven times in a day, and turns to you seven times and says, I repent [I am sorry], you must forgive him (give up resentment and consider the offense as recalled and annulled). (Luke 17:4 AMPC)

But you walked away from your *first love*—why? What's going on with you, anyway? Do you have any idea how far you've fallen? A Lucifer fall! Turn back! Recover your dear *early love.* No time to waste, for I'm well on my way to removing your light from the golden circle. (Revelation 2:4–5 MSG; emphasis mine)

The best way to respond to sin is to sincerely and quickly repent. If you delay the reset in your mind and resist the Holy Spirit, things will only get more difficult. Continuous disobedience to what God is saying leads to an ever-increasing veil of deception over your conscience. Your capacity to hear from God is essentially blurred and deactivated, and your spiritual perceptual processing capacity is rendered erroneous. It's therefore important to repent not only remorsefully but also quickly. Half-hearted and delayed apologies simply fuel the downward spiral of ever-diminishing spiritual intelligence.

The wise person obeys promptly and accurately. (Ecclesiastes 8:2–7 MSG)

Those people are on a dark spiral downward. But if you think that leaves you on the high ground where you can point your finger at others, think again. Every time you criticize someone, you condemn yourself. It takes one to know one. Judgmental criticism of others is a well-known way of escaping detection in your own crimes and misdemeanors. But God isn't so easily diverted. He sees right through all such smoke screens and holds you to what *you've* done. (Romans 2:1–2 MSG)

Without a clear conscience, genuine faith, and a lifestyle of quick repentance, your ability to spiritually perceive and sync your mind with the mind of God becomes virtually impossible. Our prompt obedience to Him is also a reflection of our genuine love for Him and a sign of how much we really fear Him.

> But if one loves God truly [with affectionate reverence, *prompt obedience*, and grateful recognition of His blessing], he is known by God [recognized as worthy of His intimacy and love, and he is owned by Him]. (1 Corinthians 8:3 AMPC; emphasis mine)

> Look carefully then how you walk! Live purposefully and worthily and accurately, not as the unwise *and* witless, but as wise (sensible, *intelligent* people). (Ephesians 5:15 AMPC; emphasis mine)

> Whoever does not persevere *and* carry his own cross and come after (follow) Me cannot be My disciple. For which of you, wishing to build a farm building, does not first sit down and *calculate the cost* to see whether he has sufficient means to finish it? (Luke 14:27–28 AMPC; emphasis mine)

The purer our consciences, the clearer His message of love and restoration will be ministered through us. We are merely the dispensers of His goodness and carriers of His glory. We may have innumerable weaknesses but with first love, quick repentance, and pure consciences, our connection to God's heart and mind are optimized. This is when we're most helpful to Him and most representative of who He really is. As clean conduits who carry our own cross, we are able to dispense His goodness, carry His glory, and love and lead intelligently.

Before we proceed to the next chapter on the importance of mind renewal for spiritual intelligence, let's pray.

God, forgive me for any spiritual blind spots and any calluses on my conscience. Cleanse and restore my conscience so I can maintain a strong connection to Your heart and mind. Thank You that as I maintain a healthy conscience,

I will be able to more accurately perceive what You are communicating and avoid things that grieve You. Help me to conduct regular self-examinations and develop a lifestyle of quick repentance. Grant me the capacity to diligently maintain a clear conscience so I can love and lead intelligently and represent You well. In the preeminent name of Jesus. Amen.

CHAPTER
12

Mind Renewal to Advance Spiritual Intelligence

And be constantly renewed in the spirit of your mind
[having a fresh mental and spiritual attitude].

—Ephesians 4:23 (AMPC)

The sanest person today is one who knows God the most.

—A.W. Tozer (1897-1963)

MIND RENEWAL AND STRENGTHENING OUR SYNCING CAPACITY WITH GOD'S MIND

Have you ever wondered how the Word of God could place such emphasis on the transformative power of mind renewal? Perhaps you've contemplated how a renewed mind can have such profound influence over our capacity to perform God's perfect will. We looked at Romans 12:2 earlier, but let's ponder it further for a moment. Think about the ramifications of what this verse means. "Do not be conformed to this world (this age), fashioned after and adapted to its external, superficial customs, but be transformed by the *entire renewal* of your *mind* by its new ideals and its new attitude, so that you may prove for yourselves what is the good and acceptable and perfect will of God" (Romans 12:2 AMP; emphasis mine).

Transformation in change management theory and practice denotes radical rethinking and reconceptualization of the status quo. This is also referred to as gamma change or tectonic change. This verse instructs (not suggests) us to be dramatically changed through the entire reconstruction and repair of our minds. Dramatic change is noticeable at every level and affects every part of our makeup—spirit, mind, and body. Interestingly, the Amplified Bible mentions the word *spirit* 839 times, the word *mind* 344 times, and the word *body* 262 times. It's not surprising since we know spiritual transformation precedes mental renewal, and mental renewal is an antecedent to physical transformation.

Constant mental renewal, as Ephesians 4:23 emphasizes, is essential for sustained mental health and well-being. "And be constantly renewed in the spirit of your mind [having a fresh mental and spiritual attitude]" (Ephesians 4:23 AMPC). The Passion Translation says we need to be made *new* by every *revelation*. "Now it's time to be made new by every revelation that's been given to you" (Ephesians 4:23 TPT).

In both Ephesians 4 and Romans 12 of the Amplified Bible, notice, too, the "re" before "new," which suggests that the original design and capability of the mind needs to be restored. It is essential that our minds become reconditioned to the point that we indeed have the mind of Christ (1 Corinthians 2:16).

We can't have the mind of Christ without sharing the same headspace with Him, right? We can't have His spiritual intelligence without this union, right? When the Bible instructs us to have His mind, it means we are truly capable of doing so through *intimacy* with Him. Knowing Him *personally* makes it possible. The Bible also assures us that constantly renewing our minds will dramatically change us. It will give us His perceptions and thoughts toward us and for this world.

Be on guard for false teachers and deceived pastors, who subtly embrace a theology of Christian perfectionism that diminishes the importance of ongoing mental renewal through the maintenance of a personal relationship with God. Be especially on guard against pseudoscientists who seek to present rapid mental renewal solutions that offer "new" revelation beyond the scope of the Bible. Even if the "new" revelation is disguised under a shroud of quantum physics or neuroscientific jargon, don't be duped into thinking it's from God unless it lines up with His written Word. Remember, genuine transformation of the mind can only come through a transformed spirit and sustained intimacy with God.

One heeded thought from God alone has the power to revolutionize our lives. The key to accessing His mind isn't through following a formula-driven process or thinking technique; it is intricately wrapped up in a genuine relationship and frequent interaction with Him. We don't just seek access to it to get secret information and solutions for our personal benefit or merely for things that concern us. We seek Him and Him alone, and the rest follows. If your motive is for selfish gain and ambition, you'll never actually get to share "headspace" with Him. Pursue Him, seek to know the innermost depths of who He is, and you will find Him. This promise is articulated over sixty times in the Bible. Here's just a snapshot, but the pattern is the same. When we seek Him, then we find Him; when we draw close to Him, then He draws close to us. Notice who needs to take the first move! Yes, He loved us first, but when seeking intimacy with God and drawing closer to Him, He explicitly instructs us to be the initiators.

> But if from there you seek the Lord your God, you will find him if you seek him with all your heart and with all your soul. (Deuteronomy 4:29 NIV)

> But first *and* most importantly seek (aim at, strive after) His kingdom and His righteousness [His way of doing and being right—the attitude and character of God], and all these things will be given to you also. (Matthew 6:33 AMP)

> Move your heart closer and closer to God, and he will come even closer to you. But make sure you cleanse your life, you sinners, and keep your heart pure and stop doubting. (James 4:8 TPT)

Have you ever wondered how the apostle Paul could issue such an extravagant directive to believers to glorify God with one mind and one mouth (Romans 15:6) and that we be joined together in the same mind (1 Corinthians 1:10)? Don't these words sound a little too like an impractical dream? Paul was inspired by the Holy Spirit to write these words because they are true and possible. Once we share Christ's mind personally and experientially, we naturally become unified with others who share His mind. It's not something that's regulated or contrived. Our unity with each other, our like-mindedness, is a natural (and supernatural) product of us each being individually connected to the mind of Christ. We don't first unite with each other and force a single-mindedness. We first establish a personal intimacy with Him, and *then* the unity between believers is the outcome. Do you see the difference? That's why we can meet strangers who love and know God intimately and instantly feel a connection and sense of unity with them. It's not because we're trying to desperately follow a "rule" to be in unity; it's because we both intimately know Jesus. This is why Jesus could pray that His followers would be one as He is one with the Father (John 17:21).

UNITY THROUGH SHARING THE MIND OF GOD

Knowing the importance of being unified, Paul pleaded with the believers in Corinth to have the same mind and judgment. His words were inspired instruction from the Holy Spirit and are still relevant today. He pleaded with them to have no divisions and to be perfectly joined together in the same mind (1 Corinthians 1:10). He also instructed them to glorify the God and Father of our Lord Jesus Christ in one mind (Romans 15:6). Notice that Paul didn't say they were to aim for unity centered around a man-made vision or strive for a common organizational culture. He said to be joined together in the same mind (1 Corinthians 2:16).

As we believers draw close to God and develop high spiritual intelligence through an intimate relationship with Him, we progressively access more and more of the mind of Christ. This is how genuine, sustained unity and mental well-being is established among believers. All the team-building activities and fun get-togethers in the world will never achieve the level of unity Paul is pleading with the Corinthians to attain. However, any size group of believers, all possessing the mind of Christ, will make this a reality.

The Bible doesn't exaggerate, and God never gives us instructions we cannot obey. Having one mind isn't just referring to a single goal or a unitary mindset; otherwise the Bible would have said that. We together have one mind as a product of our individual intimacy with God. He is the focus of our affections, and as our minds are constantly being renewed and increasingly hardwired to His mind, the body of believers around the world becomes perfectly joined together with the mind of Christ.

You can see why much of the lack of genuine unity and mental struggles in the global body of "believers" is a product of people not engaging the mind of Christ because they don't actually know the real Him; they know *about* Him or a version of Him but not Him *personally*. He wants to share His mind with us and wants His innermost thoughts and understandings to be unified with ours. In His immaculate design of our minds, He created them with the capacity to connect to His so we could truly know and understand Him. His desire for us to access His thoughts in the deepest way is almost too profound to fathom. It compels us to better appreciate the depths of His lavish generosity and the scope of His limitless love.

It is incredible to think that He designed our minds in such a way that they would be compatible with His, much like our electronic devices can pair using Bluetooth. So by design, the potential capacity exists, but the access is conditional. This is comparable to how our devices don't automatically sync; the pairing is restrictive. In the same way Bluetooth searches for a connection, we need to have our spiritual intelligence enabled and open for revelation from God. He designed our minds so there would be a powerful syncing capacity with His mind.

He wants us to have His Word impressed on our minds, even to our innermost thoughts. "I will imprint My laws upon their *minds*, even upon their *innermost thoughts and understanding*, and engrave them upon their hearts; and I will be their God, and they shall be My people" (Hebrews 8:10 AMP; emphasis mine).

I love how The Message captures the importance of putting our minds in gear so we are ready to receive and welcome the Messiah (today and when He returns). This enables our mental receptors and puts our minds in a posture to receive downloads and regular installations of God's intelligence, thereby enhancing our spiritual intelligence and the fruits associated with it.

> So roll up your sleeves, put your *mind in gear*, be totally *ready to receive* the gift that's coming when Jesus arrives. Don't lazily slip back into those old grooves of evil, doing just what you feel like doing. You didn't know any better then; you do now. As obedient children, let yourselves be pulled into a way of life shaped by God's life, a life energetic and blazing with holiness. God said, "I am holy; you be holy." (1 Peter 1:13–16 MSG; emphasis mine)

STAYING CONNECTED AND IN SYNC FOR DIVINE DOWNLOADS

Just as our electronic devices receive downloads, updates, and installations as we sleep, so too God wants to download solutions, ideas, and faith to us. However, nightly updates on our devices are conditional on our providing password access and making sure our devices are plugged in to the power source. Similarly, our minds need to be in gear, connected, and open to receive "downloads" from God to be fueled daily with fresh revelation. The parable of the connection between the True Vine, the Vinedresser, and the branches illustrates this picture brilliantly.

> I am the *Real* Vine and my Father is the Farmer. He cuts off every branch of me that doesn't bear grapes. And every branch that is grape-bearing he prunes back so it will bear even more. You are already pruned back by the message I have spoken. Live in me. Make your home in me just as I do in you. In the same way that a branch can't bear grapes by itself but only by being joined to the vine, you can't bear fruit unless you are joined with me. I am the Vine, you are the branches. When you're joined with me and I with you, the relation *intimate* and organic, the harvest is sure to be abundant. Separated, you can't produce a thing. Anyone who separates from me is deadwood, gathered up and thrown on the bonfire. But if you make yourselves at home with me and my words are at home in you, you can be sure that *whatever you ask* will be listened to and acted upon. This is how my Father shows who he is—when you produce grapes, when you mature as my

disciples. I've loved you the way my Father has loved me. Make yourselves at home in my love. If you keep my commands, you'll remain *intimately* at home in my love. That's what I've done—kept my Father's commands and made myself at home in his love. I've told you these things for a purpose: that my joy might be your joy, and your joy wholly *mature*. This is my command: Love one another the way I loved you. This is the very best way to love. Put your life on the line for your friends. You are my *friends* when you do the things I command you. I'm no longer calling you servants because servants don't understand what their master is thinking and planning. No, I've named you *friends* because I've let you in on everything I've heard from the Father. (John 15:1–12 MSG; emphasis mine)

In these verses, Jesus reveals the key to staying vitally connected to Him (the Real Vine). He is showing us that God the Father is the Farmer who cuts off any branch that doesn't bear fruit and who cleanses and repeatedly prunes any branch that does bear fruit to ensure it produces even more fruit. Jesus also emphasizes the importance of remaining attached to Him so our prayers will be answered. Did you see that? This kind of pairing and unity provides us with endless access to God's ear and absolute assurance that He will listen to and act upon whatever we *ask*.

Living this kind of life that is connected and synced to God empowers us to produce fruit that otherwise would've been entirely impossible. The spiritual and practical implications are limitless. When we exhibit or manifest natural and spiritual fruit (for example, kindness, love, patience, and so forth), God is honored, and we display and prove ourselves to be genuinely connected to Him.

That's how we get to live out the great commandment to love God with all our passion, prayer, and intelligence—and to love our neighbor as ourselves (Luke 10:27). It isn't that we first love Him, and then we get plugged in. No, we first get connected; *then* we access His love so we can obey Him. Can you see the difference? Jesus also clarifies why He told us these things. The reason? So His joy and happiness may be in us and that they may be so full that they overflow. This is how we get to truly love one another exactly as He loves us.

Once you're personally connected to God in this way, He can install and download His love, His joy, and His thoughts and perceptions to us (even while we sleep in the form of night visions or dreams). By appropriating these downloads, we are then empowered to display and prove we are His children. Without the connection, however, our relationship remains dormant and deactivated, and we remain defeated and devoid of spiritual growth and maturity.

Let us use another technology illustration. It's like when you're trying to pair devices and transfer capability across devices, and the pairing fails. So, too, this pairing capacity God designed for us to have with Him can be incapacitated, disabled, or deactivated. We need to remain activated and attached to Him, even in environments where we might be the only people who have a connection to Him. It takes a devoted heart and a renewed and well-balanced mind, intimately connected to God, to stay and remain "paired" to His love, thoughts, and perceptions.

Similar to how our received signal strength indication (RSSI) on our devices will highlight the power level we're receiving from an access point or router; likewise, our spiritual intelligence signal strength will have varying levels of power and accessibility. Let us continue with this analogy: our spiritual signal strength will reveal how well we can hear a signal or perceive a message from God. When the power is diminished, the data throughput is slower and lower. When conditions are optimal, when we're in right standing, when our hearts and minds are congruent with God's, immense power is made available.

The Holy Spirit not only counsels, heals, and restores us but, as 2 Timothy 1:7 points out, gives us sound judgment and abilities, which result in a well-balanced mind. Anything less than this level of mental well-being is contrary to God's Word and will for us. "For God did not give us a spirit of timidity (of cowardice, of craven and cringing and fawning fear), but [He has given us a spirit] of power and of love and of calm *and* well-balanced mind *and* discipline *and* self-control" (2 Timothy 1:7 AMPC).

I know this verse in Timothy is usually associated with overcoming fear and we will look at it again in the final chapter, but allow me to also focus in on a *well-balanced mind*. Since we were made in God's image and His mind is balanced and whole, our minds too by design should be whole. If we have inherited God's mind (1 Corinthians 2:16), then we should be progressively accessing this part of our inheritance in a balanced manner. Let's stop saying I am a left-brain or right-brain thinker, and let's start activating the whole mind. Moreover, since patterns of thinking, rather than left-brain or right-brain propensities, drive behavior and decision-making, we can further understand why God is as much a mathematician as He is an artist. He is as much a systematic, analytic thinker as He is a creative thinker. Let's also recognize and remember the power of our thought patterns in determining our decisions and behavior. This is entirely biblical (Proverbs 23:7).

MAINTAINING A HEALTHY THOUGHT LIFE FOR MENTAL WELL-BEING

The thoughts we repeatedly and habitually contemplate or meditate on are the ones that will eventually direct our decisions and behavior. For example, if our thoughts are typically directed toward worry, fear, and anxiety, we will inevitably make decisions and act in a way that reflects those fears and worries. Similarly, if our thoughts are directed toward the truth, we will make decisions and act in ways consistent with that.

> Whatever is true, whatever is worthy of reverence and is honorable and seemly, whatever is just, whatever is pure, whatever is lovely and lovable, whatever is kind and winsome and gracious, if there is any virtue and excellence, if there is anything worthy of praise, think on and weigh and take account of these things [fix your minds on them]. (Philippians 4:8 AMPC)

This is why it's so important to cultivate a vibrant and intimate relationship with the Holy Spirit. Not only does He help us develop sound judgment and a well-balanced mind, but He also gives us the grace to face each day without fear and worry, and He gives us the guarantee that we indeed belong to God.

> He has also appropriated and acknowledged us as His by putting His seal upon us and giving us His Holy Spirit in our hearts as the security deposit *and* guarantee of the fulfillment of His promise. (2 Corinthians 1:22 AMPC)

> *And this is no empty hope,* for God himself is the one who has prepared us for this wonderful destiny. And to confirm this promise, he has given us the Holy Spirit, like an engagement ring, as a guarantee. (2 Corinthians 5:5 TPT)

If you read verse 5 of 2 Corinthians 5 in context, you will find apostle Paul is speaking to the Corinthians about the fact that while they were still in their bodies with its challenges, they could always be *full* of hope and confident courage because their mortal bodies would one day be engulfed by eternal life through the guarantee provided by the Holy Spirit. The same words apply to us today.

If people find solace in having a certificate of guarantee for a product or service they purchase, how much more can we rest assured and find great hope and confidence in the fact that we will live forever with God? The Holy Spirit gives us that assurance. He is the One who enables us to perceive that Jesus abides in us. He gives us the perceptual awareness to grasp and comprehend what cannot be understood merely by natural intelligence and the natural senses. He empowers us to increasingly come to know God experientially. He is the One who gives us the capacity to use our spiritual senses and discern with accuracy who He is and who we are in relation to Him. Without close intimacy with Him as believers, our perceptual senses will be dull, and our overall spiritual intelligence will remain undeveloped and dormant. Look at how the Amplified Bible confirms this. "By this we come to know (*perceive,* recognize, and *understand*) that we abide (*live* and *remain*) in Him and He in us: because He has given (imparted) to us of His [Holy] Spirit" (1 John 4:13 AMPC; emphasis mine).

It is through the Holy Spirit that we come to grow in our perceptual awareness of God. It is therefore vital that we have a close relationship with Him to develop spiritual intelligence. It's the close friendships that influence our lives. The Holy Spirit longs to have that acquaintance with us, so let's respond with open hearts and minds, and commit to intentionally walking in a closer fellowship with Him.

MEMORY CULTIVATION AND WHY IT'S VITAL FOR SPIRITUAL INTELLIGENCE

All intelligence demands memory. Memory is among the most impressive of capabilities God, the Creator of our minds, designed. Imagine life without it. Nothing would have meaning because what someone or something means to us is a product of remembered history of our relationship with that person or thing. So, too, spiritual intelligence needs good memory to facilitate the accurate processing and interpretation of spiritual data. It is our capacity to remember that allows us to recognize patterns and meanings associated with people, things, and events. It is a key to progressively improving our ability to discern larger and more complex volumes of spiritual data with precision.

God knows our propensity to forget things, though. Sometimes forgetting is a wonderful thing, if we have horrendous recollections. Forgetting the pain of the past and feelings associated with the loss of a loved one can be a good thing. However, when it comes to our relationship with God, we want to try to remember everything.

> But they quickly forgot His works; They did not patiently wait for His counsel *and* purpose to be revealed regarding them. (Psalm 106:13 AMP)

> I'll never forget the trouble, the utter lostness, the taste of ashes, the poison I've swallowed. I remember it all—oh, how well I remember—the feeling of hitting the bottom. But there's one other thing I remember, and remembering, I keep a grip on hope. (Lamentations 3:19–21 MSG)

The Bible says to "remember" approximately 227 times, depending on the version. God knows we need to work at our memory to progressively grow in our spiritual intelligence and knowledge of Him (the kind of knowledge that is personal, intimate, and ensures we have eternal life). Forgetfulness and loss of memory can therefore play a role in diminishing our spiritual intelligence over time.

The etymological origins of the word *memory* are closely associated with the roots of the word *mind*. *Mind* and *remembrance* in Latin are "memory."[68] These associations highlight the importance of memory to the mind and any mental experience. In other words, memory is essential for a well-functioning mind. Without any memory, nothing would have much meaning. People, places, experiences, and things that mean something to us are based on the remembered history of our interactions. Without that memory, the meaning is lost.

For new information to get stored in our long-term memory for later retrieval, a variety of pathways are possible. One way is through repeating items in our working memory (for example, repeating what we read and speaking it aloud). Another is through rehearsing items in working memory (for example, diligently studying for later recitation when sharing). A third way is through reviewing information (for example, checking over notes before a presentation). Repeating, rehearsing, and reviewing all assist in encoding information into our long-term memories. The effect and capacity of our brains to possess even ordinary memory are remarkable. This capability should inspire us to cultivate extraordinary memory of God's Word and all He communicates with us each day. Therefore, habits like reading, studying, meditating on, listening to, and journaling God's Word are essential for strengthening our memory and advancing our spiritual intelligence.

Forgetting (information retrieval failure), even when it's something as small as a momentary lapse of memory of a name you may previously have known, can happen to anyone. This is because stored, long-term memory can be lost or decay if it isn't reviewed, rehearsed, or repeated regularly over time. Having some kind of hint or related information can trigger or revive the memory, but even these triggers can decline in effectiveness if not reviewed. So, too, spiritual intelligence is fueled and maintains vitality through the recollection and remembrance of revelation knowledge. Recollection of what God's Word says about us, for example, influences the way we respond to, handle, and confront all new life experiences and all new revealed knowledge. Similarly, persistent recollection, repetition, and rehearsing of past hurts and negative life experiences keep toxic memories alive when we should be allowing them to dissipate. It is the unhealthy memories we want to forget and the healthy, God-inspired memories we want to retain. This is why diligent study, meditation, and memorization of the Bible, consistent journaling, and regular repetition and confession of God's words (past and present) are so vitally important to enhance healthy memory and promote optimal spiritual intelligence.

Here are just a few of the many verses in the Bible that exhort us not to forget God's goodness, teachings, and words. Not only are they promises, but they fuel healthy thoughts, feelings, and accurate perceptions, thereby sharpening our spiritual intelligence. I've italicized words for emphasis.

> Yahweh, you are my soul's celebration. How could I ever *forget* the miracles of kindness you've done for me? (Psalm 103:2 TPT)

> Get wisdom, get understanding; *do not forget* my words or turn away from them. (Proverbs 4:5 NIV)

> Only pay attention and watch yourselves closely so that you *do not forget* the things which your eyes have seen and they do not depart from your heart all the days of your life. Make them known to your children and your grandchildren [impressing these things on their mind and penetrating their heart with these truths]. (Deuteronomy 4:9 AMP)

The Bible is also great at encouraging us to let go of and indeed forget the things associated with our past that are negative. Dismissing and constantly replacing negative thoughts from our past with truth are imperative for growth in spiritual intelligence.

> *Forget* the former things; do not *dwell* on the past. (Isaiah 43:18 NIV)

> Brothers and sisters, I do not consider myself yet to have taken hold of it. But one thing I do: *Forgetting what is behind* and straining toward what is ahead. (Philippians 3:13 NIV)

I've italicized the words *forget, dwell,* and *forgetting what is behind* in the verses above. These are explicit commands drawn from both the Old and New Testament, not suggestions. The Creator of our minds knows we can renew and rejuvenate our cognitive processes by replacing old toxic thoughts with new thoughts that line up with the truth. The prophet Isaiah, under the inspiration of the Holy Spirit, instructs us to forget the past and not to dwell on it. When thoughts dwell in us, they take up residence and form mental strongholds due to repeated meditation on them. Worry has the same effect. Repeated negative thoughts about a possible situation or scenario, or painful past experiences, eventually become mindsets in our long-term memory. A brief thought that is negative simply goes through our working memory, but repeated recollecting and pondering it move it into our long-term memory. That's why we need to think about, ponder, and meditate on things that are excellent and admirable—not because we are trying to convince ourselves of a false reality but so we replace old mindsets and memories with new, healthy ones. These more vibrant mindsets subsequently promote healthier relationships and advance the relationship dimension of spiritual intelligence.

The word *stronghold,* translated *Misgab* in Hebrew, means "a secure height and refuge."[69] By accessing the mind of our Messiah and consequently having more and more of God's thoughts, we begin to increasingly perceive things as He does and secure those thoughts into understandings inaccessible by negative thoughts. This enables us to quickly discern and distinguish between toxic thoughts, our imagination, and inner thoughts congruent with truth. That's why God said in Hebrews 8:10 that He would imprint His teachings on the hearts *and* minds of His people, even upon their innermost thoughts and understanding. He knows the importance of our having His words (past and present) embossed on our innermost thought lives so we develop strong minds capable of doing incredible exploits for Him. Notice the words *imprint* and *engrave* in the Amplified version. "I will imprint My laws upon their minds [even upon their innermost thoughts and understanding], and engrave them upon their hearts [effecting their regeneration]. I will be their God, and they shall be My people" (Hebrews 8:10 AMP).

That's also why God told us to make His words *penetrate* and to impress them on the hearts and minds of our children. To "impress" means to make a permanent mark on others, to ensure the information they receive goes deep into their long-term memory. Notice the words *sharpen* and *diligently* in the next verse. "You shall whet and sharpen them so as to make them penetrate, and teach and impress them diligently upon the minds and hearts of your children, and shall talk of them when you sit in your house and when you walk by the way, and when you lie down and when you rise up" (Deuteronomy 6:7 AMPC).

Similarly, the Bible encourages us to think about things that are true, noble, right, and pure, not to escape reality but to develop and maintain a healthy thought life. It explicitly emphasizes this because we eventually act out and become what we repeatedly think. Instead of developing and maintaining toxic mindsets, generated by repeated worrisome thoughts, we develop healthy mental strongholds solidified by the truth.

> Finally, brothers and sisters, whatever is true, whatever is noble, whatever is right, whatever is pure, whatever is lovely, whatever is admirable—if anything is excellent or praiseworthy—think about such things. (Philippians 4:8 NIV)

> For as he thinks in his heart, so is he [in behavior]. (Proverbs 23:7 AMP)

Now that we know how vital repeating and reviewing God's Word are for encoding truth into our thought lives and long-term memory, it's important to focus more closely on the spiritual disciplines of prayer and meditation in the next chapter.

Before we proceed, let's pray.

God, thank You for creating humans with spectacular minds and the ability to renew them. Help me to progressively come to have the mind of my Messiah. Help me to play my part in accessing Your revealed truth and help me to grow in my capacity to perceive You. Let my old mindset not get in the way of my relationship with You. It's almost beyond comprehension how generous You are

Prayer and Meditation for Spiritual Intelligence

> Keep on asking and it will be given you; keep
> on seeking and you will find; keep on knocking
> [reverently] and [the door] will be opened to you.
>
> —Matthew 7:7 (AMPC)

> If any of you is deficient in wisdom, let him ask of the giving
> God [Who gives] to everyone liberally *and* ungrudgingly,
> without reproaching *or* faultfinding, and it will be given him.
>
> —James 1:5 (AMPC)

HOW CRUCIAL THE DISCIPLINE OF PRAYER IS FOR SPIRITUAL INTELLIGENCE

Prayer is an act of worship in which we humbly seek God with all our hearts. Whether individually during private times or in groups with others, prayer is one of the most powerful and life-changing spiritual exercises that lays a foundation, on which to build a strong and intimate relationship with God. A word search in the Amplified Bible yields 471 instructions to pray. No other spiritual discipline in the Bible yields that many directives. *Praise* is mentioned 346 times, and we all know how important that is. *Teach* is mentioned 345 times. *Fast* is mentioned 146 times, and *preach* comes up 126 times. While this illustration isn't all inclusive and the exact numbers aren't the point, it does highlight the relative significance of prayer as a fundamental discipline for all believers to remain connected to God. Prayer is a crucial spiritual necessity. It is too imperative a discipline to delegate. It is too vital an activity to pass on or pass off for another day.

God wants humankind to be acquainted with and genuinely know Him, and prayer is the mechanism to begin and maintain an ongoing dialogue with Him. In this two-way exchange, we not only speak and ask God for His help, but we hear and heed what He is saying to us. The clarity of our hearing and perceptual awareness, how we process what we hear, and the translation of what we hear into life-enhancing action reflect a spiritually intelligent prayer life. Jesus modeled a life of prayer and instructed us to do likewise.

> Also [Jesus] told them a parable to the effect that they ought always to pray and not to turn coward (faint, lose heart, and give up). (Luke 18:1 AMPC)

> But when you pray, go into your [most] private room, and, closing the door, pray to your Father, Who is in secret; and your Father, Who sees in secret, will reward you *in the open*. And when you pray, do not heap up phrases (multiply words, repeating the same ones over and over) as the Gentiles do, for they think they will be heard for their much speaking. Do not be like them, for your Father knows what you need before you ask Him. Pray, therefore, like this: Our Father Who is in heaven, hallowed (kept holy) be Your name. Your kingdom come, Your will be done on earth as it is in heaven. Give us this day our daily bread. And forgive us our debts, as we also have forgiven left, remitted, and let go of the debts, and have given up resentment against) our debtors. And lead (bring) us not into temptation, but deliver us from the evil one. For Yours is the kingdom and the power and the glory forever. Amen. (Matthew 6:6–13 AMPC; emphasis mine)

God's desire and delight are in establishing and maintaining a strong connection with us so we can become thoroughly acquainted with Him, understand Him more completely, and be continually conformed to His likeness. Just as the bandwidth strength of our connections to the internet is essential for accessing information, so too our connection strength with God and our personal acquaintance with Him will determine the effectiveness of our prayers.

> And this, so that I may *know* Him [*experientially*, becoming more thoroughly *acquainted* with Him, understanding the remarkable wonders of His Person more completely] and [in that same way experience] the power of His resurrection [which overflows and is active in believers], and [that I may share] the fellowship of His sufferings, by being *continually conformed* [inwardly into His likeness even] to His death [dying as He did]; (Philippians 3:10 AMP; emphasis mine)

One of the primary drivers to pray should be because it pleases and delights God. *Merriam-Webster's Dictionary* defines *delight* as "a high degree of gratification or pleasure."[70] If you love someone, you naturally want to bring them pleasure. This alone should be reason for us to pray often and earnestly.

I like how The Passion Translation says that *every* prayer of His godly lovers pleases His heart. Notice too how it highlights how loathsome counterfeit worship is to Him. "It is despicable to the Lord when people use the worship of the Almighty as a cloak for their sin, but every prayer of his godly lovers is pleasing to his heart" (Proverbs 15:8 TPT).

The Bible also says it's the prayers of the upright that bring Him pleasure, not just the act of prayer. The word *upright* implies being "right-minded, ethical, honest, honorable, conscientious, true, and virtuous."[71]

People love to quote the latter part of James 5:16, which emphasizes that the prayers of a righteous person make tremendous power available. However, let's also pay attention to the beginning of James 5:16, which directs us to confess our faults and pray for each other so we may be healed and restored to a spiritual tone of mind and heart. Notice the coupling of confession with prayer. The act of repenting and turning from our ways through confession is an antecedent to generating healing and restoration, which in turn aids in the renewing of the mind and the healing of the heart. The pattern is simple yet profound. While certain religious doctrines have overcomplicated this and made confession out to be such a lofty, mysterious activity, God simply wants us positioned to produce powerful prayers from a place of right standing with Him. Maintaining a lifestyle of quick repentance and forgiveness toward others causes our prayers to move from ineffective to powerful.

> Confess to one another therefore your faults (your slips, false steps, offenses, sins) and pray [also] for one another, that you may be healed *and* restored [to a spiritual tone of mind and heart]. The earnest (heartfelt, continued) prayer of a righteous man makes tremendous power available [dynamic in its working]. (James 5:16 AMPC)

> For if you forgive other people when they sin against you, your heavenly Father will also forgive you. But if you do not forgive others their sins, your Father will not forgive your sins. (Matthew 6:14–15 NIV)

> If we confess our sins, he is faithful and just and will forgive us our sins and purify us from all unrighteousness. If we claim we have not sinned, we make him out to be a liar and his word is not in us. (1 John 1:9–10 NIV)

PRAY FOR SPIRITUAL INTELLIGENCE

> Jesus said, "'Love the Lord your God with all your passion and prayer and intelligence.' This is the most important, the first on any list. But there is a second to set alongside it: 'Love others as well as you love yourself.' These two commands are pegs; everything in God's Law and the Prophets hangs from them." (Matthew 22:37–40 MSG)

We looked at Matthew 22:37 earlier, as it pertains to intelligence, but notice the reference to passion *and* prayer too, both of which enhance spiritual intelligence. So, the question becomes, what has God not recently been able to do for you because you didn't pray or because your prayer lacked power because you were holding on to an offense? When last did you pray for your enemies, as the Word instructs us? "But I tell you,

Love your enemies and pray for those who persecute you" (Matthew 5:44 AMPC).

When Jesus commanded us to love our enemies, He knew the power forgiveness would generate as well as the mental freedom it would grant us from those who may have hurt us. Heed His words and watch your prayers get answered and your mind get restored.

Isaiah was inspired by the Holy Spirit to prophesy and write that God's house would be called a house of prayer for all peoples (Isaiah 56:7). Jesus reiterated this in Mark 11:17 when He emphasized that His house would be a house of prayer for all nations. It's noteworthy to pay attention to the verses Jesus quoted from the Old Testament, and this is one of them. Since our bodies represent a place of habitation for the Holy Spirit, we too need to be "houses" of prayer, not just our local congregation.

> Do you not know that your bodies are temples of the Holy Spirit, who is in you, whom you have received from God? You are not your own; you were bought at a price. Therefore, honor God with your bodies. (1 Corinthians 6:19–20 NIV)

> All these I will bring to My holy mountain and make them joyful in My house of prayer. Their burnt offerings and their sacrifices will be accepted on My altar; for My house will be called a house of prayer for all peoples. (Isaiah 56:7 AMPC)

> And He taught and said to them, Is it not written, My house shall be called a house of prayer for all the nations? But you have turned it into a den of robbers. (Mark 11:17 AMPC)

So, both the local congregation and we as individuals need to have prayer as a priority. Jennifer Eivaz, in her book *The Intercessors Handbook*, says, "Prayer is the first ministry of the modern-day Church. We govern our world with prayer. Prayer is the most powerful exercise of godly authority on the earth. A praying church overturns demonic plans, puts angels on assignment, cleanses atmospheres and creates conditions for the visible invasion of the Word of God into the nations."[72]

In his book *Prayer That Brings Revival: Interceding for God to Move in Your Family, Church, and Community,* Dr. Cho says, "Before I do or say anything, I pray. This is the difference between acting and reacting. As I study the life of Christ, I notice that Jesus always acted; He never reacted … As I live my life in prayer, I know that I have the mind of Christ. Then when I make a decision, I know it is the will of God and can stand firm in the assurance that I am acting for God."[73] Notice his spiritual intelligence. He perceives a need and responds appropriately by taking that need to God in prayer, then makes a spiritually intelligent decision that is consistent with the will of God. Dr. Cho knows God, and He does His will. He perceives accurately, knows the mind of Christ, manages the revelation he receives and his relationship with God well, and responds appropriately with God-centered action, not self-centered reaction. Dr. Cho says, "Our problem has been that we have thought about prayer, read about prayer, even received teaching regarding prayer—but we just have not prayed."[74]

In her book *Lioness Arising: Wake Up and Change Your World,* Lisa Bevere poignantly captures the importance of prayer. "Prayer is our most powerful reason for gathering … prayer paves the way for provision, purpose, and strategies."[75]

Jesus paid the price and endured many hardships and disciplines so we wouldn't have to endure them. Prayer isn't one of those things He did (and still does) so we don't have to. He spent all night in prayer before He made decisions regarding His disciples (Luke 6:12). Why then would we think we could get away with quick, microwave-type prayers? The answer is that prayer takes discipline, it takes an investment of time, it takes personal sacrifice, and it takes humility and perseverance to keep doing it effectively. Unfortunately, those who only sporadically practice genuine prayer are unable to effectively sustain a lifestyle of prayer and also inevitably struggle to maintain high spiritual intelligence. That is why the Bible says on numerous occasions that our prayer lives need to be constant.

> Be unceasing in prayer [praying perseveringly]. (1 Thessalonians 5:17 AMPC)

> I thank God Whom I worship with a pure conscience, in the spirit of my fathers, when without ceasing I remember you night and day in my prayers. (2 Timothy 1:3 AMPC)

The ongoing theme in this book is the importance of being closely acquainted with God. If prayer involves both speaking and hearing, we must develop an intimate relationship with God for a robust prayer life. Persistent, continuous prayer keeps our perceptual awareness and perceptual processing capacity accurate and engaged. It not only strengthens our relationship with God but also increases the effectiveness of our relationships with others and how we handle and deal with change. Prayer fortifies our perceptual awareness, our capacity to process revelation knowledge, and our relationship management. We were born to establish and maintain a strong prayer life, built on an intense connection with God, so let's endeavor to do so.

> Be earnest *and* unwearied *and* steadfast in your prayer [life], being [both] alert *and* intent in [your praying] with thanksgiving. (Colossians 4:2 AMPC)

> Pray at all times (on every occasion, in every season) in the Spirit, with all [manner of] prayer and entreaty. To that end keep alert and watch with strong purpose *and* perseverance, interceding in behalf of all the saints (God's consecrated people). (Ephesians 6:18 AMPC)

At the end of every chapter and in the appendices of this book, numerous prayers have been compiled, based on Scripture, to help advance your spiritual intelligence. Again, take the opportunity to pray them aloud as you make progress in your spiritual journey.

THE VALUE OF MEDITATION FOR MIND RENEWAL AND ADVANCING SPIRITUAL INTELLIGENCE

What is the most important activity we can engage in to make our lives prosperous and successful? It's none other than meditating on the Word of God and doing what it says. Notice how the Amplified Bible links meditation with success. "This Book of the Law shall not depart out of your mouth, but you shall meditate on it day and night, that you may observe and do according to all that is written in it. For then you shall make your way prosperous, and then you shall deal wisely and have good success" (Joshua 1:8 AMPC).

Knowing this, let's explore some of the key verses in the Bible that encourage us to meditate on God. I have italicized the word *meditate* for emphasis in the verses that follow:

> Open up my understanding to the ways of your wisdom and I will *meditate* deeply on your splendor and your wonders. (Psalm 119:48 TPT)

> Sing to Him, sing praises to Him; *meditate* on and talk of all His wondrous works and devoutly praise them! (1 Chronicles 16:9 AMPC)

> One thing have I asked of the Lord, that will I seek, inquire for, and [insistently] require: that I may dwell in the house of the Lord [in His presence] all the days of my life, to behold and gaze upon the beauty [the sweet attractiveness and the delightful loveliness] of the Lord and to *meditate*, consider, and inquire in His temple. (Psalm 27:4 AMPC)

> When I remember You upon my bed and *meditate* on You in the night watches. (Psalm 63:6 AMPC)

> I call to remembrance my song in the night; with my heart I *meditate* and my spirit searches diligently. (Psalm 77:6 AMPC)

> I will *meditate* also upon all Your works and consider all Your [mighty] deeds. (Psalm 77:12 AMPC)

> Sing to Him, sing praises to Him; *meditate* on and talk of all His marvelous deeds and devoutly praise them. (Psalm 105:2 AMPC)

> I will *meditate* on Your precepts and have respect to Your ways [the paths of life marked out by Your law]. (Psalm 119:15 AMPC)

Princes also sat and talked against me, but Your servant *meditated* on Your statutes. (Psalm 119:23 AMPC)

Let the proud be put to shame, for they dealt perversely with me without a cause; but I will *meditate* on Your precepts. (Psalm 119:78 AMPC)

My eyes anticipate the night watches and I am awake before the cry of the watchman, that I may *meditate* on Your word. (Psalm 119:148 AMPC)

I remember the days of old; I *meditate* on all Your doings; I ponder the work of Your hands. (Psalm 143:5 AMPC)

On the glorious splendor of Your majesty and on Your wondrous works I will *meditate*. (Psalm 145:5 AMPC)

Practice and cultivate and *meditate* upon these duties; throw yourself wholly into them [as your ministry], so that your progress may be evident to everybody. (1 Timothy 4:15 AMPC)

But his delight and desire are in the law of the Lord, and on His law (the precepts, the instructions, the teachings of God) he habitually *meditates* (ponders and studies) by day and by night. (Psalm 1:2 AMPC)

The Hebrew word for *meditate* is *hagah* and denotes to ponder, imagine, mutter, study, or utter.[76] Note that it includes imagining and studying. How often do you ponder God's Word and personally imagine all its implications for your life? Imagine, for example, actually possessing the very perceptions of God and sharing His thoughts on a subject or person you are praying for? How radically different the outcome of the prayer becomes.

Biblical meditation is the original, God-designed, practice of focusing on God and the Word of God day and night. It isn't the fabricated, counterfeited version of meditation associated with people seeking "peace" or "stress relief" through emptying their minds.

Biblical meditation is centered on God and the Word of God (recalling, repeating, reciting, and reviewing it), while counterfeit meditation focuses on the inner self, your feelings, your own self-actualization, and your breathing. Counterfeit meditation focuses on people being in control and relies on "self" as the agent to bring peace.

Biblical meditation promotes the renewing of the mind for life transformation through God. It entails filling our minds with thoughts of God and His Word and pondering them repeatedly. Counterfeit meditation involves emptying one's mind and focusing on oneself. Biblical meditation turns our focus toward God and His Word, whereas counterfeit meditation turns the focus on self. Counterfeit meditation seeks higher levels of consciousness and altered mindsets so those practicing it can escape from reality to relieve stress. Biblical meditation, on the other hand, doesn't offer an escape from reality but rather helps people solve problems and challenges associated with their reality.

Meditating on God's Word, pondering and imagining Him, and communing with Him are the endeavors that activate dramatic change in the spiritual realm. No wonder the enemy of our souls copied it for his counterfeit pursuits. Notice in the two verses below how meditation can be used for activities contrary to God's will and purpose. Counterfeit practices that employ meditation techniques aren't a new phenomenon. The propensity and accelerated use of them are what's new, including the use of counterfeit meditative practices by people who should know better.

> They also that seek and demand my life lay snares for me, and they that seek and require my hurt speak crafty and mischievous things; they meditate treachery and deceit all the day long. (Psalm 38:12 AMPC)

> Your mind will meditate on the terror: [asking] Where is he who counted? Where is he who weighed the tribute? Where is he who counted the towers? (Isaiah 33:18 AMPC)

God wants His children to use this tool as it was designed for them for a reason. If you meditate on the truth, your life will line up with it. If you meditate on Scripture associated with health and well-being, your body, mind, and spirit will realign themselves in that direction. If you meditate on Scripture associated with life and restoration, you will begin finding answers in prayer that simply begging God will never generate. When you meditate on God's promises and things that are pleasing to Him, they become a reality in your life. Look at how David prayed that his meditation would be pleasing to God. "May these words of my mouth and this meditation of my heart be pleasing in your sight, Lord, my Rock and my Redeemer" (Psalm 19:14 NIV).

You don't need to get into a weird position or confined place to meditate. Nor do you need to start saying certain peculiar words, making bizarre sounds, or chanting strange utterances. Remember what biblical meditation is: to ponder, imagine, speak, study, or mutter. Think back on a time you studied for an exam. In preparing, you likely found yourself pondering some of the content and speaking out some of the critical definitions. All that should have helped you to better remember the content and gain a better outcome on the exam. There is nothing weird or paranormal about rehearsing or repeatedly saying something you are trying to get into your long-term memory.

As we explored previously, contemporary versions of counterfeit spiritual intelligence have their roots in pantheism. Many people engage in these alternate forms of meditation as a means of finding stress relief and relaxation. As children of God, we don't need to seek peace anywhere else other than from the Prince of Peace (Isaiah 9:6), the Lord Himself. The Bible mentions "peace" over four hundred times, and it is a vital component of spiritual, emotional, and physical well-being. By the grace of God, we can appropriate the genuine power to overcome stress and anxiety in our lives, and truly get to experience God's peace and tranquility. The Bible also tells us quite explicitly not to have any anxiety about anything but rather to pray and make our wants known to God.

> Do not fret or have any anxiety about anything, but in every circumstance and in everything, by prayer and petition (definite requests), with thanksgiving, continue to make your wants known to God. And God's peace [shall be yours, that tranquil state of a

> soul assured of its salvation through Christ, and so fearing nothing
> from God and being content with its earthly lot of whatever
> sort that is, that peace] which transcends all understanding shall
> garrison and mount guard over your hearts and minds in Christ
> Jesus. (Philippians 4:6–7 AMPC)

> Therefore, I tell you, stop being perpetually uneasy (anxious and
> worried) about your life. (Matthew 6:25 AMPC)

God has also provided us with magnificent things He created for our enjoyment and relaxation in nature, from the sound of crashing waves to the sound of birds on a spring day, to the fresh smell of a rose garden or a romantic evening with one's spouse. God knows we need rest, relaxation, and peace in this stressful world, but the ultimate source of that genuine peace is always Him. No amount of massages and vacation getaways, as wonderful as they are, can ever generate the kind of peace and undisturbed composure the Spirit of God provides. The Bible says it surpasses all understanding for a reason. That means it exceeds logical reason and is beyond our comprehension. Meditating on our Creator and His Word will provide the only true and lasting peace.

Praying, studying, speaking out, and repeating the Word of God, are profoundly powerful life-transforming practices. If your only exposure to the Word of God is brief and non-meditative, it may easily be unintentionally forgotten, and it won't transform your life to the level it was intended to. Biblical meditation will cause the Word of God to be infused into your long-term memory, thereby supercharging your spiritual intelligence. The more you do it, the stronger your perceptual awareness will grow, and the more accurate your discernment will be. Do not neglect it and don't settle for the counterfeit version of it.

Before we proceed to the next chapter on the importance of having first love for God, let's pray.

God, thank You that You made it very explicit in Your Word that I need to pray to You directly and often. Thank You for creating the capacity for me to communicate with You real time. Help me to develop a lifestyle of faith-filled and fervent prayer that touches Your heart. May my prayers bring You gratification and pleasure. You said Your house will be a house of prayer for the nations. May the global church return to its knees. May houses of worship not just be places where people pray, but let prayer define and distinguish them. Forgive me for prayerlessness and prayers devoid of faith. Forgive me for seeking peace through counterfeit meditation and activities contrary to Your Word. May my meditation and thought life be pleasing and acceptable to You. Help me to develop a lifestyle of prayer and meditation so I remain continuously supercharged with spiritual intelligence. In Jesus' beautiful name. Amen.

CHAPTER
14

The Ultimate Fruit of Spiritual Intelligence

But I have this [one charge to make] against you:
that you have left (abandoned) the love that you had
at first [you have deserted Me, your first love].

—Revelation 2:4 (AMPC)

WITHOUT GENUINE LOVE, FAITH IS USELESS, AND IGNORANCE THRIVES

While a word search for "pray" in the Amplified Bible yielded 471 directives, not surprisingly the command to "love" surpassed that with 566 mentions. As we continue to advance in spiritual intelligence and progressively adopt God's mindset, we increasingly gain greater revelation of His love, which we're then able to extend back to Him and share with others. We are able to love Him, because He first loved us (1 John 4:19), and we can tell who is strongly connected to God by the fruit of love they generate (1 John 2:9–11). Love is absolutely essential to achieving high spiritual intelligence. Where love is deficient, deception and ignorance thrive. Where love abounds, knowledge and discernment increase correspondingly. Notice how closely aligned these virtues of love and knowledge are in the Scriptures.

[God Is Love] Those who are loved by God, let his *love* continually pour from you to one another, because God is love. Everyone who loves is fathered by God and experiences an *intimate knowledge* of him. (1 John 4:7 TPT; emphasis mine)

And if I have prophetic powers (the gift of interpreting the divine will and purpose), and understand all the secret truths *and* mysteries and possess all knowledge, and if I have [sufficient] faith so that I can remove mountains, but have not love (God's love in me) I am nothing (a *useless* nobody). (1 Corinthians 13:2 AMPC; emphasis mine)

That their hearts may be encouraged, being knit together in *love,* and attaining to all riches of the full assurance of understanding, to the *knowledge* of the mystery of God, both of the Father and of Christ. (Colossians 2:2 NKJV; emphasis mine)

And this I pray, that your *love* may abound still more and more in *knowledge* and all *discernment.* (Philippians 1:9 NKJV; emphasis mine)

You may have heard the saying "People don't care about how much you know until they know how much you care." Why should anyone want to listen to someone teach, preach, lecture, or share if they didn't think that person genuinely cared about them first? What's empowered me to impart knowledge to thousands of students I've taught over the past two decades is the fact that I love and care about them. That genuine love builds assurance in them that as I guide them and help them learn and improve their competencies for success in their careers, they can trust that I have their best interests at heart. Love fosters learning, and learning fosters knowledge generation and creativity. My students know I care about them, and from that platform, I am then able to instruct them in a way that generates sustainable learning.

God wants us to love Him with *all* our passion, prayer and intelligence—and others as ourselves (Matthew 22:37). We've looked at this verse numerous times throughout this book in the context of intelligence and prayer, but how about passion? We love Him with all our musical, teaching, linguistic, or artistic passions and give Him pleasure, glory, and honor as we excel in these things. However, when we consider having *first* love for God, we are referring to Him being our greatest passion, the highest of our priorities, and our vital necessity above all else. The question then becomes, what is your primary passion? Is it your ministry or the Master? Is it connecting with people or with the High Priest? Notice that none of the secondary passions I've offered as examples are insignificant. In fact, you should be passionate about all of them. However, to attain intimate oneness with God and high spiritual intelligence, He needs to be our *chief* passion. As we seek Him as our first necessity, He pours out His endless grace and power to do His will. Being with God is always the first call.

Love enables faith, which we know is essential to please God (Hebrews 11:6). God's love, not counterfeit worldly "love," activates and energizes faith. Without it, faith is rendered useless. God's love is perfect and real. It endures all things, it is never self-seeking, and it keeps no records of a suffered wrong. It believes the very best of everyone and remains unwavering in challenging times. Love for God and all people is absolutely essential for the accurate transference of what God wants to be communicated and in the manner He wants it communicated.

> When you're joined to the Anointed One, circumcision and religious obligations can benefit you nothing. All that matters now is living in the faith that works and expresses itself through love. (Galatians 5:6 TPT)

> Love never fails [it never fades nor ends]. But as for prophecies, they will pass away; as for tongues, they will cease; as for the gift of special knowledge, it will pass away. If I speak with the tongues of men and of angels, but have not love [for others growing out of God's love for me], then I have become only a noisy gong or a clanging cymbal [just an annoying distraction]. And if I have the gift of prophecy [and speak a new message from God to the people], and understand all mysteries, and [possess] all knowledge; and if I have all [sufficient] faith so that I can remove mountains, but do not have love [reaching out to others], I am nothing. If I give all my possessions to feed the poor, and if I surrender my body to be burned, but do not have love, it does me no good at all. (Corinthians 13:1–3 AMP)

If others think they've come to know and understand much of divine spiritual things without God's love, they are deceived. Without God's love, it is impossible to strongly and clearly perceive and understand or even recognize anything we really ought to know. Even if people have a form of spirituality and faith, if they deny and resist the love of God, they render conditions impossible to have true spiritual intelligence. If they continue to pursue spiritual things devoid of God, who is love (1 John 4:8), what they are left with is counterfeit intelligence, a copy of the real thing but with vastly different immediate and long-term outcomes.

> If anyone imagines that he has come to know and understand much [of divine things, without love], he does not yet *perceive* and recognize and *understand* as strongly and clearly, nor has he become as *intimately acquainted* with anything as he ought or as is necessary. (1 Corinthians 8:2 AMPC; emphasis mine)

FIRST LOVE IS KEY

Jesus rebuked five of the seven churches in the book of Revelation. However, the church that is strikingly applicable to the subject of first love is the church in Ephesus. Jesus acknowledged and complemented this church for its industry and activities, laborious toil and trouble, its patient endurance, and how it tested and critically appraised impostors. If you'd asked the church in Ephesus whether they loved God, they would have insisted they did. However, Jesus charged them for abandoning their *first* love and commanded them to repent and do the works they had when the first knew Him (Revelation 2:1–5). He instructed them to do the things they had when they previously were more closely acquainted with Him, not necessarily things associated with ministry. So not only is the rebuke very striking, but the warning is even more alarming.

If the church didn't return to its first love and do the things it previously had done when it knew God intimately, He would remove His lampstand from it. A lamp, biblically speaking, has several related meanings. The Word of God is a lamp to our feet and a light to our path (Psalm 119:105). A lampstand is also something that holds oil, and oil is symbolic of the Holy Spirit (Zechariah 4:6), as we saw earlier in the parable of the ten virgins. Samuel described God as the Lamp (2 Samuel 22:29). The Word of God is described as a lamp and the teaching of it as the light that emitted from it (Proverbs 6:23). The lamp needs a lampstand so others can see the light (Luke 11:33).

This rebuke and warning should generate a healthy fear of God in any believer who has walked with the Lord for a substantial period and may well have once had high spiritual intelligence but, unbeknownst to them, drifted into low or moderate spiritual intelligence. By assuming they were still developing spiritually because they were working hard and patiently in ministry, they unintentionally lost their *first* love for God. God wanted them to love Him intensely and to know Him intimately as their primary priority, not as a secondary or tertiary priority after ministry.

> I know all that you've done for me—you have worked hard and persevered. I know that you don't tolerate evil. You have tested those who claimed to be apostles and *proved* they are not, *for they were imposters.* I also know how you have bravely endured *trials and persecutions* because of my name, yet you have not become discouraged. But I have this against you: you have abandoned the *passionate love* you had for me at the beginning. Think about how far you have fallen! Repent and do the works *of love* you did at *first.* I will come to you and remove your lampstand from its place *of influence* if you do not repent. (Revelation 2: 2–5 TPT)

THE MENTALLY LIBERATING POWER OF BEING HUMBLE AND LOVING YOUR ENEMIES

Humility is an essential ingredient to activating and maintaining a strong connection to God. Pride and arrogance instantly deactivate or temporarily disable that connection, just as quickly as a power outage can disconnect an electrical appliance. Just as faith without action is dead, perceptual awareness with pride stifles spiritual intelligence. People may perceive things in the spiritual realm about others, for example, but if they aren't humble while processing that information, the relationship management dimension of spiritual intelligence will be completely undermined.

For example, someone may perceive that someone is struggling with a particular sin. Instead of processing that information with accuracy and compassion, the person becomes judgmental and proud. The perceptual processing capacity is jeopardized, and the flow of accurate interpretation that would typically be provided from the Holy Spirit is diluted or entirely compromised. This, in turn, affects how they relate to the struggling individual, and the person may respond in a critical or judgmental way with words that may be condescending and discouraging.

The fruit of this encounter would be damaging rather than encouraging and life giving. Consistent with this, Dr. James Goll, a bestselling author, says in his book *The Discerner: Hearing, Confirming, and Acting on Prophetic Revelation*, "As we begin to hear God's voice more clearly through our senses, there is the risk that we may slip into pride, which will immediately start to shut down the flow from heaven. If that happens, we find that we must manufacture feelings and thoughts that used to bubble up from the Holy Spirit. We tend to turn off the checks and balances and rely on ourselves."[77]

God is no respecter of persons, so anyone who is prideful will experience the disabling effect thereof. God gives enabling power to the humble but resists the proud.

> And Peter opened his mouth and said: Most certainly and thoroughly I now perceive and understand that God shows no partiality and is no respecter of persons. (Acts 10:34 AMPC)

> God resists you when you are proud but continually pours out grace when you are humble. (James 4:6 TPT)

Whoever wants to grow in wisdom and spiritual intelligence needs to put on unassuming humility, remembering that the fear of God is the beginning of true wisdom.

> Who is there among you who is wise and intelligent? Then let him by his noble living show forth his good works with the unobtrusive humility which is the proper attribute of true wisdom. (James 3:13 AMPC)

The Message translation paints a clear illustration of true wisdom, and like oil and water, wisdom and pride don't mix.

> I am Lady Wisdom, and I live next to Sanity; Knowledge and Discretion live just down the street. The Fear-of-God means hating Evil, whose ways I hate with a passion—pride and arrogance and crooked talk. Good counsel and common sense are my characteristics; I am both Insight and the Virtue to live it out. With my help, leaders rule, and lawmakers legislate fairly; With my help, governors govern, along with all in legitimate authority. I love those who love me; those who look for me find me. Wealth and Glory accompany me—also substantial Honor and a Good Name. My benefits are worth more than a big salary, even a *very* big salary; the returns on me exceed any imaginable bonus. You can find me on Righteous Road—that's where I walk—at the intersection of Justice Avenue, Handing out life to those who love me, filling their arms with life—armloads of life! (Proverbs 8:12–21 MSG)

As we grow in spiritual intelligence and accurately sense and know what God is saying through our perceptual awareness, it is absolutely crucial that we remain humble for the perceptual processing and relationship management components of spiritual intelligence to be optimal. Any form of intelligence is admirable and may invoke praise and accolades, but let that praise always belong to God, the Source of true spiritual intelligence. We should have the same attitude and humble mind as Jesus. We can do nothing of eternal value without Him (John 5:19; 8:28), but with Him, *all* things are possible (Matthew 19:26; Mark 9:23; 10:27).

> Let this same attitude *and* purpose *and* humble mind be in you which was in Christ Jesus. Let Him be your example in humility. (Philippians 2:5 AMPC)

> With tender humility and quiet patience, always demonstrate gentleness and generous love toward one another, especially toward those who may try your patience. (Ephesians 4:2 TPT)

> So, chosen by God for this new life of love, dress in the wardrobe God picked out for you: compassion, kindness, humility, quiet strength, discipline. Be even-tempered, content with second place,

quick to forgive an offense. Forgive as quickly and completely as the Master forgave you. And regardless of what else you put on, wear love. It's your basic, all-purpose garment. Never be without it. (Colossians 3:12–14 MSG)

Jesus radically subverted the conventional thinking of His day when He commanded us to love our enemies. He knew that even our natural enemies were subject to and victims of the real foe's devices.

You're familiar with the old written law, "Love your friend," and its unwritten companion, "Hate your enemy." I'm challenging that. I'm telling you to love your enemies. Let them bring out the best in you, not the worst. When someone gives you a hard time, respond with the energies of prayer, for then you are working out of your true selves, your God-created selves. This is what God does. He gives his best—the sun to warm and the rain to nourish—to everyone, regardless: the good and bad, the nice and nasty. If all you do is love the lovable, do you expect a bonus? Anybody can do that. If you simply say hello to those who greet you, do you expect a medal? Any run-of-the-mill sinner does that. (Matthew 5:44–48 MSG)

Do not judge others, and you will not be judged. Do not condemn others, or it will all come back against you. Forgive others, and you will be forgiven. Give, and you will receive. Your gift will return to you in full—pressed down, shaken together to make room for more, running over, and poured into your lap. The amount you give will determine the amount you get back. (Luke 6:35–38 NLT)

Submit yourselves, then, to God. Resist the devil, and he will flee from you. (James 4:7 NIV)

Our spiritual enemy is to be resisted, but natural enemies are to be loved, not condemned. This is why so many self-righteous know-it-alls struggle so much with offense because they are always looking down on others and have an elevated opinion of themselves. They judge and condemn anyone who isn't like them. They will associate only with people at their "level," and if anyone "below" them ever challenges them or treats them as an "equal," they immediately criticize them.

We see in both Matthew 19:17 and Luke 18:19 that Jesus shows us how we should respond if we ever begin to erroneously think we are good outside of God. Without God there is no one who is good. This fact should strip us of any self-righteousness and remind us that without God, our so-called "righteousness" is soiled. The Holy Spirit inspired prophet Isaiah to pen this very explicitly.

> All of us have become like one who is unclean, and all our righteous acts are like filthy rags; we all shrivel up like a leaf, and like the wind our sins sweep us away. (Isaiah 64:6 NIV)

> Why do you ask me about what is good?" Jesus replied. "There is only One who is good. If you want to enter life, keep the commandments. (Matthew 19:17 NIV)

> Why do you call me good?" Jesus answered. "No one is good— except God alone. (Luke 18:19 NIV)

These verses also highlight the importance of not assuming credit when in fact it is only by and through God that we can do anything great and worthwhile. It is quite liberating if you meditate on this reality. It makes you recognize and acknowledge that God *alone* deserves all the glory for anything truly good we do or accomplish in life. When we are living with the highest form of spiritual intelligence, it is a product of our being most submitted to His authority and will. In our weaknesses, His power is perfected, and when we surrender our ambitions, desires, and thoughts to Him, that's when His life-giving power invigorates and propels us to the true abundant life talked about in John 10:10.

> For *My* strength and power are made perfect (fulfilled and completed) and show themselves most effective in your weakness. (2 Corinthians 12:9 AMPC)

> For to me, to live is Christ and to die is gain. (Philippians 1:21 NIV)

I love how The Message captures the apostle Paul's assertion.

So how am I to respond? I've decided that I really don't care about their motives, whether mixed, bad, or indifferent. Every time one of them opens his mouth, Christ is proclaimed, so I just cheer them on! And I'm going to keep that celebration going because I know how it's going to turn out. Through your faithful prayers and the generous response of the Spirit of Jesus Christ, everything he wants to do in and through me will be done. I can hardly wait to continue on my course. I don't expect to be embarrassed in the least. On the contrary, everything happening to me in this jail only serves to make Christ more accurately known, regardless of whether I live or die. They didn't shut me up; they gave me a pulpit! Alive, I'm Christ's messenger; dead, I'm his bounty. Life versus even more life! I can't lose. (Philippians 1:21 MSG)

The Bible says everyone has fallen short of the grace of God, lest anyone boast. It is only through God that we gain victory over the enemy and his devices. Even though our hearts and flesh may fail, God is the strength of our hearts and eternally sustains us. "My flesh and my heart may fail, but God is the Rock and firm Strength of my heart and my Portion forever" (Psalm 73:26 AMPC).

God's love and forgiveness are so powerful that anyone with counterfeit spiritual intelligence can be radically changed and eventually develop high spiritual intelligence if they turn to God. There is no exception; we have all, to varying degrees, fallen short of God's best for us.

This righteousness of God comes through faith in Jesus Christ for all those [Jew or Gentile] who believe and trust in Him and acknowledge Him as God's Son. There is no distinction, since *all have sinned and continually fall short of the glory of God*, and are being justified [declared free of the guilt of sin, made acceptable to God, and granted eternal life] as a gift by His [precious, undeserved] grace, through the redemption [the payment for our sin] which is [provided] in Christ Jesus, (Romans 3:22–24 AMP; emphasis mine)

Before we proceed to the next and final chapter, which explores prerequisites to authentic spiritual intelligence, let's pray.

God, thank You for loving me so much that You sent Your Son to die in my place so I can experience forgiveness of all my sins and live eternally with You. Thank You that the suffering He endured before His death on the cross also paid a hefty price for my physical and mental well-being. Thank You that every stripe on my High Priest's back gives me power to overcome any disease. Thank You that the thorns of His crown, which painfully penetrated His head, paid a weighty price for my mental health and wellness. Thank You that the blood He shed from His hands and feet gives me power to stand and serve as a conduit for His enabling power. Thank You that the emotional trauma He endured through the mockery and slander against Him paid the price for my emotional well-being and peace.

Thank You that by following You wholeheartedly, I have access to Your mind. Your generosity is almost too amazing to fathom. Help me to always remain humble so my spiritual broadband connection to You remains strong. May You remain my greatest passion, my highest priority, and my first love throughout my life. Help me to remain humble and relentless as I grow toward spiritual maturity and high spiritual intelligence. May my lifestyle, habits, and behavior reflect and confirm my relationship with You. Let me not squander Your amazing grace or limit the boundless power it provides. I look forward to a life of ongoing progress, continuous learning, increasing strength in the face of suffering, and greater intimacy with You. I love You and want nothing more than to be close to You and to know You better. In Jesus' wonderful name. Amen.

Prerequisites for Authentic Spiritual Intelligence

O worship the Lord in the beauty of holiness; tremble
before *and* reverently fear Him, all the earth.

—Psalm 96:9 (AMPC)

The fear of the Lord *is* the beginning of wisdom, and
knowledge of the Holy One *is* understanding.

—Proverbs 9:10 (NIV)

HOLINESS AND THE FEAR OF THE LORD SUPERCHARGE YOUR SPIRITUAL CONNECTIVITY TO GOD

Two exquisite spiritual blessings we get from being united with God are holiness and a reverent fear of Him. The more we get to know Him personally, the more we appreciate and profoundly respect Him. The fear of God and holiness are spiritual commodities that boost our connection strength to the heart and mind of God. Irreverence and lack of holiness stunt spiritual growth, generate spiritual deception, and downgrade our spiritual intelligence. We should regularly pray for both commodities and seek to genuinely understand their meaning and significance.

In both Hebrew and Greek, the word *holy* denotes being set apart. *Merriam-Webster's Dictionary* refers to the word as "having a divine quality," "worthy of complete devotion."[78] For some the word *holiness* may seem ultrareligious or old fashioned, but it is really quite practical and an essential condition necessary to draw close to God. Without holiness and a genuine reverence for God, the ability to "see" and "hear" God will be difficult, if not out of reach. Linking this to spiritual intelligence, the capacity to receive, review, and release revelation will be rendered impossible without real respect for God.

In Hebrew, the *fear* of God denotes "awesome" and "reverence."[79] *Merriam-Webster's Dictionary* differentiates between various types of fear and describes fearing God as "reverential awe of God."[80] It is precisely this humble admiration and appreciation of God that is so vital to authentic spiritual intelligence. When the Bible talks about the *fear* of God it is not referring to a spirit of fear that generates anxiety and horror. The world is plagued with such fear and the Scriptures remind us that God has *not* given us a spirit of fear (2 Timothy 1:7).

Don't be duped into diluting the true meaning of the fear of God or misrepresenting it's value simply because the counterfeit triggers panic. There is a huge difference between fearing God and fearing humans. The former draws us to Him and the latter offends Him. Scripture instructs us not to fear anything or anyone other than God. Just as it very definitively instructs us to worship Him exclusively (Deuteronomy 6:13). The Bible makes it clear that those who fear and worship God *will* acquire wisdom and righteousness. Notice how the Bible links the fear of God with the capacity to deal responsibly with *all* of reality. "It's best to stay in touch with both sides of an issue. A person who fears God deals responsibly with all of reality, not just a piece of it" (Ecclesiastes 7:18 MSG).

The Scriptures very lucidly highlight that God wants us to fear Him alone, and to regard Him as holy *and* awesome. This isn't because He wants to be a stickler for punishment or to enforce rules that keep us from enjoying life. To the contrary, He wants us to be positioned away from the things of this world that could harm and defile us, and He wants us to experience true freedom from all the nastiness, heartlessness, and perverseness of this world. He wants us to walk in His presence and in intimacy with Him. He cannot inhabit an unholy sanctuary that doesn't respect Him. He wants us to be holy and in awe of Him so He can abide in us and share the secret thoughts of His mind with us. The secrets of God are with those who fear Him (Psalm 25:14).

I like how the Amplified Bible puts it, because it challenges us to prepare our minds for action, to *be holy* as He is holy, to conduct ourselves in *reverent fear* of Him, and to show Him *profound respect.*

> So prepare your *minds for action*, be completely sober [in spirit—steadfast, self-disciplined, spiritually and morally alert], fix your hope completely on the grace [of God] that is coming to you when Jesus Christ is revealed. [Live] as obedient children [of God]; do not be conformed to the evil desires *which governed you* in your *ignorance* [before you knew the requirements and transforming power of the good news regarding salvation]. But like the Holy One who called you, *be holy* yourselves in all *your* conduct [be set apart from the world by your godly character and moral courage]; because it is written, "You shall be holy (set apart), for I am holy." If you address as Father, the One who impartially judges according to each one's work, conduct yourselves in [*reverent] fear [of Him] and* with *profound respect* for Him throughout the time of your stay *on earth.* (1 Peter 1:13–17 AMP; emphasis mine)

Notice Peter's emphasis on holiness in *all* our conduct. He was essentially saying that we need to elevate our morals, ethics, and ideals to God's standards of morality. We need to imitate Him in our thought lives, words, and actions. We need to conform to His lifestyle. This seems like an impossible feat but not according to the Bible. With God, all things are possible (Mark 10:27), and as we renew our minds and attitudes (Romans 12:2) and progressively take on the mind of Christ (1 Corinthians 2:16), this higher life increasingly becomes a reality. God's intention is for His people to be perfected and fully equipped. He wants us to attain a full and accurate knowledge of Him so we genuinely spiritually mature. This seems like an astounding objective. Our Father in heaven wants His people to be like Jesus. When He wants something from us, He always makes it possible.

> His intention was the perfecting and the *full equipping* of the saints (His consecrated people), [that they should do] the work of ministering toward building up Christ's body (the church), [That it might develop] until we all *attain oneness* in the faith and in the comprehension of the [*full and accurate*] *knowledge* of the Son of God, that [we might arrive] at *really mature* manhood (the *completeness* of personality which is nothing less than the standard height of Christ's own perfection), the measure of the stature of the *fullness* of the Christ and the *completeness* found in Him. (Ephesians 4:12–13 AMPC; emphasis mine)

In a nutshell, when we imitate the lifestyle of Jesus, when we're really mature and possess high spiritual intelligence, we will stay away from *anything* that would undermine our relationship with Him. When you are truly in love with someone, you want nothing more than to please that person and show them what they mean to you; you will avoid anything that may be off putting or offensive to them. You will also go out of your way to find out what the person likes and dislikes, and make accommodations and adjustments to better suit theirs, right? You essentially put the person's interests and desires above your own, even if you don't necessarily understand why they have certain preferences or ideals.

To have high spiritual intelligence, we need an intimate companionship with the Lord, in which He reveals His deep inner thoughts and shares secrets with us. To really draw near to God—to perceive Him, hear Him, and truly know Him—we need to regard Him as holy and treat Him with the deepest respect.

> The Lord of hosts—regard Him as holy *and* honor His holy name by regarding Him as your only hope of safety], and let Him be your fear and let Him be your dread lest you offend Him by your fear of man and distrust of Him. (Isaiah 8:13 AMPC)

> By those who come near Me
> I must be regarded as holy;

> And before all the people
> I must be glorified. (Leviticus 10:3 NKJV)

Notice that the Scriptures make it emphatically clear that nearness to God is a product of regarding Him as holy. Esteeming and revering Him above anyone or anything are what propel us closer to Him. Those who fear Him lack *nothing*. We ought to be even more motivated to make certain the fruits in our lives reflect and confirm our genuine awe and profound respect for Him.

> I sought the Lord, and he answered me;
>> he delivered me from all my fears.
> Those who look to him are radiant;
>> their faces are never covered with shame.
> This poor man called, and the Lord heard him;
>> he saved him out of all his troubles.
> The *angel* of the Lord *encamps* around those who *fear* him,
>> and he delivers them.
> Taste and see that the Lord is *good*;
>> blessed is the one who takes refuge in him.
> *Fear* the Lord, you his *holy* people,
>> for those who *fear* him lack *nothing*. (Psalm 34: 4-9 NIV;
>> emphasis mine)

HOW LACK OF HOLINESS AND IRREVERENCE INHIBITS INTIMACY WITH GOD AND DOWNGRADES SPIRITUAL INTELLIGENCE

Solomon is an example of someone who initially had a very intimate relationship with God. God appeared to him twice (1 Kings 11:9) and gave him exceptional wisdom, understanding, and breadth of mind (1 Kings 4:29).

In 2 Chronicles, we see how God gladly responded to Solomon's request for wisdom and intelligence.

> Give me now chochmah and *intelligence*, that I may go out and come in before HaAm Hazeh, for who can judge this Thy people, that is so great? (2 Chronicles 1:10 OJB; emphasis mine)

Give me wisdom and knowledge, so that I may go out and come in [performing my duties] before this people, for [otherwise] who can rule and administer justice to this great people of Yours?" God replied to Solomon, "Because this was in your heart and you did not ask for riches, possessions or honor and personal glory, or the life of those who hate you, nor have you even asked for long life, but you have asked for wisdom and knowledge for yourself so that you may rule and administer justice to My people over whom I have made you king, wisdom and knowledge have been granted you. I will also give you riches, possessions, and honor, such as none of the kings who were before you has possessed nor will those who will come after you." (2 Chronicles 1:10–12 AMP)

Having been granted wisdom and intelligence, Solomon was able to manage people with profound discernment, equity, and justice. His leadership demonstrated extraordinary spiritual intelligence and wisdom in action. Later in Solomon's life, however, he unfortunately began to get involved in counterfeit spiritual activities. His downfall came about due to his sexual relations with pagan women. This entanglement with the counterfeit wasn't just physical but also spiritual.

Solomon understood the value of wisdom and intelligence; he appreciated that one's conscience is the lamp of the Lord (Proverbs 20:27), and he knew the importance of fearing God (Ecclesiastes 12:13). He had distinct revelation knowledge of this at first but failed to maintain intimacy with God for the duration of his life. His revelation knowledge deteriorated, and he flirted with paganism and those who practiced it. He replaced his closeness with God with being intimate with pagan women. Symbolically, he exchanged the authentic for the counterfeit. His "lamp" may have looked intact, but it was no longer illuminated with spiritual insight. It had the capacity for understanding but lacked oil to keep the revelation flowing. He fell for the bait and lost His awe for God. His downgraded spiritual intelligence increasingly made it difficult for him to recognize his spiritual vulnerabilities and how far his viewpoint had shifted from God's.

God warned Solomon of the consequences of pagan entanglement, but He never manipulated or forced him to obey. This exemplifies the nature of God; He guides and warns but allows people to have their own free will. In His sovereignty, He chooses to allow humans to have free choice. Solomon was no exception. God is still warning humankind to stay far from paganism. "Buyer, beware" of the lure and attractiveness of the fake brand. So many continue to take the bait though. Only by seeking God as our *first* love and fearing Him (not people) will we avoid being enticed by evil (Proverbs 16:6).

> If you seek Him [inquiring for and of Him, craving Him as your soul's *first* necessity], He will be found by you; but if you [become *indifferent* and] forsake Him, He will forsake you (2 Chronicles 15:2 AMPC; emphasis mine)

When Solomon lost his fear of God, he lost his ability to accurately discern between good and evil. He appeared to be confused and to lack discernment unlike in his former days. It's as though the Spirit of God was warning him when he wrote these words: "The backslider in heart from God and from fearing God shall be filled with the fruit of his own ways, and a good man shall be satisfied with the fruit of his ways with the holy thoughts and actions which his heart prompts and in which he delights" (Proverbs 14:14 AMPC).

This verse also powerfully illustrates how backsliding isn't just outright rejection of God (which Solomon didn't do) but a backsliding from fearing God. Like the old adage, familiarity breeds contempt, so, too, Solomon lost His fear and reverence for God, assuming he could live life his own way and that God's grace would simply cover his sin. The reality, however, was that Solomon's life deteriorated, his relationship with God faded, and his once-profound spiritual intelligence was seriously downgraded.

While people can grow in spiritual intelligence and progress from no spiritual intelligence to high spiritual intelligence, Solomon's experience also highlights that people can slide backward from high spiritual intelligence to low spiritual intelligence, or sadly, even counterfeit spiritual intelligence, if they don't fear God and keep Him as their first priority and greatest passion.

After everything Solomon went through, read how he concluded the book of Ecclesiastes. He essentially summed up the bottom line to the entire duty of humankind and the foundation for all happiness into two things: fear God and obey His commands. Since we know God's commands are summed up in the command to love, the two most important duties we have are to love God and to fear Him. People who achieve high spiritual intelligence have and maintain both.

> Now all has been heard; here is the conclusion of the matter: Fear God and keep his commandments, for this is the duty of all mankind. (Ecclesiastes 12:13 NIV)

The Bible couldn't be clearer in its assertion that the fear of the Lord is the beginning of wisdom, the *prerequisite* to truly knowing God. Fearing God is a genuine reverence for and acknowledgment of your insignificance in comparison to His majesty.

> The [reverent] fear of the Lord is the beginning (the *prerequisite*, the absolute essential, the alphabet) of wisdom; A good understanding *and* a teachable heart are possessed by all those who do *the will of the Lord*; His praise endures forever. (Psalm 111:10 AMP; emphasis mine)

> The fear of the Lord *is* the beginning of knowledge, *But* fools despise wisdom and instruction. (Proverbs 1:7 NIV)

Why should the Lord grant us a private, intimate audience with Him when we ignore what He has already told us in His Word? Why would He contradict His Word by making exceptions for us that are more in line with our culture? The fear of God protects us from deception and hypocrisy (2 Corinthians 3:16). The fear of man is a snare and offensive to God (Proverbs 29:25). God's salvation is close to those who fear Him (Psalm 85:9), and by the fear of the Lord, people avoid evil (Proverbs 16:6). In these last days, with deception so rampant and counterfeit spiritual intelligence so evident, holiness and the fear of the Lord will keep God's children from backsliding and help them maintain blameless consciences amid a spiritually warped generation.

> For then you will be seen as innocent, faultless, and pure children
> of God, even though you live in the midst of a brutal and perverse
> culture. For you will appear among them as shining lights in the
> universe. (Philippians 2:15 TPT)

> And he said to the human race, "The fear of the Lord—that is
> wisdom, and to shun evil is understanding." (Job 28:28 NIV)

Jesus also warned us in Matthew 24:12 that in the last days, the love of
many will grow cold because of the multiplied lawlessness and iniquity.
Without love, deception gains ground, spiritual intelligence diminishes,
and the ability to discern between good and evil becomes increasingly
difficult. The apostle Paul said the end-times would be one of the most
difficult times to be a believer because of deception. You may wonder
how deception could increase in an age when knowledge is exploding and
ignorance should be decreasing as a result. The reason is that counterfeit
knowledge (knowledge that contradicts truth) is widespread. God wants
His people to know Him intimately, share the mind of Christ, and possess
high spiritual intelligence so they won't be easily deceived and fall for
something that appears to be of God but actually isn't.

In 2 Timothy 3:1–6, the apostle Paul was in effect warning all believers
that the last days will be times of great stress and trouble, when people will
be narcissistic and self-focused boasters. He warned of false accusers, haters
of good, and betrayers inflated with self-conceit. He described people in the
last days as being unholy lovers of sensual pleasures and vain amusements
rather than lovers of God. He said they will have a form of religion but
deny the power thereof. If you're not yet convinced we are living in those
very days, let's take note of some more of his warnings. Notice how many
of these characteristics are consistent with fruits associated with low or no
spiritual intelligence, which we examined earlier.

> But understand this, that in the last days dangerous times [of
> *great stress* and trouble] will come [difficult days that will be
> hard to bear]. For people will be lovers of self [*narcissistic, self-
> focused*], lovers of money [impelled by greed], boastful, arrogant,
> revilers, disobedient to parents, ungrateful, unholy *and* profane,
> [and they will be] unloving [devoid of natural human affection,

calloused and inhumane], irreconcilable, malicious gossips, devoid of self-control [intemperate, immoral], brutal, haters of good, traitors, reckless, conceited, lovers of [sensual] pleasure rather than lovers of God, holding to a form of [outward] godliness (religion), although they have denied its power [for their conduct nullifies their claim of faith]. Avoid such people *and* keep far away from them. (2 Timothy 3:1–6 AMP; emphasis mine)

MAINTAINING CLOSENESS TO GOD IN A CULTURE OF SELF-OBSESSION

We're undoubtedly living in a generation and at a time when people are obsessed with themselves and their own self-righteousness, where many aren't standing with God and are hence falling for anything. Self-confidence is now the order of the day rather than God confidence. Even seemingly harmless distractions can sap people's energy and drain their time when they could be developing a strong and intimate relationship with God, and gaining access to His creative strategies and solutions for a world in crisis. Anyone focusing mainly on their self-promotion, marketing, and ministry, even if well intentioned, ends up thinking more about themselves than about God. That person pays less attention to who God is and what He is doing. God isn't pleased with being snubbed or pushed to second place. Lack of intimacy with God stunts our growth, makes us spiritually sluggish, and dulls our perceptual awareness and the accuracy with which we process spiritual data and translate it into productive action. God needs us to be sharp, spiritually smart, and knowledgeable.

> Those who think they can do it on their own end up obsessed with measuring their own moral muscle but never get around to exercising it in real life. Those who trust God's action in them find that God's Spirit is in them—living and breathing God! *Obsession with self* in these matters is a dead end; attention to God leads us out into the open, into a spacious, free life. Focusing on the self is the opposite of focusing on God. Anyone completely absorbed in *self* ignores God, ends up thinking more about *self* than God. That person ignores who God is and what he is doing. And God isn't pleased at being ignored. (Romans 8:5–8 MSG; emphasis mine)

God isn't American, nor should He be approached in the same way as you would approach a human dignitary or leader. He is the Most High, the Greatest, the Supreme One, His Majesty, the most honorable, glorious King. Unlike our earthly leaders, He is perfect and blameless.

The Bible (depending on the version) refers to God as the "Most High" 64 times. Seventy-seven times the Scriptures declare "Glory to God." He is referred to as the "Great God" 192 times. His majesty is mentioned at least 32 times. The Bible says to honor God 77 times. Human talent and giftedness pale in comparison to God, yet if we examine the credence given to God in comparison to the honor and spotlight on humans in this world, we should be ashamed. No wonder He is inhibited from revealing Himself and constrained in demonstrating His power in our midst. Irreverence and lack of holiness deflect His glory and refract His power.

Sometimes believers start out revering God but over time they begin to get familiar with Him. This familiarity and irreverence also translates into a disrespect for spiritual authority and a propensity to trivialize, underestimate, or neglect things associated with His kingdom. It's no wonder so many struggle with developing *and* maintaining a genuine closeness to the Lord.

John Bevere's book *The Fear of the Lord: Discover the Key to Intimately Knowing God* captures this scenario perfectly. "Often the messages we have preached over the past twenty years via pulpits and airwaves have given God the appearance of the 'Sugar Daddy in the sky' whose desire is to give us whatever we want, whenever we want it ... Spoiled children lack true respect for authority, especially when they do not get *what they want when they want it*. Their lack of reverence for authority sets them up to be easily offended with God."[81]

True holiness through the fear of God may seem like an impossible feat for believers, given the constant and rampant temptations continually bombarding our lives. However, by God's grace, of which holiness is a product, we can overcome any sin we may be tempted by with total success. Moreover, in an age where we are witnessing so much blatant lack of fear of God, growing deception, self-centeredness, and counterfeit intelligence, God is countering this by raising up a generation of humble, God-centered believers with high spiritual intelligence. God is close friends with those who fear Him (Psalm 25:14) and gives empowering grace to the humble (James 4:6).

The prophet Joel declared that in the last days, God will pour out His Spirit upon *all* humankind. Prophetic activity will dramatically increase and more people, young and old, male and female, will prophesy. People will increasingly see visions and have dreams, telling forth the divine counsels and predict future events pertaining especially to God's kingdom (Joel 2:28). This not just for a group of super-spiritual elites but for everyday people like you and me. This is God's promise, and we are on the precipice of this magnificent outpouring of extraordinary revelation knowledge, and things have already begun. God's kingdom will come, and *His* will shall be done on earth as it is in heaven.

> This is what I will do in the last days—I will pour out my Spirit on everybody and cause your sons and daughters to prophesy, and your young men will see visions, and your old men will experience dreams *from God*. The Holy Spirit will come upon all my servants, men and women alike, and they will prophesy. (Acts 2:17–18 TPT)

We are living in the greatest time in history, and for those of you reading this book, God wants you to get ready for your role in the paramount expression of His Spirit the world has yet experienced. He wants you to grow in *authentic* spiritual intelligence and to be on guard against what's counterfeit. The *original* is part of our inheritance and birthright as His children. God desires *all* people to know Him intimately, to love Him with a *first* love, to profoundly revere Him, to have a lifestyle of *quick* repentance, and to possess *high* spiritual intelligence. He needs people who, because they genuinely know Him through *personal* experience, prove themselves strong and do great exploits for Him (Daniel 11:32). Let's be those people, who will manifest His presence and carry His glory. Let's be people who truly love God with *all* our passion, prayer, *and* intelligence.

Let's accurately and honorably represent Him, and *intelligently* demonstrate His love to our broken humanity.

In conclusion, let's pray.

God, thank You for Your amazing love for me. Thank You for creating in me the capacity to love You and profoundly respect You. I now know that they are keys to practical wisdom and genuine spiritual intelligence. Help me to embrace them, to employ them well, and to avoid the counterfeit. Help me to remain humble and holy so I may stay closely connected to You. I acknowledge that without You, I can do nothing. Thank You that through You, anything is possible. Let me be unceasing in my prayer life and help me to pray powerful prayers that advance Your kingdom and perpetuate Your purposes on the earth. I surrender my heart and mind to You, Holy Spirit. Help me to grow in my intimacy and revelation knowledge of You so I can bring forth fruit associated with high spiritual intelligence throughout my life. To You be all the glory forever. In Jesus' supreme name. Amen.

As final encouragement, I extend this prayer to the God of the universe on your behalf:

Amazing Father, may the readers of this book be among the highly spiritually intelligent ones in these last days. May they become all You have called them to be. Activate, elevate, and accelerate the development of their spiritual intelligence. May Your enabling power and love remain with them, and may their lives be forever changed for Your glory. May the spiritual seeds that have been planted as they've read and reread this book bear much fruit that will not only determine the course of their destinies but also greatly influence the destinies of those they lead. May Your overwhelming love for them increasingly become more real to them, and may it continue to activate and eternally energize their faith in You. May Your kingdom come and Your will be done in their lives, as You've destined in heaven. To You alone be all the glory and honor forever. In the awe-inspiring name of Jesus. Amen.

APPENDIX A

Get Activated or Reactivated

A precondition to spiritual intelligence is to be spiritually transformed by God through faith in our Messiah, Mediator, and High Priest, Jesus. Once we are spiritually reborn, we can begin the journey of developing spiritual intelligence and a genuine partnership with the Holy Spirit in searching out things far beyond our natural human understanding. Jesus made it clear that a person must be born again (spiritually reborn) to ever perceive the kingdom of God (John 3:3).

Long before God created the earth, He had us in mind. He planned for us to be adopted into His family and to enter into His presence and have a relationship with Him. "How blessed is God! And what a blessing He is! He's the Father of our Master, Jesus Christ, and takes us to the high places of blessing in Him. Long before He laid down earth's foundations, He had us in mind, had settled on us as the focus of His love, to be made whole and holy by His love. Long, long ago He decided to adopt us into His family through Jesus Christ. (What pleasure He took in planning this!) He wanted us to enter into the celebration of His lavish gift-giving by the hand of His beloved Son" (Ephesians 1:3–6 MSG).

God isn't asking you to put your spectacular mind aside in your relationship with Him but to be childlike in your openness to learning.

> Truly I tell you, anyone who will not receive the kingdom of God like a little child will never enter it. (Luke 18:17 NIV)

> You, however, are not in the realm of the flesh but are in the realm of the Spirit, if indeed the Spirit of God lives in you. And if anyone does not have the Spirit of Christ, they do not belong to Christ. (Romans 8:9 NIV)

When you truly surrender your life to the lordship of Jesus, you will gain an assurance of your new identity as a child of God. God's Spirit will affirm your spirit, reassuring you that you are indeed a child of God. This isn't a mental assurance based on works or benevolent activities. This assurance is something your spirit will sense, when your heart truly believes in Jesus and demonstrates its belief through a verbal declaration of that faith.

> The Spirit himself testifies with our spirit that we are God's children. Now if we are children, then we are heirs—heirs of God and co-heirs with Christ, if indeed we share in his sufferings in order that we may also share in his glory. (Romans 8:16–17 NIV)

> Because if you acknowledge *and* confess with your lips that Jesus is Lord and in your heart believe (adhere to, trust in, and rely on the truth) that God raised Him from the dead, you will be saved. (Romans 10:9 AMPC)

This new reality, moving from spiritual blindness to a state of spiritual rebirth, won't materialize if you simply repeat a religious-sounding prayer you felt pressured to pray because someone obliged you to repeat it. Nor will this rebirth become a reality if your motive is to get a quick ticket to heaven or a quick eternal life insurance policy without genuine repentance from your past and a sincere turning over of your life to Jesus. Jesus would rather you stay cold than say a false prayer and sit on the fence between a life lived for Him and a life lived for yourself.

This initial spiritual rebirth and transformation is a free gift from God for anyone who chooses to follow Jesus. It isn't something that can be achieved through our own striving but something to receive with thanks.

> For it is by grace you have been saved, through faith—and this is not from yourselves, it is the gift of God.
> (Ephesians 2:8 NIV)

> For *everyone* who calls upon the name of the Lord [invoking Him as Lord] will be saved. (Romans 10:13 AMPC; emphasis mine)

It is quite amazing to imagine the intensity of God's love for humankind that would motivate Him to make a way for us to become His children and to share in the inheritance of His Son no matter what we have done, who we are, or where we are from. His heart's desire is for *all* to be saved and to come into a relationship with Him.

> This is good, and pleases God our Savior, who wants all people to be saved and to come to a knowledge of the truth. For there is one God and one mediator between God and mankind, the man Christ Jesus, who gave himself as a ransom for all people. This has now been witnessed to at the proper time. (1 Timothy 2:3–6 NIV)

> See what great love the Father has lavished on us, that we should be called children of God! And that is what we are! The reason the world does not know us is that it did not know him. (1 John 3:1 NIV)

Here is a prayer to become a child of God and to begin the journey of growing in spiritual intelligence.

> *God, I acknowledge that I have done things my own way and admittedly the wrong way. Forgive me for falling short of Your righteous standards and for thinking I could do life without You. Thank You for sending Your Son, Jesus, to die on a cross for me and to bear my judgment. I believe He was born of the virgin Mary, and that He rose from the dead and is now seated at Your right hand as King of kings and Lord of my life. I offer my life to You.*

> *Jesus, I confess You as my Savior, my King, and my Lord. Come into my life, into my heart, and transform my mind through Your Spirit. Transfer me into the kingdom of light, empowering me by Your Spirit to become all You have called me to become. I renounce the kingdom of darkness and everything I have been involved in that's associated with that kingdom.*

> *Thank You, Lord, for rescuing my life and for giving me the privilege of becoming a child of God! I look forward to developing a deep and intimate friendship with You. Help me to grow in spiritual intelligence and to truly get to know You. My life is no longer my own, and I am so thankful I am now Yours forever. Amen.*

APPENDIX B

Get Filled or Refilled

Like becoming spiritually renewed and born again, the experience of being filled with the Holy Spirit doesn't come through a formal ritual but rather through prayer and a genuine heart's desire to experience everything God intended for us. It is a real and distinct experience that will invigorate your spiritual journey and empower you to operate in the supernatural at a level you could otherwise not achieve naturally. The experience will draw you infinitely closer to the Holy Spirit and give you a renewed capacity to hear Him and follow Him more succinctly. The experience isn't a precondition to salvation, but it is vital for high spiritual intelligence. The Holy Spirit is the Comforter, our ultimate Service Provider—the Counselor, Helper, Intercessor, Advocate, Strengthener, and Standby (John 14:16). Much like when our Wi-Fi connection speed is slow or our broadband signal strength is weak, without a strong acquaintance and intimacy with the Holy Spirit, we struggle to hear what God is saying to us. The experience of being filled or refilled with the Holy Spirit enhances that connection strength and access speed to the heart and mind of God. Jesus is the One who baptizes us with the Holy Spirit (Matthew 3:11). You can trust Him to perform the baptism safely and lovingly, since you know Him. The time between our spiritual rebirth and the baptism can be days, months, or years. For me, it was eight years. Irrespective of how long it takes, the experience is unique and powerful. Once You are truly baptized with the evidence of speaking in other tongues, you will certainly know it. You will also appreciate the increased access to God's enabling power and enhanced capacity to perceive Him.

> I baptize you with water for repentance. But after me comes one
> who is more powerful than I, whose sandals I am not worthy to

carry. He will baptize you with the Holy Spirit and fire. (Matthew 3:11 NIV)

All of them were filled with the Holy Spirit and began to speak in other tongues as the Spirit enabled them. (Acts 2:4 NIV)

For they heard them speaking in tongues and praising God. (Acts 10:46 NIV)

For anyone who speaks in a tongue does not speak to people but to God. Indeed, no one understands them; they utter mysteries by the Spirit. (1 Corinthians 14:2 NIV)

But you, dear friends, carefully build yourselves up in this most holy faith by praying in the Holy Spirit, staying right at the center of God's love, keeping your arms open and outstretched, ready for the mercy of our Master, Jesus Christ. This is the unending life, the *real* life! (Jude 1:20–21 MSG)

The Bible makes it clear that all believers should speak in tongues (1 Corinthians 14:5) and not forbid or hinder the speaking of tongues (1 Corinthians 14:39). Why? So that God's children would be built up and make progress, remaining right at the center of God's love (Jude 1:20–21). After you are filled with the Spirit, be sure to stay filled. Just like our Wi-Fi connection strength and speed can weaken and slow down, so, too, our ability to clearly hear from and perceive the Holy Spirit can dwindle over time due to busyness or carelessness. We need to endeavor to go on being filled and stimulated with the Spirit (Ephesians 5:18). The one-time experience will require additional "refills" that come through spending time with Him, much like your devices need regular updates and downloads. So don't wait for a formal baptismal event or religious ceremony to be filled or refilled. Simply ask God and mean it.

Here is a prayer to be filled or refilled in the Holy Spirit to advance your spiritual intelligence.

Father, thank You that I have been spiritually reborn and am Your child. I want to know You better and to receive the baptism of Your Spirit with the evidence of speaking with new tongues. Forgive me for resisting a more intimate relationship with You and for being hesitant to go deeper with You. Your Word shows that You want all Your children to be filled with the Spirit and to stay filled so they can be encouraged and developed. Help me to receive the infilling with childlike faith and to trust in You and what Your Word says. Jesus, please fill me afresh with the Holy Spirit.

Holy Spirit, I receive Your infilling. I commit to remaining filled with You. I commit to investing in my relationship with You. Help me to follow You well and to be a friend You can confide in and rely on. I love You and trust You want only the best for me. Show me what grieves You about things I do and say, and help me to make the necessary adjustments so our relationship can thrive. You are my Source of intelligence, my Counselor, my Helper, my Intercessor, my Advocate, my Strengthener, and my Standby. Continue to free my body, mind, and spirit from everything contrary to what You desire for me. Fill me to overflowing with Your presence and transform my life, heart, and mind. In Jesus' awesome name. Amen.

APPENDIX C

Prayers to Develop Spiritual Intelligence

Below is a compilation of 70 prayers that have been developed from various versions of the Bible to help you advance your spiritual intelligence. The Bible verse that served as the inspiration for each prayer is indicated.

Fill me with the Your Spirit God, with wisdom and ability, with understanding and intelligence, with knowledge and all kinds of expertise. (Exodus 31:3 AMPC)

Grant me a spirit of intelligence and let Your breath give me understanding. (Job 32:8 AMPC)

Create in me a clean heart, O God, and renew a right and steadfast spirit within me. (Psalm 51:10 AMP)

Open my eyes so I can see what You show me of Your miracle-wonders. (Psalm 119:18 MSG)

Grant me wisdom, great insight, and breadth of understanding. (1 Kings 4:29 NIV)

Help me to grow a wise heart and keep a clear head. (Proverbs 19:8 MSG)

Give me wisdom and intelligence that I may lead well. (2 Chronicles 1:10 OJB)

Grant me a spirit of wisdom and revelation, of insight into mysteries and secrets, in the deep and intimate knowledge of You. (Ephesians 1:17 AMPC)

Help me to tune my ears to wisdom and to set my heart on a life of understanding. Help me to make insight a priority. Help me to understand the fear of the Lord, so I can personally know You. (Proverbs 2:1–6 MSG)

What the world calls smart, You call stupid. Keep me from foolish ignorance. (1 Corinthians 3:18–20 MSG)

May I increasing have the mind of Christ and hold the thoughts, feelings and purposes of His heart. (1 Corinthians 2:16 AMPC)

Help me to progressively become more intimately acquainted with Jesus, and know Him more definitely, accurately and thoroughly. (Colossians 2:2 AMPC)

May I constantly be renewed in the spirit of my mind, continuously having a fresh mental and spiritual attitude. (Ephesians 4:23 AMPC)

Let me not conform to the pattern of this world, but let me be transformed and progressively changed by the renewing of my mind so that I may personally prove what Your will is—Your good, acceptable, and perfect plan and purpose for me. (Romans 12:2 AMP)

May Your Spirit rest upon me—the Spirit of wisdom and understanding, the Spirit of counsel and might, the Spirit of knowledge and the fear of the Lord. Make me of quick understanding, and may I delight in fearing and obeying You. (Isaiah 11:2–3 AMPC)

Let me love You more and more with all my passion, prayer, muscle, and intelligence, and help me to love those around me as well as I do myself. (Luke 10:27 MSG)

Give me a wise mind and spirit attuned to Your will, so I can acquire a thorough understanding of the ways in which You work. Let me live well for You. (Colossians 1:9–10 MSG)

Great are You and highly to be praised. Help me to increasingly grasp Your greatness and make Your greatness known. (Psalm 145:3 AMP)

Help me to be informed and knowledgeable, and to understand how Your Spirit gets worked into our lives. Help me to use my intelligence and my head, to seek to gain understanding. (1 Corinthians 12:1–3 MSG)

Let the eyes of my heart be flooded with light, so I can know and understand the hope to which You have called me and how rich Your glorious inheritance is. (Ephesians 1:18 AMPC)

Help me to have a lifestyle of quick repentance and to give heed to Your reproof, so that wisdom will be poured out upon me, and Your words made known to me. (Proverbs 1:23 AMPC)

Since eternal life is to know (to perceive, recognize, become acquainted with, and understand) You, the only true and real God, help me to know You well. (John 17:3 AMPC)

Help me to answer people like You do, clear-cut and accurate. May I love You with all my passion, intelligence, and energy, and others as myself. (Mark 12:32–33 MSG)

I recognize it's better to be wise than strong and that intelligence outranks muscle any day. Help me to grow in intelligence, wisely using strategic planning and good counsel to win in life. (Proverbs 24:5–6 MSG)

Help me to imitate You. May I copy You and follow Your example. (Ephesians 5:1 AMPC)

May I acquire skillful and godly wisdom, since it's preeminent! With all my acquiring, let me get understanding, and actively seek spiritual discernment, mature comprehension, and logical interpretation. (Proverbs 4:7 AMP)

Help me to know and understand the immeasurable and unlimited and surpassing greatness of Your power in and for us who believe. (Ephesians 1:19 AMPC)

Generous in love, God, give me grace. In Your mercy, purify my conscience. Scrub away my guilt and soak out my sins in Your laundry. (Psalm 51:1–3 MSG)

Help me to grow up spiritually and to use my head—my mature adult head. Let me have a childlike unfamiliarity with evil but give me mature and well-exercised spiritual intelligence to save me from falling into gullibility. (1 Corinthians 14:20–25 MSG)

May I be invigorated and strengthened with all power according to the might of Your glory, and may I exercise every kind of endurance and patience, perseverance and forbearance with joy. (Colossians 1:11 AMPC)

Help me to pray at all times (on every occasion, in every season) in the Spirit, with all manner of prayer and entreaty. Let me keep alert and watch with strong purpose and perseverance, interceding on behalf of all God's people. (Ephesians 6:18 AMPC)

May we develop and attain oneness in the faith and in the comprehension of the full and accurate knowledge of the Son of God, that we may really mature and come to the measure of the stature of the fullness of Jesus and the completeness found in Him. (Ephesians 4:13 AMPC)

Let the signs of Your power be revealed to me and my children. (Psalm 90:16 AMPC)

Help me to work out my salvation with reverence, serious caution, tenderness of conscience, and watchfulness against temptation. May I refrain from whatever might offend You and discredit Your name. (Philippians 2:12 AMPC)

You are a God in heaven who reveals secrets. Lord, reveal secrets to me through dreams and visions that appear in my mind. (Daniel 2:28 AMPC)

Help me understand and utter unknown and unattainable things that have been hidden from humankind since the foundation of the world. (Matthew 13:35 AMP)

Thank You that nothing is hidden, except to be revealed; nor has anything been kept secret, that will not come to light. Let the hidden things continue to be made manifest. (Mark 4:22 AMP)

Help me by Your Holy Spirit to speak mysteries, secret truths, and hidden things. (1 Corinthians 14:2 AMP)

Let me speak excellent and noble things. May the opening of my lips reveal right things. (Proverbs 8:6 AMP)

Send me the Comforter, Counselor, Helper, Intercessor, Advocate, Strengthener, Standby, the Holy Spirit, to teach me all things and help me to remember everything You tell me. (John 14:26 AMPC)

Develop in me moral and spiritual integrity that places me in constant right standing with You. (Psalm 97:12 AMP)

Thank You that You did not give us a spirit of fear, but You have given us a spirit of power, love, sound judgment, and personal discipline. Grant me a calm, well-balanced mind, and self-control. (2 Timothy 1:7 AMP)

May illumination, understanding and wisdom from Your Spirit be found in me. (Daniel 5:11 AMP)

Help me to reveal the interpretation of dreams with accuracy, for the Spirit of God is in me. (Daniel 4:18 AMP)

May our hearts be braced (comforted, cheered, and encouraged) as they are knit together in love. May we come to have all the abounding wealth and blessings of assured conviction of understanding. Help us to progressively become more intimately acquainted with Jesus, and know Him more definitely, accurately and thoroughly. (Colossians 2:2 AMPC)

Thanks for always leading me in triumph in Christ, and for helping me spread and make evident the fragrance of the knowledge of You everywhere I go. (2 Corinthians 2:14 AMPC)

Shine in our hearts and give us the light of the knowledge of Your glory. (2 Corinthians 4:6 NIV)

May I refute arguments, theories, reasonings, and every proud thing that sets itself up against the true knowledge of You, bringing every thought captive to the obedience of Christ. (2 Corinthians 10:5 AMPC)

You said to call on You and You would answer me, and show and tell me great and mighty things which have been confined and hidden, and which I do not know or understand. Let it be. (Jeremiah 33:3 AMP)

Father, I openly and joyfully acknowledge Your great wisdom that You have hidden from the worldly-wise and so-called intelligent, and revealed to those seeking Your will and purpose. (Matthew 11:25 AMP)

Help me to set my mind on what gratifies the Holy Spirit, for the mind of the Holy Spirit is life and soul peace both now and forever. (Romans 8:5–6 AMPC)

May I be eager and ambitious to possess spiritual gifts and manifestations of the Holy Spirit, striving to excel in ways that will build up Your people. (1 Corinthians 14:12 AMPC)

Confirm and establish me, and anoint me with the gifts of the Holy Spirit. (2 Corinthians 1:21 AMPC)

Help me to receive spiritual gifts and to employ them well in serving others. (1 Peter 4:10 AMP)

Confirm the message of salvation by signs and wonders, and various miracles and gifts of the Holy Spirit according to Your will. (Hebrews 2:4 AMP)

May I be exceedingly enriched in You, in everything, in all speech empowered by the spiritual gifts and in all knowledge with insight into the faith. (1 Corinthians 1:5 AMP)

Let my spiritual ears be attentive to skillful and godly wisdom, and may my heart be applied to understanding. May I seek it conscientiously and strive for it eagerly. (Proverbs 2:2 AMP)

May I continue to grow in grace so that I can still bring forth fruit associated with high spiritual intelligence in old age. Let me be full of the sap of spiritual vitality, and rich in the verdure of trust, love, and contentment. (Psalm 92:14 AMPC)

Give me courage and grace, and may I stand before You with a clear conscience. (Luke 21:36 TPT)

Help me to love You with all my heart and with all my understanding, intelligence, discernment, and strength, and to love my neighbor as myself. (Mark 12:33 AMPC)

May my love flourish so that I not only love much but well. Help me to learn to love appropriately. Let my love be sincere and intelligent, not sentimental gush. Help me to live a life bountiful in fruits, making Jesus attractive to all. (Philippians 1:9–11 MSG)

Grant me a mind that is packed with wisdom and intelligence. May I adopt Your mode of thinking and judging of thoughts, feelings, and purposes. (Revelation 17:9 AMPC)

Empower me to hear Your voice in dreams and visions. (Job 33:15 NIV)

Help me to have a lifestyle of quick repentance and to give heed to Your reproof, so Your words will be made known to me. (Proverbs 1:23 AMPC)

You see everything I do, and observe every single habit I have. Heal any scars on my conscience so that they don't become the ropes that tie me up. (Proverbs 5:21-22 TPT)

May I love You with all my passion, prayer, and intelligence, and others as well as I love myself. (Matthew 22:37–40 MSG)

Let the words of my mouth and the meditation of my heart be acceptable in Your sight, O Lord, my Rock and my Redeemer. (Psalm 19:14 AMPC)

Fill me with Your Spirit, with ability and wisdom, with intelligence and understanding, and with knowledge and all kinds of skills. (Exodus 35:31 AMPC)

Thank You that Your word says that anyone deficient in wisdom should ask You for it. Thank You for so liberally and ungrudgingly giving it to those who ask. (James 1:5 AMPC)

Let Your rays of revelation-light shine from Your people and pierce the conscience of those who don't know You. (Psalm 94: 1 TPT)

Lord, my determined purpose is that I may know You. May I progressively become more deeply and intimately acquainted with You. Help me to perceive, recognize, and understand the wonders of Your Person more strongly and more clearly. (Philippians 3:10 AMPC)

ENDNOTES

1   Lexico Dictionary, s.v. "intelligence," accessed July 7, 2020, https://www.lexico.com/definition/intelligence.

2   *Merriam-Webster*, s.v. "intelligence," accessed July 7, 2020, http://www.merriam-webster.com/dictionary/intelligence.

3   Bible Hub, s.v. "7919a.sakal," accessed July 7, 2020, https://biblehub.com/hebrew/7919a.htm.

4   Bible Hub, s.v. "5429.phronimos," accessed July 10, 2020, https://biblehub.com/greek/5429.htm.

5   Lee Strobel, *The Case for Christ: A Journalist's Personal Investigation of the Evidence for Jesus* (Grand Rapids: Zondervan, 2017).

6   Josh McDowell and Sean McDowell, *Evidence That Demands a Verdict: Life-Changing Truth for a Skeptical World* (Nashville: Thomas Nelson, 2017).

7   Daniel Goleman, *Emotional Intelligence: Why It Can Matter More Than IQ* (New York: Bantam, 1995).

8   David A. Livermore and Chap Clark, *Cultural Intelligence: Improving Your CQ to Engage Our Multicultural World* (Grand Rapids: Baker Academic, 2009).

9   Howard Gardner, *Frames of Mind* (New York: Basic Books, 1983).

10 Jennifer Palthe, "Multiple Intelligences in Change Leadership: Exploring the Diversity," *Management and Organizational Studies* 6, no. 1 (2019).

11 Goleman, *Emotional Intelligence*, 43.

12 David Livermore, *Leading with Cultural Intelligence: The Real Secret to Success* (American Management Association, 2015).

13 Bible Hub, s.v. "3045.yada," accessed July 10, 2020, https://biblehub.com/hebrew/3045.htm.

14 Bible Hub, s.v. "1108.gnosis," accessed July 10, 2020, https://biblehub.com/greek/1108.htm.

15 Bible Hub, s.v. "1922.epignosis," accessed July 10, 2020, https://biblehub.com/greek/1922.htm.

16 *Merriam-Webster*, s.v. "revelation," accessed July 10, 2020, https://www.merriam-webster.com/dictionary/revelation.

17 Bible Hub, s.v. "1540.galah," accessed July 10, 2020, https://biblehub.com/hebrew/1540.htm.

18 Bible Hub, s.v. "602.apokalupsis," accessed July 10, 2020, https://biblehub.com/greek/602.htm.

19 Jewish Encyclopedia, s.v. "revelation," accessed July 10, 2020, http://www. jewishencyclopedia.com/articles/12713-revelation.

20 Bolz, *God Secrets*, 43.

21 *Merriam-Webster*, s.v. "perceive," accessed July 15, 2020, http://www.merriam-webster.com/dictionary/perceive.

22 *Merriam-Webster*, s.v. "awareness," accessed July 15, 2020, http://www.merriam-webster.com/dictionary/awareness.

23 Bible Hub, s.v. "3798.horao," accessed July 20, 2020, https://biblehub.com/greek/3708.htm.

24 Bible Hub, s.v. "2940.taam," accessed August 5, 2020, https://biblehub.com/hebrew/2940.htm.

25 Dave Williams, *Skill for Battle: The Art of Spiritual Warfare* (Decapolis Publishing, 2009), 68.

26 Williams, *Skill for Battle*, 70.

27 David Yonggi Cho, *Prayer that Brings Revival: Interceding for God to Move in Your Family Church, and Community* (Lake Mary, FL: Charisma House, 1998), 13.

28 Cho, *Prayer that Brings Revival*, 23.

29 Ibid., 24.

30 Jennifer Eivaz, *Seeing the Supernatural: How to Sense, Discern and Battle in the Spiritual Realm* (Minneapolis, MN: Chosen, 2017), 32.

31 Ibid., 40 - 41.

32 Bible Hub, s.v. "374.ephah," accessed July 10, 2020, https://biblehub.com/hebrew/374.htm

33 Bible Hub, s.v. "1431.dorea," accessed July 20, 2020, https://biblehub.com/greek/1431.htm.

34 *Merriam-Webster*, s.v. "gratuity," accessed July 20, 2020, http://www.merriam-webster.com/dictionary/gratuity.

35 Shawn Bolz, *God Secrets: A Life Filled with Words of Knowledge*, (ICreate: 2017), 43.

36 *Merriam-Webster*, s.v. "nothing," accessed July 21, 2020, http://www.merriam-webster.com/dictionary/nothing.

37 Guillermo Maldonado, *How to Walk in the Supernatural Power of God* (New Kensington, PA: Whitaker House, 2011), 134.

38 Lexico Dictionary, s.v. "counterfeit," accessed July 30, 2020, https://www.lexico.com/definition/counterfeit.

39 *Merriam-Webster*, s.v. "counterfeit," accessed July 30, 2020, http://www.merriam-webster.com/dictionary/counterfeit.

40 Sid Roth, *It's Supernatural,* sidroth.org

41 Pew Research surveys conducted December 4–18, 2017.

42 Illicit Trade, Trends in Trade in Counterfeit and Pirated Goods, OECD: iLibrary, accessed July 30, 2020.

43 Steven Bancarz and Josh Peck, *The Second Coming of the New Age*, (Crane, MO: Defender Publishing, 2018), 139.

44 Bancarz and Peck, *The Second Coming of the New Age*, 140 - 141.

45 *Merriam-Webster*, s.v. "yoga," accessed July 30, 2020, http://www.merriam-webster.com/dictionary/yoga.

46 Bancarz and Peck, *The Second Coming of the New Age*, 311.

47 Phil Mason, *Quantum Glory: The Science of Heaven Invading Earth*, (Quantum Ministries, 2010), 27.

48 Mason, *Quantum Glory*, 220.

49 Jennifer LeClaire, *Discerning Prophetic Witchcraft: Exposing the Supernatural Divination That is Deceiving Spiritually Hungry Believers* (Shippensburg, PA: Destiny, 2020).

50 LeClaire, *Discerning Prophetic Witchcraft*, 94.

51 *Merriam-Webster*, s.v. "manipulation," accessed July 30, 2020, http://www.merriam-webster.com/dictionary/manipulation.

52 Dave Williams, *The Jezebel Spirit: Freeing Yourself form the Spirit of Control* (Decapolis Publishing, 2002).

53 *Merriam-Webster*, s.v. "divination," accessed July 30, 2020, http://www.merriam-webster.com/dictionary/divination.

54 Michael L. Brown, *The End of The American Gospel Enterprise* (Shippensburg: PA, Destiny Image, 1989), 75.

55 Brown, *The End of The American Gospel Enterprise*, 77.

56 John Bevere, *Breaking Intimidation* (Lake Mary, FL: Charisma House, 1999), 161.

57 Phil Mason, *The New Gnostics: Discerning Extra-Biblical Revelation in the Contemporary Charismatic Movement* (Quantum Ministries: 2019), 11.

58 Mason, *The New Gnostics,*104.

59 Michael Brown, *Hyper-Grace: Exposing the Dangers of the Modern Grace Message* (Lake Mary, FL: Charisma Media, 2014), 221.

60 Susana Wesley, letter to her son John Wesley dated June 8, 1725, accessed August 5, 2020, https://www.wesleyan.org.

61 *Merriam-Webster*, s.v. "conscience," accessed August 5, 2020, http://www.merriam-webster.com/dictionary/conscience.

62 Bible Hub, s.v. "4893.suneidesis," accessed August 5, 2020, https://biblehub.com/greek/4893.htm.

63 Lexico Dictionary, s.v. "conscience," accessed August 5, 2020, https://www.lexico.com/en/definition/conscience.

64 *Merriam-Webster*, s.v. "intellect," accessed July 7, 2020, http://www.merriam-webster.com/dictionary/intellect.

65   John Bevere, *Driven by Eternity: Making Your Life Count Today and Forever* (New York, NY: FaithWords, 2006), 202.

66   Bevere, *Driven by Eternity,* 90.

67   Ibid., 91 - 92.

68   *Merriam-Webster*, s.v. "memory," accessed August 5, 2020, http://www.merriam-webster.com/dictionary/memory.

69   Bible Hub, s.v. "4869.misgab," accessed August 5, 2020, https://biblehub.com/hebrew/4869.htm.

70   *Merriam-Webster*, s.v. "delight," accessed August 18, 2020, http://www.merriam-webster.com/dictionary/delight.

71   *Merriam-Webster*, s.v. "upright," accessed August 18, 2020, http://www.merriam-webster.com/dictionary/upright.

72   Jennifer Eivaz, *The Intercessors Handbook: How To Pray with Boldness, Authority & Supernatural Power* (Minneapolis, MN: Chosen, 2016), 168.

73   Cho, *Prayer that Brings Revival,* xxvii.

74   Ibid., 21.

75   Lisa Bevere, *Lioness Arising: Wake Up and Change Your World* (Colorado Springs CO: Waterbrook Press, 2010), 221.

76   Bible Hub, s.v. "1897.hagah," accessed August 18, 2020, https://biblehub.com/hebrew/1897.htm.

77   James Goll, *The Discerner: Hearing, Confirming, and Acting on Prophetic Revelation* (New Kensington PA: Whitaker House, 2017), 108.

78   *Merriam-Webster*, s.v. "holy," accessed August 18, 2020, http://www.merriam-webster.com/dictionary/holy.

79   Bible Hub, s.v. "3374.fear," accessed August 18, 2020, https://biblehub.com/hebrew/3374.htm.

80   *Merriam-Webster*, s.v. "fear," accessed August 18, 2020, http://www.merriam-webster.com/dictionary/fear.

81   Bevere, *The Fear of the Lord: Discover the Key to Intimately Knowing God* (Lake Mary FL: Charisma House, 1998), 23.

Printed in the United States
by Baker & Taylor Publisher Services